HABITS OF THE HEARTLAND

Habits of the Heartland

Small-Town Life in Modern America

Lyn C. Macgregor

Cornell University Press

Ithaca and London

Copyright © 2010 by Cornell University

First published 2010 by Cornell University Press
First printing, Cornell Paperbacks, 2010
Printed in the United States of America

Library of Congress Cataloging-in-Publication Data

Macgregor, Lyn Christine, 1973–
    Habits of the heartland : small-town life in modern America / Lyn C.
Macgregor.
        p. cm.
    Includes bibliographical references and index.
    ISBN 978-0-8014-4836-2 (cloth : alk. paper) — ISBN 978-0-8014-7643-3
(pbk. : alk. paper)
    1. Viroqua (Wis.)—Social life and customs.   2. Viroqua (Wis.)—
Commerce—Social aspects.   3. Community life—Wisconsin—Viroqua.
4. City and town life—Wisconsin—Viroqua.   I. Title.
F589.V57M33   2010
977.5'73—dc22   2009045343

Cornell University Press strives to use environmentally responsible
suppliers and materials to the fullest extent possible in the publishing of
its books. Such materials include vegetable-based, low-VOC inks and
acid-free papers that are recycled, totally chlorine-free, or partly composed
of nonwood fibers. For further information, visit our website at
www.cornellpress.cornell.edu.

Cloth printing   10 9 8 7 6 5 4 3 2 1
Paperback printing   10 9 8 7 6 5 4 3 2 1

This book is dedicated to the people of Viroqua

Contents

ACKNOWLEDGMENTS

This book would not have been written were it not for William Sewell Sr., who appeared in my office one day in 1998 with a map of Wisconsin, spread the map out on my desk, and began circling towns he knew had been included in surveys conducted by members of the University of Wisconsin's sociology and rural sociology departments in the 1940s. He had hoped for a long time, he said, that an ethnographer would someday return to one of these towns and conduct a community study. We talked about the possibility of such a project for a while, and when he turned to go I reminded him to take his map. "Hold on to it," he said. I had not adequately thanked Bill for entrusting me with this project before he passed away in 2001, and frankly, I am not sure I could have found any way to do so had I had more time.

It turned out that there were a number of researchers who studied Viroqua before I did, and I owe them a tremendous debt: Arthur Vidich, Virginia Vidich, Arnold Strickon, Lynne Heasley, Jacob Hundt, and Amy Lake. Robert Jackall and Herbert Lewis alerted me to the existence of the work of the Vidiches and Strickon, respectively, and Dr. Vidich was kind enough to read some chapter drafts. The project received generous financial support from the National Science Foundation (SES 0117753) and the Social Science Research Council Fellowship in the Program on Social Science and the Arts.

Over the years, many mentors and colleagues contributed to the development of this book. I owe a special thanks to Mitch Duneier, who made me realize that I wanted to be an ethnographer in the first place and who nurtured this project early on. His support took diverse forms—from hosting marathon writing sessions in Santa Barbara to calling me from restaurants to tell me that produce from Viroqua was featured on the cover of the menu. Other important influences include Gianpaolo Baiocchi, Kelly Besecke, Japonica Brown-Saracino, Matt Desmond, Jeremy Freese, Art Goldberger, Stephen Kalberg, Paul Lichterman, Doug Maynard, and Erik Wright. Larry Bumpass and Bob Hauser were my advocates at a critical juncture. The participants in the ethnography conferences at the University of California, Los Angeles, in 2001 and the University of Pennsylvania in 2003, particularly Jack Katz and Eli Anderson, were also important in the formative stages of this book. I am grateful for the collegial support of Mary Campbell, Jennifer Eggerling-Boeck, Steve Hitlin, Molly Martin, Alair McLean, Ann Meier, Diane Soles, Kelley Strawn, and Jim Yocom. I have particularly benefitted from feedback from Mike Bell, Nina Eliasoph, Pam Oliver, and Bob Ostergren. Nina Eliasoph and Daniel Monti were instrumental in shaping the final product. I thank my colleagues and administrators at the University of Montana, who made it possible for me to take maternity and research leaves. Ruth Amundsen helped me keep up with current events in Viroqua after I left, and R. Patrick Bixler provided much-needed research assistance. Chris Chekuri inspired the title. Finally, at Cornell University Press I thank acquisitions editor Peter Wissoker, editor in chief Peter Potter, Susan Specter, Katy Meigs, Rachel Post, and the anonymous reviewers.

I am more grateful than I can say for the continuous support of every kind provided by my parents, Alan and Barbara Macgregor, and my sister Nancy Macgregor. This book would have been much less fun to write were it not for my husband Ted Halsted and my daughters, Caroline and Jillian, who make each day a joy.

HABITS OF THE HEARTLAND

INTRODUCTION

Viroqua, population 4,335,[1] sits among the many hills and ridges of southwest Wisconsin's Driftless Area, so called because of the hills left in place when the last wave of Ice Age glaciers passed the area by. Viroqua is the seat of Vernon County, and it lies about twenty miles from the Mississippi River, directly east of the Iowa-Minnesota border on the river's opposite shore. It is a two-hour drive northwest from Madison, Wisconsin's state capital, and three hours from the Twin Cities in Minnesota, though residents advise allowing four hours if you are catching a flight at the St. Paul–Minneapolis airport.

Viroqua's economic history is primarily agricultural, driven until the 1970s by dairy and tobacco farming. While there are still dairy farms in the countryside and a few farmers still line up at the town's tobacco building each winter to sell their bundles of cured leaves, today only about 5 percent

---

1. U.S. Census, 2000.

of the town's rural residents work in agriculture or related fields. Instead, both town and rural residents are employed primarily in health care, education, and other service fields. The median age of residents is about forty-four. Most live modestly. The median family income in 1999 was $35,475 (compared to over $50,000 nationally). But most residents (two-thirds of them) own their own homes, and the rate of families living below the poverty level was 12.4 percent, about the same as the national rate.

In December 2000 I visited Viroqua for the first time, to find out whether it would make an appropriate site for a community study of contemporary small-town life. I moved to Viroqua the following August to begin my research. My time there began and ended with two events of uncanny symmetry that suggested that, despite the franchises and the satellite dishes perched on the roofs of some of the homes, some things about small towns never do change.

Moving Violations

On the first Sunday evening of September 2001, I was making the last in a series of car trips from my former home in Madison. The car was loaded with boxes of books and household items destined for my new home at 322½ Independence Street. As I was driving north on Highway 14 and about fifteen miles south of Viroqua, I was pulled over by a member of the Vernon County sheriff's department, who had noticed that my license plate lacked a current registration sticker. Because the registration had only recently expired, the officer said he was willing to let me off without a ticket, as long as I provided proof to the Sheriff's Office within a week that I had renewed it. To my dismay, he found that I had allowed my driver's license to expire as well. Though he could have taken me to jail for driving without a valid license, the officer kindly stuck to his original plan: I was allowed to go as long as I promised not to drive once I arrived in Viroqua and renewed both the license and registration within a week.

My first response was one of horror, mostly at the idea that my name would appear in the sheriff's report in the next week's issue of the local newspaper, the *Vernon County Broadcaster.* At least, I thought, as I pulled off the road's shoulder and continued on to Viroqua, there was some comfort in the knowledge that I did not yet know anyone there. If my name were listed in the paper, no one would yet be able to connect the violations with me.

Two days later, I went to the optometry department at Viroqua's Wal-Mart Supercenter. A very pleasant woman with blond hair, who appeared to be in her early to mid-twenties, greeted me at the optometry counter, and she located my name on her list of appointments. She repeated my name as if she were thinking aloud, then looked up at me with raised eyebrows and asked, "Did you get pulled over the other night?"

I do not know how well I hid the degree to which her question stunned me. I told her I had, and explained why, attempting to manage my embarrassment by explaining that I had forgotten to make the appropriate renewals in the chaos of moving. Not only was I floored that she knew about the episode, but I could not imagine how she knew about it. The newspaper containing the Sheriff's Report would not even appear until the following afternoon.[2] "How did you know?" I asked her. "I haven't even lived in Viroqua for two days."

"I'm on the ambulance [squad]," she said. "I heard it on the scanner."

"Welcome to Viroqua," I thought to myself, and considered getting back into my illegal car and leaving immediately.

"Everyone knows your business," was a statement that many Viroquans made to me over the course of my time there. It was incidents like these that had compelled me to leave the small Connecticut town in which I was raised for the largest, most urban college campus I could find. Unlike many of the people I met in Viroqua, I did not choose to live there because I longed to return to a small-town community. Viroqua attracted me because it promised to be an interesting case for a community study.

My sociological interest in Viroqua overrode my impulse to flee, though that was not the last time I was tempted to do so. But by the time I did leave two years later, I had also witnessed a number of events illustrating the good that comes from being embedded in small-town social networks. As often as everyone knowing one's business prevented individuals from keeping their troubles secret, it helped them to avoid certain kinds of trouble. It was this side of small-town community that I experienced in my

---

2. Because the officer who pulled me over did not issue an official citation, my name did not appear in the newspaper after all.

next encounter with the law, which occurred while I was in the process of my moving away from Viroqua when my fieldwork was nearly finished.

On the last Sunday afternoon of March 2003, I was driving north on Highway 14 again. This time, I was driving a minivan generously lent to me by one of the families in town I had gotten to know reasonably well.[3] The couple who owned the van were widely known in the community. They were professionals whose jobs brought them into contact with many residents, and they were deeply involved in numerous community and civic activities. This time, I was pulled over for speeding by a Wisconsin state trooper, nearly thirty miles outside Viroqua.

The trooper informed me that I had been going seventy-four miles per hour in a fifty-five mile-per-hour zone. In Wisconsin, this offence carried a $166 fine. Where was I going, the trooper wanted to know, and was there any reason I was driving so fast?

Squinting into the late afternoon sun, I handed over my license. "Independence Street…where's that?" asked the trooper, reading my address on the license. Assuming that the trooper must be familiar with Viroqua to have asked the question this way, I answered that Independence paralleled Highway 56, two blocks north of the Vernon County Courthouse, and I asked if the trooper was familiar with the area.

"I live in Viroqua," the officer responded, and he strode back to the police car to "run" my license and tags. On returning, he asked, "How do you know the [family who owns this car]?" After I explained our connection, the trooper said curtly that I was driving much too fast and that I needed to "drive the limit." He added, "But [the owner of the van] is a friend of mine, and I'm going to let you off with a warning." I signed a form the trooper handed me, and he asked if I had any questions. I did not. "You really deserve a ticket," the officer finished. Then he turned abruptly and stalked back to the patrol car. The parting shot reminded me that I was getting off easy—that I was being singled out to receive exceptional help in staying out of trouble—because of who my friends were.

Again, my first response was embarrassment. I had been driving poorly in a car that was not even mine. My next thought was that I'd prefer that

---

3. Though they may or may not be named elsewhere in this book, I will not identify this family or the trooper because when I returned the van and told the owner this story, she suggested that it might not look good for any of the individuals involved.

the owners of the van not learn about the incident lest they realize they had lent their van to a bad driver. I knew, however, that the incident might come up in conversation if the trooper and the van owners saw each other in town, and it would behoove me to tell the owners about the event myself. The same social connections that were getting me off the hook in one sense kept me on it in another. Luckily, when she heard my story, the van's owner laughed, and joked that she was pleased to learn that she and her husband were the kind of people whose friendship could get people out of speeding tickets.

Small-Town Stuff in the Twenty-First Century

This pair of events illustrated two things everyone thinks they know about small-town social life. First, everyone in a small town knows everyone else's business. It is nearly impossible to get away with anything or keep much private. Second, everyone in a small town knows everyone else, so when one does get away with something, it is because of one's personal connections. Conventional wisdom suggests that the detailed personal knowledge people have of one another is a unique feature of small-town community life—that residents' knowledge of one another plays an important role in integrating individuals into a cohesive social order.

This conventional wisdom extends to sociological thinking about small towns. In his preface to Albert Blumenthal's (1932) study of "Mineville," Montana, E. W. Burgess identified precisely these principles as the essence of small-town life. While the characteristics of particular small towns might vary, he argued:

> The main characteristics of small-town life stand out in clear perspective: close acquaintanceship of everyone with everyone else, the dominance of personal relations, and the subjection of the individual to continuous observation and control by the community. These are essentially what are referred to [by Blumenthal] by the phrase "small town stuff." (Burgess 1932, xii)

Though Burgess's words were over seventy years old, my brushes with the law suggested that they still captured important features of small-town social life.

Such instances of "small-town stuff" as I have just described may seem mundane enough that Viroquans, and perhaps residents of other small towns, will not find them especially telling. They may even find it somewhat obnoxious that an outsider should try to inflate their significance for the sake of making an obvious point and then call it scholarship. People who have less direct experience with small towns may also wonder what the point is. Isn't this sort of thing exactly what one expects in a small town—and, more broadly, in any *real* community?

It is just such assumptions that make small-town life worth investigating. For one thing, we can no longer expect most Americans to have had direct experience with small-town social life. Throughout the nineteenth and well into the twentieth century, most Americans spent at least some part of their lives in rural areas or in small towns in rural areas (Pedersen 1992). By 2000, less than one quarter of the U.S. population lived in places the U.S. Census Bureau classified as rural.[4] Despite this lack of direct experience with rural life, and perhaps because of it, images of small-town and rural life remain "among the most powerful, persistent, and pervasive myths shaping many Americans' sense of their past and national identity" (Pedersen 1992, 3). The power of these images comes from the extent to which they continue to shape the ways that Americans think about communities more generally.

Evidence of the continuing significance of these images of small-town social life is everywhere. As I was beginning the study that led to this book, a cell phone dealer ran a radio advertisement touting its ability to provide customers with "big-city selection and small-town service."[5] The popularity of writers like Garrison Keillor, the storyteller whose radio program "A Prairie Home Companion" put the fictional small town of Lake Wobegon, Minnesota, on the map; the recent explosion of interest in the work of Norman Rockwell, as well as American folk art and bluegrass; and the wide circulation of magazines like *Country Living* testify to a certain amount of longing for small-town life and "stuff."[6] When asked about

---

4. According to the 2000 Census, 21% of the population of the United States lived in rural areas. This statistic includes both metropolitan and nonmetropolitan rural areas.

5. I heard this ad a number of times during September 2000 on WMMM, 105.5 FM, in Madison.

6. A representative of Hearst Magazines, the Iowa-based publisher of *Country Living*, told me that more than 1,300,000 Americans read this magazine each month.

their perceptions of rural life, Americans overwhelmingly describe idealized, even nostalgic, versions, actively rejecting more negative stereotypes
of small towns and rural places and the people who live in them (Willits, Bealer, and Timbers 1990). Though we are surrounded by evidence
that life in small communities is changing—whether they are declining
or booming—we remain focused on a timeless idealization of village life.
Keillor's Lake Wobegon is, after all, "the little town that time forgot and
the decades cannot improve."

These images are not just inert concepts that hang in our cultural air.
They have important ramifications for the ways we think about what constitutes "community" and for the ways we go about making community.
Americans have a long tradition of worrying about the quality of our communities (see Bender 1978; Bellah et al. 1985). We see community as an
essential source of meaning in the lives of individuals yet fear that it has
been depleted by a variety of powerful changes associated with modernity.
These changes—often articulated in terms of concerns about excessive individualism or excessive material consumption, or a focus on private over
public goals—presumably undermine our ability to develop meaningful
ties to other people. The small-town stuff that is the basis of communal
life that Ferdinand Tönnies called *gemeinschaft* has become a benchmark
against which we measure other forms of social order (or any apparent
lack thereof). Like the earliest sociologists and urban planners, we implicitly compare "disorganized" cities and alienating suburbs to our image of
the close-knit relationships that are fashioned from small-town stuff.

We care about community because we believe that communities provide material, social, and even psychological benefits to their members. But
what do we mean by community? Sociologists, psychologists, planners,
and many others have tried endlessly to formulate a definition of community and have not been especially successful (see Hillery 1977; McMillan
and Chavis 1986). In addition to the apparent futility of attempting to formulate a comprehensive definition of community by which we might be
able to measure the "quality" of it at different times and places, there are at
least two major problems with this kind of evaluative approach. First, such
normative projects inevitably draw on and reinforce analytic categories of
community (some familiar examples include urban versus rural, *gemeinschaft* versus *geselleschaft,* face-to-face versus "imagined") that are at best
historically contingent and, at worst, oversimplifications that don't make

much sense in the real world. Second, such measurement approaches to the study of community cannot account for practices outside of the ones their own instruments are designed to capture. We cannot learn much about community, especially about changes in the ways people create communities over time, if we do not take seriously the significance of community to the people we study.

The principal lesson I learned in Viroqua was that there are myriad ways to understand and cultivate community. The town's residents taught me that while traditional ideas about "community," especially as connected with living in a small town, still provided an important organizing logic for peoples' lives, there were a variety of ways to understand community, and a number of ways to go about creating it. Rather than try to evaluate the success of Viroquans' efforts at community, I examined what Viroquans said and did about making their lives together, and used field data to discern what *their* ideas about community were. Drawing on the tools of a cultural approach to community, I investigated how the taken-for-granted ways in which people operated encouraged some forms of individual and collective action while discouraging others. Rather than asking whether residents' community making in Viroqua measured up to some arbitrary definition, I examined the cultures of community in Viroqua and the ways that residents' assumptions about and connections to community enabled and constrained them in a variety of ways.

How does one study cultures of community? Basically, a researcher who studies culture pays careful attention to what people say and do, and the contexts in which they say and do things.[7] She then looks for recurring patterns in these words and deeds. In these patterns, she begins to discern the ideas, meanings, and assumptions that matter to residents, the logics that inform their perceptions of themselves and others, and of the range of actions available to them at any given moment.

When I paid attention to the patterns in what Viroquans said and did, it was clear that Viroquans had differing ideas about how community worked and—more important—how it *ought* to work. These differences in ideas were not unique to individuals: certain constellations of practices and assumptions occurred together, making it relatively likely, for example, that

---

7. For a detailed, technical understanding of the ways I gathered and analyzed data, consult the methodological appendix at the end of this book.

the same Viroquans who did most of their grocery shopping at the Viroqua Food Cooperative enrolled their children at the Pleasant Ridge Waldorf School, while the children of workers at the fertilizer plant attended the local public schools. Taking a cultural approach to questions about how people make community makes it possible to see that the important question is not whether one set of practices results in a version of community that is more authentic or successful than others. Instead, there were at least three principal patterns in the ways that Viroquans approached community. Each was tied to a set of moral orientations toward it, and each came with a specific set of possibilities and constraints. These three orientations were also important markers of social distinction in Viroqua, resulting in the existence of three social groups within the town—groups I came to call the Alternatives, the Main Streeters, and the Regulars.

How do Americans in a small town make community today? I found that despite the continued importance of small-town stuff traditionally associated with face-to-face communities, it makes no sense to think that contemporary technological, economic, and cultural shifts have had no impact on the ways Americans practice community life. Instead, different Viroquans took different approaches to making community that reflected different confluences of moral logics—their senses of obligation to themselves, to their families, to Viroqua, and to the world beyond it, and their views on the importance of exercising personal agency. The biggest surprise was that these ideas about obligation and agency, and specifically about the degree to which it is necessary or good to try to bring one's life into precise conformance with a set of larger goals, turned out to have replaced more traditional markers of social belonging, such as occupation or ethnicity, in separating Viroquans into social groups.

The residents of Viroqua were generous in their willingness to assist me with my research. Nearly everyone I asked graciously allowed me into their places of work, the organizations to which they belonged, and even into their homes and family lives. I hope that in these pages they find their town rendered honestly, and perhaps find some new ways to think about and understand one another.

Of course this book is not just for Viroquans. I hope that other readers will find here ideas that resonate with their experiences in the communities—of all sizes—of which they are a part. I hope that this research provides an example of a way to understand community making that places agents' understandings of it at the forefront of research questions. Doing so allows a researcher to ask about the relative strengths and weaknesses of a variety of styles of community making, and the way different cultures of community sometimes promote cooperation and sometimes create barriers to working together. Such a cultural approach promises to bear more sociological fruit than attempting to measure all communities against an arbitrary standard.

Why Study Viroqua?

Of the thousands of small towns in the United States, why did I choose Viroqua to study? One reason was that it had been studied before. Sociologists from the University of Wisconsin conducted surveys in a number of towns in the state during the late 1930s and early 1940s. Based primarily on survey data, the studies examined a variety of questions about rural life, family background, youths' occupational aspirations, and status attainment.[8]

The towns where surveys were conducted were chosen in part for their ethnic composition, on the logic that families of different ethnic and sociolinguistic backgrounds used different child-rearing methods

8. These studies were precursors to a larger body of work on attainment, including the large ongoing Wisconsin Longitudinal Survey. It would have been ideal to use the original survey data to add to my understanding of Viroqua's residents and history. This was not possible, as the original data were no longer available. A number of dissertations and master's theses based on these studies provided me with an important sense of the social climate of Wisconsin's rural areas seventy years ago. Thanks to Robert Jackall of Williams College, I found one thesis that was not in the University of Wisconsin library archives: an interview study conducted in Viroqua in 1946 by Arthur J. Vidich, who, with coauthor Joseph Bensman, later wrote one of the country's most famous and influential small-town community studies, *Small Town in Mass Society*.

As it turned out, sociologists were not the only people who had studied Viroqua. The late Arnold Strickon, a University of Wisconsin anthropologist who specialized in racial and ethnic identities in South America, also studied Viroqua and surrounding towns in the mid-1970s, though he never published any work based on his research there. His colleague and friend Herbert Lewis alerted me to the extensive collection of field notes, interviews, photographs, and survey data that that he had turned over to the Wisconsin Historical Society on Strickon's death. This archive turned out to be very useful, and I have incorporated some of what I learned from it in this book. I owe an enormous debt to Arnold Strickon's work and to Herbert Lewis, without whom I might not have located it. Finally, just before I arrived in Viroqua, Lynne Heasley, a student in the University of Wisconsin Forestry Department, had completed a dissertation about land use in the Kickapoo Valley area, which was useful.

and transmitted different ideals of success to their children.[9] Most of the surveyed towns were near the city of Madison, but some were sprinkled throughout the state, particularly in areas to the north and west of the university, where, in the 1930s, the researchers found towns with high concentrations of Norwegian, Polish, German, or Italian families. In 1999 William Sewell Sr. of the University of Wisconsin Department of Sociology provided me with a map with circles around the towns where he knew for certain early research had been conducted.

When I investigated the towns that had been included in those surveys, I found that a number would not be suitable sites for an ethnography of a small town, for reasons that reflect some of the broad changes that have affected rural areas across the country. Towns adjacent to Madison, such as Stoughton and Fitchburg, were no longer small towns at all but had mushroomed into suburban bedroom communities for the capital city. There were also a small number of towns from the original studies that had disappeared altogether due to depopulation. If I was going to study a small town to learn about community, I wanted to find the kind of place where we think community is easiest to have—the iconic small town. Viroqua fit the bill perfectly, not only in its appearance, but by its reputation. One of the reasons Viroqua's downtown looked as iconic as it did was because of the enormous efforts that residents had made to preserve and restore it. In the early 1990s, Viroqua became one of the smallest communities to successfully compete for a spot in the state's Main Street Program, the state-level arm of a program run by the National Trust for Historic Preservation. The state did not provide any funds to towns that entered the program, but it did provide access to consultants with expertise in planning, tourism, and architecture. The Main Street Program was just one part of the significant effort made by local residents to keep the downtown vital when Wal-Mart opened a store on the north side of town. Viroqua's relative success drew attention from national media, including *Smithsonian Magazine* and CBS news.

In other words, Viroqua was not a typical small town. It was partly the town's uniqueness that prompted me to select it. Viroqua was known

---

9. Norwegian-American families, for example, were found to encourage children, especially boys, to continue in farming, while German-American families were more likely to encourage boys to seek higher education as a way of attaining a better career.

throughout and beyond Wisconsin for another reason as well. Its growing alternative community and the businesses and institutions it spawned had broad connections across the country. As one of the few Waldorf schools located in a rural area in the United States, Pleasant Ridge was highly visible in the national Waldorf school community. In addition, Viroqua was well known in the Twin Cities and Madison because of the Viroqua-area farmers who sold produce, meats, and cheeses at the farmers markets and food co-ops, and directly to local consumers through community-sponsored agriculture (CSA) programs. The same farms provided ingredients to restaurants such as L'Etoile and Harvest in Madison, whose nationally known owners and chefs were leaders in the Slow Food movement. This movement, which began in the 1970s, aimed at developing a socially and environmentally responsible cuisine based on locally grown, organic seasonal foods from small farms.[10] Some of Viroqua's farmers had themselves developed national reputations as family-farm activists and as leaders in the community of small-scale organic farmers.

There was lots going on in Viroqua. How was it that Viroqua was able to not only retain but increase the number of jobs in its downtown and maintain the size of its hospital and other local institutions when other small towns were losing theirs altogether? How could the population of a small town support a public school, a Waldorf school, a Christian school, and have a large home-schooling community as well? How did this small town manage to refurbish its old theater? To build an expensive community amenity such as an indoor ice rink?

Viroqua's residents were getting things done, and they seemed to be accomplishing a variety of tasks that usually cannot be accomplished by individuals but must be the result of collective—that is communal—efforts. I wanted to study how Americans made community, and Viroqua was clearly a place where people were getting things done together. More interestingly, it was also clear that it was a complicated place—which I later learned was attributable in part to the variety of styles of community that residents pursued.

---

10. Odessa Piper opened L'Etoile in 1976. Jeff Orr and Tami Lax, both former L'Etoile employees, opened Harvest in 2000. Lax has been a principle organizer of area chapters of Slow Food. Founded in Italy, Slow Food is an international organization that promotes sustainably produced foods and local food traditions.

Part I

Cultures of Community

The first feature of Viroqua to make a deep impression on me was the larger-than-life fiberglass bull that stared sternly out over drivers on Highway 14 as they entered the town from the south. The bull advertised what was, at the time of my first visit in December 2000, a restaurant called Ricky's. Passing the bull and heading into the downtown proper, I passed the VFW hall on the right, the Century 21 real estate office on the left and, shortly after that, the Latter-day Saints church, the optometry office, the Vernon County Historical Society Museum, and Vernon Memorial Hospital, before entering the designated historic section of the downtown. These two blocks of Main Street were lined with brick one- and two-story buildings that housed shops at the street level with apartments and offices above. The first block was home to Gary's Rock Shop, Dairyland Printing, Clark/Peterson Motors, Dahl Pharmacy, Buzzy's Furniture and Buzzy's Country across the street (specializing in "country"-style furnishings and décor), and a long, low building housing an IGA supermarket that later became a branch of the Western Wisconsin Technical College. At the end of this block, a traffic light stopped travelers at the intersection of Highway 14 and Jefferson Street. A right on Jefferson led to Viroqua's post office and the MacIntosh Public Library.

Continuing north on Main Street, I passed Rockweiller Appliance, the Bramble Press bookstore, Bonnie's Wedding Center, Art Vision, two banks (Citizens First Bank and the Bank of Virginia), and the Viking Inn restaurant. Across the street were the Temple Theatre, the Common Ground coffee shop, Box Office Video, Center Stage clothing, a second-hand shop called Second Time Around, Felix's clothing store, and Soda Jo's diner. The marquee over the Temple Theatre heralded a film festival to raise money for the theater's $2 million renovation that was eventually completed in 2002. The city's second traffic light stopped me at the intersection with State Highways 56 and 82. Taking a right on Highway 82 leads the traveler to the parking lot of Nelson's Agri-Center and the American Legion hall and bar. Turning around and following Highway 56 in the other direction took me toward the courthouse and the public schools and into the residential neighborhood where I would eventually live.

The afternoon that I visited Viroqua for the first time, I ate lunch at Soda Jo's diner, which then occupied the space that later housed Bella Luna, an Italian restaurant. The waitresses at Soda Jo's wore saddle shoes, and they sometimes sang along with the oldies broadcast over the restaurant's sound system. The walls were cluttered with 1950s and 1960s memorabilia, including 45 records and LP album jackets. A pair of penny loafers was affixed to the wall at the bottom of a pair of black pants and a white T-shirt that were stapled to the wall in a way that suggested a two-dimensional dancer frozen in mid Twist.

After finishing my slice of banana cream pie and paying the waitress at the diner's vintage cash register, I stepped outside and spent a moment surveying Viroqua's main street. I was struck, as I would be again and again, by the quintessential Midwest downtown aura of the shop fronts, the knots of laughing kids, and the patient dogs lounging in the backs of parked pickup trucks. The lunchtime crowd was slowly trickling out of the diner and out of the Viking Inn, diagonally across the street. A little girl struggled to pile into a minivan with her older siblings while remaining in command of a dripping ice cream cone. Down the street a Buick sedan pulled into the IGA parking lot (by the building that later became the Tech College). Its elderly driver alighted and made his way around the car's wide front end to open the passenger-side door for a woman I assumed to be his wife.

On the surface at least, Viroqua had the timeless character that many Americans associate with small towns. The pastiche of historic eras represented in the downtown by features like the reproduction 1930s lamps lining the street, the 1920s theater, and the 1950s diner did not give the sensation of stagnation in any particular era. Instead, it gave the impression of stepping out of time, and suggested that time was perhaps not the most important consideration there. Timelessness is an important feature of the way Americans think about small towns, especially those in the Midwest. The rest of the world may be cruising down the fast lane, but the small towns of the heartland never seem to be in any such hurry.

A visitor might be able to maintain this illusion of timelessness if he or she did not continue traveling north, past the downtown area, where there are familiar franchise restaurants and stores: Country Kitchen, Pizza Hut, McDonalds, Wal-Mart. There is also an entrance to the town's industrial park and to the large steel building housing a National Cash Register company factory that specialized in producing labels.

In this book I examine the variety of ways that the citizens of this quintessential yet unique small Midwestern town make community together. The first four chapters, which make up part 1, explore in depth the three principle orientations that Viroquans had to making community and how differences in the fundamental commitment to Viroqua itself and the sense that community is something to deliberately create led to important social distinctions. These differences also led to residents having different sets of practices as community members in an everyday sense. In chapter 1 I present an overview of the three different groups I encountered in Viroqua and the ways they celebrated a major cultural holiday. I begin looking at the groups in more detail in chapter 2 with a consideration of those I call the Alternatives, not because they are the most important residents, or even the largest group of residents, but because they were so visible as a group and their presence was somewhat surprising. In chapters 3 and 4 I analyze the cultures of community in the Main Street and Regular groups respectively.

In part 2 I examine the ways that residents' different ideas about community manifest themselves in a number of aspects of commercial life.

Viroquans' ethics of agency and logics of commitment guided their actions when it came to mundane decisions about exchanging goods and services, and in these arenas we can see how the different models of making community played out in everyday life.

The book's concluding chapter examines some of the opportunities and constraints each group faced in Viroqua. It extends the idea that community making anywhere might be fruitfully understood through cultural analysis of the logics of commitment and ethics of agency.

1

Three Halloweens, Three Viroquas

By three-thirty in the afternoon, it was nearly impossible to walk down Main Street without being poked by a witch's broomstick or swatted with a fairy's magic wand. Small Spider-Men darted among ghosts wearing plastic *Scary Movie* masks with flashing red lights. A giggling chain of Snow Whites and Cinderellas snaked out of Felix's clothing store holding hands and ran (as fast as possible considering the crowds) up the sidewalk to the next store on the block. The sidewalks were swarming with children of all ages, including some teenagers. It was a scene of unmitigated collective glee.

The kids did not seem to care (or even notice) that many other kids were dressed in Halloween costumes identical to their own. When two Incredible Hulks passed each other on the sidewalk, they did not even glance at each other. The vast majority of children were wearing store-bought costumes representing familiar commercial characters. The Snow Whites were obviously Snow Whites because their costumes evoked Disney's animated Snow White. Children did vary in the degree to which their parents had mandated concessions to the late-fall temperatures, so some of the Hulks' "muscles" were clearly augmented by sweaters, while others remained lean. Costume originality, however, was not the point of the event. Candy was.

Some of the Main Street business owners who were on hand to provide the candy attempted to keep the hordes of marauding trick-or-treaters out of their stores by standing just outside the entrances of their shops to distribute it. They looked a little like trees hanging tenuously onto the banks of a river flooding with X-Men, Bob the Builders, and Dora the Explorers and in danger of being swept under at any moment. At other shop entrances, eddies of children formed where they entered and hustled out as quickly as possible to move on to the next shop for more treats. Some of the adults were dressed in costumes. Most, however, were wearing workaday clothes but had added signifiers of costumes, such as rubber noses or funny hats.

Like many cities and towns across the country, Viroqua had attempted to bring some order to the Halloween ritual of trick-or-treating both for children's safety and to try to curb the potential for chaos on a holiday that sometimes invited rule breaking. The planned and advertised Halloween celebration on Main Street served an additional purpose: it was one of a number of events throughout the year designed by the Viroqua Partners, a group formed when the Chamber of Commerce and the Viroqua Revitalization Association merged in 1995. In order to promote local businesses, the Partners organization was always looking for ways to bring residents into the downtown to have a good time, with the ultimate goal of encouraging them to think of the downtown and the shops located there as the heart of the community.

But Main Street's was not the only public observance of Halloween in town. After watching the activity there for a while, I went home and donned my own Halloween costume[1] and went to meet Bjorn Leonards, a furniture maker, and his wife Brie Lamers, an artist, who were taking their two kids to what turned out to be a rather different Halloween event. As we walked from their house on Rock Street toward the Landmark Center, Brie explained that the event we were about to attend had

---

1. I used a red-and-white hat and a rubber cat nose to suggest Dr. Seuss's Cat in the Hat.

been spearheaded largely by Paula Greneier, a chiropractor and parent of children who attended Pleasant Ridge Waldorf School.[2] "She thought we should try to make Halloween about something other than just kids eating tons of junk food," Brie explained from behind a clown-size pair of cat's-eye glasses, which she was wearing with a silver dress, go-go boots, and a pair of wings made of fabric and wire. As we neared the Landmark Center building, we could see lots of other kids and parents, almost all in home-made costumes.

As on Main Street, there were princesses and witches and ghosts, but there were also pirates and gypsies and woodcutters and armored knights and parrots and farmers. It was not always easy to tell exactly what some of the children's costumes represented, as they were clearly the work of the children themselves. Adults took advantage of such ambiguities to engage children in conversation. Exclaimed one woman to a little girl wearing a bright dress (several sizes too big) along with many strands of plastic beads and a winter hat made of synthetic fleece, "You look great! Tell me about your costume!" The woman had knelt down on the ground to the child's eye level, and though they were standing too far away for me to hear the child's response, I was struck by the little girl's poise and the confidence with which she addressed this adult who was not her parent.

Three parents were collecting donations of a dollar per person in front of the Landmark Center, a three-story brick building that had once housed Viroqua's public high school. The building was now owned by Nancy Rhodes, a local businesswoman who had purchased the building from the city in hopes of preserving it by finding new uses for it. She had turned the

---

2. Developed by Austrian Rudolf Steiner (1861–1925) after the First World War, Waldorf education is premised on Steiner's belief in the need for a type of education that engages the child's spirit, body, and mind in a manner appropriate to each of three developmental stages: early childhood, when adults must cultivate an environment that encourages children to imitate desirable tasks and behaviors; middle childhood, when children develop cognitive skills through the use of their imagination; and adolescence, when the young adult emerges as an individual capable of thinking and acting independently while retaining the curiosity and sense of wonder cultivated earlier. Ideally, classroom teachers remain with their students from first through eighth grade on the assumption that doing so cultivates a sense of community among students and their parents. Steiner hoped that an experiential type of learning that developed children's imaginations, cognitive abilities, and a sense of themselves as spiritual beings would become the basis for social and cultural renewal in the modern world. Though Steiner and the approach he developed have critics, there are currently 800 Waldorf Schools in forty countries around the world, 150 of which are in North America.

old gymnasium into a health club and had rented out much of the rest of the space. The Landmark Center housed a Waldorf kindergarten, several offices (including the Greneiers' chiropractic practice), and the Youth Initiative High School, a high school with a Waldorf-inspired curriculum. YIHS was founded by graduates of the Pleasant Ridge Waldorf School, which was located next door in the midcentury building that was once Viroqua's public elementary school. Paula Greneier was dressed in a green hat, tights, and tunic. We formed a group with about fifteen other adults and kids who had arrived at the same time, and Paula explained that she would lead us to an enchanted forest. We followed her a block and a half to the wooded lot that the Pleasant Ridge school had purchased to use as an outdoor classroom.

The forest had indeed been enchanted, thanks to Pleasant Ridge's seventh and eighth graders. These older students were dressed in costumes and stationed throughout the property, acting out fairy tales and handing out treats to the younger children. As we followed a path through the trees, a student dressed as a troll emerged from beneath a small wooden bridge and explained theatrically that she was waiting for some Billy Goats Gruff, and asked the smaller children in our group if they had seen any. When the younger children replied that they had not, the troll said they had better have treats to help them on their journey through the woods. Reaching into a cloth bag, she gave every child a homemade peanut butter cookie.

A few moments later, a teenage bear emerged from behind a tree and handed out small tubes filled with honey. Periodically, a singing gingerbread man would run by, followed momentarily by an old lady who, true to the fairy tale, never caught her gingerbread man. The children eventually received edible gingerbread men of their own, however. In another part of the forest, another four students acted out the Swiss Family Robinson's life in a tree house. At the end of the trail through the forest, children were invited to select a small pumpkin to take home that was donated by a local farm. Back indoors, the final element of the event was a complex play put on by a small group of adults and children using traditional Asian shadow puppets.

This group of parents and students had produced an alternative to the Main Street Halloween celebration. While the events on Main Street were planned in part with an eye toward improving Viroqua's downtown, this second celebration attempted to improve on Halloween itself by downplaying the importance of store-bought costumes and candy and shifting the focus to kids' creating their own fun from scratch together with adults. Bjorn, Brie, their kids, and I started a slow walk back toward their home, stopping at the homes of some of their friends whose doors were open. We ate in each one: one served hot cider and handed out fresh apples; at another we ate slices of homemade bread with jam.

I also knew of children who did not participate in either organized event. The day after Halloween, I was at my part time job, tending bar at the American Legion. I asked a patron I knew only by his first name, Mark, a father of school-age children, if his kids had enjoyed the Halloween festivities. He explained that it was just too much of a hassle to get the kids home from school and then take them right back into town again for the trick-or-treating on Main Street. Mark worked at a local muffler manufacturing plant, where employees worked ten-hour shifts four days a week. Mark seemed unaware of the Enchanted Forest event, and the timing of trick-or-treating on Main Street was a problem for his family. It occurred just when he was coming home and trying to get a few things done around the house, while his wife was trying to make dinner, and, he added, the kids didn't need more candy anyway. His niece and nephews had brought over lots of candy, and the kids' grandma brought over a fair amount of it too. So at his house, Halloween was observed informally and privately. Mark's kids, their cousins, and some neighbor children ran around in their costumes, "high on sugar," and had a good time without going back into town right before dinner.

The public celebration of rituals reveals a great deal about the celebrants and the communities in which they live. There were at least three different approaches to the observance of Halloween in Viroqua, and each reflected a different way of producing community there. On one hand, the Main Street event was designed not only with the goal of marking Halloween, but with the idea of bolstering public attachment to the downtown and its commercial establishments. The event had required planning, advertising, and coordination among merchants, police, and concerned residents who believed that, for a number of reasons, it was not in anyone's interest for Halloween to remain unorganized. The result was an event that had the added bonus of bringing attention to the downtown.

Just three blocks away, members of the Pleasant Ridge Waldorf School community had gone all out to produce a Halloween event that shifted the focus of the event away from what its organizers saw as an excessive focus on unhealthy kinds of consumption. The idea was that with some creativity and elbow grease, the holiday could be celebrated in a way that would be fun both for children and adults and better than the typical observance of Halloween, because of its focus on creative activities. The event downplayed not only candy (replacing it with healthier treats) but the trappings of mass culture as well—such as Disney characters—and emphasized the homemade over the mass-produced.

There were probably some children who attended both of these events, but I did not see any. There seemed to be relatively little overlap in attendance. And in addition, for families like Mark's, it was enough just to let the children enjoy candy and costumed play at home with extended family and friends who gathered at the house spontaneously. Such observances of Halloween still brought family and neighbors together, but in a way that did not require much, if any, advance planning. In Mark's view, things didn't need to be complicated for kids to have fun—life was busy enough, and kids were good at making fun on their own.

Viroquans all shared some basic ideas about Halloween. Everyone assumed that the purpose of the event was primarily for children to have fun. Having fun entailed treats and costumes, but the nature of the treats and costumes differed. So, while lots and lots of families in Viroqua celebrated Halloween, they did not all celebrate it in the same ways. The public celebrations were executed by two distinct groups of people in town. Both invested a significant amount of planning and work in their events. One of these groups, the group responsible for the Main Street event, made the investment in part with a view toward what they thought would be good for Viroqua. The other group, a group largely, if loosely, connected to the Pleasant Ridge Waldorf School, had another kind of good in mind, one that had less to do with Viroqua per se and more to do with a larger set of goals related to raising children in ways calculated to combat "mainstream" culture, including televised entertainment and junk food. Finally, some Viroquans eschewed the formally organized events altogether, deeming them unnecessarily complicated ways of meeting the principle goal of kids' enjoyment.

The variety of ways that Viroqua's families observed Halloween exemplified a pattern I observed in the town over and over, and not only in relation to holiday rituals. Just as everyone shared some basic ideas about the meaning of Halloween, all the residents of Viroqua I knew agreed on some basic features of Viroqua that they valued—the sense of safety, the slow-lane lifestyle, the area's natural beauty. Many Viroquans, especially those I met at events like the Main Street and Enchanted Forest events, said they valued the sense of community. Indeed, these are the kinds of features that many Americans associate with small-town life. But just as the various Halloween observances reflected different ideas about the amount of work required to successfully celebrate the holiday and about a larger framework of goals that guided the planning of each event, the town's residents had different ways of producing and accessing a sense of community. They had different ideas about what community was, and how it ought to be made, and different ways of making it. These differences were the basis of some important social distinctions that played a very important role in organizing social life in Viroqua. The minimum of three communities in Viroqua was especially evident at moments like Halloween, when the occurrence of more than one celebration of the same event made Viroqua seem like "a mosaic of little worlds that touch but do not interpenetrate" (Park 1967, 40) that one would expect to find in an urban context.

Even though we more often associate such subcultural diversity with city life, it was not a complete surprise to find that one small town contained groups of people who lived rather different lives. Historically, the "structured diversity" (Varenne 1977) of American small towns has accommodated diverse populations, such that how one lived and who one knew in a small town was determined by a variety of social distinctions. Extant studies of small towns and the rural communities surrounding them provide numerous examples of the ways single towns often contained a number of distinct communities coexisting as parallel or overlapping worlds. Not surprisingly, the social distinctions in small towns that have been most studied have tended to be the social categories about which social scientists have long been concerned: race, ethnicity, national or sociolinguistic groups, and religion. In the upper Midwest, the latter two were particularly important for determining social groups within small towns (Pedersen 1992; Lingeman 1980).[3] In some small towns, especially in places that

---

3. Historically, the sources of meaningful social distinction have varied by region in the United States. In many parts of the upper Midwest, groups of primarily white immigrants formed segregated communities within new townships creating parallel sets of institutions: within one

have recently experienced waves of in-migration, such categories continue to inform social order (see Bloom 2000).

Another conventional distinction associated with small towns is the newcomer/old-timer distinction, which has often coincided with ethnic, religious, and racial lines. In addition to recurring in scholarly literatures on community (Bell 1994; Salamon 2003; Brown-Saracino 2004; Zukin 1982), numerous works of fiction and factual memoirs about American small towns provide examples of the difficulties individual newcomers have fitting in with old-timers, or the degree to which old-timers' way of life disappears if large numbers of newcomers overwhelm them. Their arrival in a small community makes them conspicuous, and old-timers are stereotypically puzzled by, if not openly hostile to, different habits or ideas newcomers bring (see Lewis 1980; Norris 1993), particularly in cases where entire groups of newcomers arrive in existing communities and are perceived to be quite different from longtime residents (Bloom 2000; Bell 1994). But, while it was clear that there were some distinct social groups in Viroqua, the familiar kinds of social distinctions listed above simply were not useful for understanding the ones that mattered. I shall consider a number of these in turn, and then suggest a set of categories that better fits this case.

The distinctions that separated Viroquans were not racial distinctions: Vernon County is, according to the 2000 Census, 98.8 percent white. This

---

town, German Lutherans and Norwegian Lutherans established separate churches and schools in which they spoke their own language. Members of extended families often purchased adjoining farm parcels, resulting in ethnic concentrations within single townships. In the days before automobiles and improved roads, the relative difficulty of transportation meant that social distinctions and spatial distinctions reinforced each other. Farm neighborhoods required their own general stores, creameries, and mills, so the neighbors one met in such public places were likely to be of similar origins. As in the South, each community within the township was likely to have parallel sets of leaders, more and less successful (wealthy) families, and networks of mutual assistance. In town, ethnicity also took on spatial dimensions, resulting in small-town ghettos analogous to larger urban ethnic neighborhoods. Class and occupational status tended to be more important in early New England communities, for example, where lands tended to be settled by existing groups of people who arrived together and established a town on a specified tract of land. The boundaries of townships in the Midwest and West were often laid out by federal statute prior to any settlement. Promoters and speculators who bought large tracts of land could only realize profits by selling plots to a willing buyer, so it was far more likely that a legal unit like a township would contain settlers of a variety of ethnic backgrounds, as well as adventurous or dissatisfied Yankees. Of course the legacy of slavery in the South has meant that race has been and continues to be a central organizing feature of social life there (Dollard 1957).

is not to say that racial categories were meaningless in Viroqua, they just were not important for understanding the distinctions Viroquans made among themselves. Residents sometimes indicated that racial categories were salient in their thinking about people who lived outside their own town, as, for example, when residents debated the possibility of a poultry plant locating in the town in 2001. A principle source of concern was that the plant might attract poor Hispanic workers, as such plants had in other communities, including nearby Norwalk, Wisconsin.

Similarly, though I met many people in the area who proudly declared that their heritage was "one hundred percent Norwegian," and the neighboring town of Westby was famous for its annual Syttende Mai celebration,[4] there was little evidence that ethnicity or national origin served as a significant source of social distinction among Viroquans. As early as the mid-1970s, many Viroquans said that the importance of ethnicity in determining who their friends were was declining.[5] Like many Americans who identify themselves as racially white, Viroquans tended to treat ethnicity as a voluntary matter of personal preference or pride (Waters 1990). I encountered few people in the area who were not native English speakers, and most of those who were not had recently emigrated from Europe.[6] Though many longtime residents could have used ethnicity and claims to Norwegian heritage to cultivate a sense of exclusivity—an identity that most newcomers could not claim—I saw no evidence they did so.

Churches were still important loci of social life for many Viroquans, but religious affiliation itself was not a social distinction that trumped any others. Of the Viroquans I interviewed who belonged to churches, many said that church was one of the principle places where they got to know other residents, and sometimes even where they made most of their friends. At the same time, the prevailing attitude toward church membership was summed up aptly by the admonition that appeared weekly in the Community Calendar section of the *Vernon County Broadcaster,* which under

---

4. Syttende Mai (May Seventeenth) is the most important national holiday in Norway. It commemorates the adoption of a national constitution on May 17, 1814.

5. According to unpublished data drawn from a survey conducted by anthropologist Arnold Strickon.

6. During my fieldwork, I met an immigrant from Germany who lived in Viroqua, as well as one each from France, Switzerland, Bulgaria, and Iceland, who lived in surrounding towns.

Sunday's heading said, "Worship at the church of your choice." As one resident put it, even for people to whom religion was important, "they don't care where you go [to church], they just want you to go."

While a handful of residents mentioned class in a strict socioeconomic sense as a source of the social distinctions that mattered to them, even my earliest data suggested that economic class and social distinction in Viroqua were not always neatly related. Income alone did not capture much of what mattered when people described themselves in relation to other residents. In addition, I observed that many Viroquans had friends and associates from socioeconomic classes other than their own. The influence of class as a source of social distinction operated in a more diffuse manner than might be expected based on the existing literature on small towns.

Initially, it seemed that the only familiar set of social categories that made sense was the newcomer/old-timer distinction. Indeed, Viroquans themselves used it often. Said one long-time resident, "There are parallel societies in Viroqua....One are the transplants, the other are the natives." The problem, however, was that when Viroquans used newcomer/old-timer categories, it seemed they usually did not mean simply whether or not someone was raised in the town. The categories of "newcomers" and "old-timers," or "transplants" and "natives," was a shorthand way of alluding to groups within the town that did not actually say very much about what really made them different from each other or why distinctions among them persisted. As one self-described "native" explained to me, there were plenty of people in Viroqua who didn't grow up there (and as such, were newcomers) who *acted* like natives. They joined existing religious and civic organizations, made friends with longtime residents, and after a period of time, became indistinguishable from "natives." In addition, there were also some lifelong residents who were deeply involved in organizations associated with "newcomers."

A patron of the American Legion bar where I worked illustrated the trickiness of these categories when he complained one evening about the influx of newcomers. It was one in the morning, and Dave was my only customer. While he talked, I picked up a damp rag and started wiping down the bar, nodding from time to time to show that I was listening. I'd heard this speech from him before, as well as variations on the theme from others in the group of men that often stopped in for beers with Dave at the end of the day shift at the Howard Johnson fertilizer plant, four blocks east of the Legion (the same plant where, Dave laughed, he had "quit five times, been fired twice, and still work[ed]").

He continued, "You know, I don't have a problem with the people who come here from cities because they want to raise their kids in a small town. I wouldn't want to raise my kids in Milwaukee or Chicago either. But as soon as they get here, they want to bring the city with them, and they start complaining that there's not enough *culture.*" He wrinkled his nose as he said the word. "And they want a fancy eating place, and they want to change everything. They don't see that that's just not the way of life here. They want everything the way *they* want it."

As a lifelong resident of the area, Dave felt that his way of life and "heritage" were threatened by the desire of newcomers to "bring the city with them." Newcomers' sense that the town could be molded into something other than what it was offended Dave's sense of what Viroqua was really like. In addition to illustrating the persistence of the use of categories like "rural" and "urban" for organizing ideas about different ways of life in the United States,[7] Dave's comments illustrated the complexity underlying the newcomer/old-timer distinction as it played itself out in Viroqua. Dave saw residents with ambitions of changing the town in ways he found distasteful as quite different from himself, and couched those differences in terms of a combination of a rural-urban distinction and one between newcomers and old-timers. The way that Dave and many other Viroquans used these categories belied the fact that many of the projects that troubled him, such as revitalizing and promoting the downtown by bringing more "culture" to it, were generally not spearheaded by newcomers but by residents with lifelong ties to the area. The residents who headed the Temple Theatre's restoration and pushed for historic preservation of many buildings in the downtown were not primarily newcomers. They did tend to be residents with more education and more professional kinds of jobs than Dave had, but they shared with Dave a sense that their personal heritage was inextricably intertwined with Viroqua and its history. The newcomer/old-timer distinction that many Viroquans used masked a difference in class status between working-class families like Dave's and middle- and upper-middle class Viroquan families who had taken charge

---

7. This is not an exclusively American phenomenon. Bell (1999) found the same thing in his research in a British village.

of, for example, preserving and renovating the historic buildings in the downtown.

A Taste for Community

Of course, simple social categories are always more complex than they seem, but the way people apply them tells us something about how they make sense of the world around them and their place in it. Dave's deployment of these categories revealed something important, even though he was not strictly accurate. People in Viroqua had some very different ideas about what made for a good town and good community. For people like Dave and like Mark, whose kids celebrated Halloween at home, living in a good community was related to a judgment that an authentic small town community was one in which people had real (that is, long-term or kinship) ties to one another, and where people did authentically rural things, not one where "city" stuff had been imported, or worse, imposed where it didn't belong. For other Viroquans, such as the members of the Viroqua Partners group who organized some of the projects that made Dave wary, having a good community was connected to ideas about working to make the town a good place—a better place than it already was. For the folks who organized and attended the Enchanted Forest, creating community in a small town was about living out one's social and political values with other people who shared them. It wasn't quite about making Viroqua better necessarily, but making things better for themselves, their children, and in some sense for society.

To think about what is good or right for people or for communities is to contemplate some deep moral questions. A great deal of what made Viroquans different from one another were matters of morality and tastes for different kinds of community-making (Bourdieu 1987). This seems consistent with ongoing discussions in national public life about whether Americans are significantly divided by their moral ideas. In the 1980s and 1990s, scholars and pundits debated the existence of a "culture war" in the United States. More recently, a similar discussion arose in the wake of the presidential elections of 2000 and 2004 about whether there are two Americas, one Red and one Blue. Red America was more religious, more concerned about issues like prohibiting gay marriage and ending abortion, and voted

Republican. Blue America was home to cosmopolitan liberal Democrats and Greens, who tended to have more education and more money, and who were more likely to care about the environment, health care, and education.

Consistent with the work of other sociologists, I found that moral boundaries play an important role in the ways that Americans draw distinctions among themselves (Lamont 1992). In Viroqua, the Red and the Blue existed side by side.[8] The town that developed a reputation for having, as one resident put it, "an herbalist on every corner" was the same town where controversy erupted in 2004 when a gay couple were slated to make a presentation at the public high school's Diversity Day program.[9] I heard Viroquans themselves reference the Red-Blue categories at times, and I believe these categories seemed compelling to them, as they were to other Americans, because the dichotomy tapped into a set of cultural distinctions that we find meaningful. These distinctions manifest themselves at the polls and in other places, such as in patterns of consumption and recreation. They appear in the different styles with which each group engages in similar activities: Blue Americans go fly fishing, while Red Americans fish for bass. Blue Americans drive foreign cars, while Red Americans choose domestic ones. Blue Americans go cross-country skiing, while Red Americans go snowmobiling.

It is certainly not news that Americans' preferences and tastes tend to occur in patterned ways. Marketing researchers have capitalized on the "clustering" of consumer preferences and identities (Weiss 1989, 2000) for a long time. Viroquans themselves often pointed to consumption patterns as a way of making sense of what made Viroquans different from one another. For example, one resident who considered himself "a native" (despite

---

8. The split is reflected in Vernon County's voting patterns in the last three national elections, in which Democratic and Green votes were slightly higher than for the rest of the state.

9. A group of parents approached the school board with a petition opposing the inclusion of the gay couple, and the school board's initial response was to cancel Diversity Day outright. When a white supremacist organization praised the cancellation on its website, another group of parents gathered signatures asking for the reinstatement of the event with the gay speakers. They pointed out that the panels and speakers at the event were all options from which students could choose—students would not be forced to hear particular speakers to whom they or their parents objected. In the end, the school board reinstated the event. Following the controversy, a private group of parents and students began organizing Diversity Day on a biannual basis. It is no longer directly supported by the school.

the fact that he was raised in another part of Wisconsin and knew Viroqua as a child only through visits to family there) talked about the number of new people moving into Viroqua. I asked him who they were. Like most Viroquans (including Dave, as we saw earlier), he puzzled over how to characterize Viroqua's newcomers and finally said, "[Recently] I went into the [People's] Food Co-op [in La Crosse] to get a sandwich . . . and I was realizing how out of place I felt in that food co-op. They didn't have any of the junk food I was used to."

"Like what?" I asked.

"Like my normal brands of Frito-Lay, the huge multinational companies that produce the stuff none of us really need. But the kind of stuff you'd see in the Kwik Trips,[10] which I'm very familiar with. And so maybe the people in the food co-op, if that's their regular [shopping] place, maybe those are like the people moving to Viroqua."

Material markers and practices such as the selection of foods really stood out to Viroquans as a way they could make some sense of their differences from one another. A second example came from one of the families I had seen at the Enchanted Forest on Halloween, who also pointed to food as something that distinguished them from their "native" neighbors, but then qualified their answer. "I think we probably eat differently from [our neighbors], but, I don't know—I mean, I bet the dinner at [our neighbors' home] is healthier than the dinner at my brother's house in suburban [large city in the Midwest]. Oh, wait—that's off the record. I mean, my *friend's* brother's house," the speaker laughed. The difference to this Viroquan was that even her "local" neighbors probably ate more fresh foods from their own farm gardens and other local producers than the processed or prepared foods she imagined other Americans eating.

Another family, one that ran an organic dairy farm, made similar references to food when they described the home-based babysitter their toddler went to two days each week to make it easier for his mother to continue to work part time from home. "We love how [the day-care provider] is with the kids," said the mom. "And the other kids who go there are not in families we would normally meet." The toddler's father agreed that the

---

10. Kwik Trip is a chain of gas stations and convenience stores with locations in Wisconsin, Minnesota, and Iowa. Viroqua has two Kwik Trips, one on the southern edge of the downtown area, and one on the northern edge. The north-side Kwik Trip is open twenty-four hours.

day-care provider took wonderful care of her charges. He added, "[Our child] eats a lot of stuff over there he doesn't get at home—that kid food, like hot dogs and chicken nuggets. But I guess we can't protect him from stuff like that forever. There's just some stuff like that you can't be so up-tight about and have to let go of." I knew plenty of Viroquans who would have agreed that hot dogs and chicken nuggets were foods they'd prefer that their children not eat. But I also knew many families for whom they were regular fare.

My own experiences supported the notion that Viroquans' practices having to do with getting and eating food illuminated some basic differences between groups of residents. Electric countertop deep fryers were common kitchen appliances in the homes of some Viroquans I knew. But when I mentioned this to other acquaintances, they laughed, and said that having deep-fried food every day was "the grossest thing [they] could think of." When I ate pasta at the home of Arvid and Sheryl Bakkestuen, whose family treated me as if I were one of them for my entire stay in town, it was served with tomato and meat sauce. A can of condensed mushroom soup was added to the sauce, making it the creamiest meat sauce I had ever eaten. We sprinkled powdery Parmesan cheese on top of our pasta, and also on our squares of buttery garlic toast. We ate our pasta while we watched the Green Bay Packers start strong but ultimately lose an exciting game on the family's large-screen television.

Bjorn and Brie, who moved to Viroqua largely so their children might attend Pleasant Ridge Waldorf School when they reached school age, did not have a TV that could be used as such. They had an older television and a VCR they used to watch movies, but the TV was not equipped to pick up broadcast programming. "Watching a movie is one thing," Bjorn once explained to me. "You have to decide to do it. It's not just there all the time, and you can just waste a bunch of time on it. You go and rent [a movie] and [after you watch it] it's over." Television did not occupy much of their family's spare time, and dinnertime was a time to be together and talk, not to watch TV.[11]

---

11. Avoiding broadcast TV was a common practice among Viroqua's Alternatives, who are discussed in detail later in the chapter. Indeed, Pleasant Ridge had a school policy suggesting that parents prohibit children from watching TV or using computers during the school week. A student at YIHS who read a draft of this chapter reported laughing when he read this section. "Yeah," he said, "that was one thing that you always wanted to do at other kids' houses, public school kids, was try to watch TV since you weren't allowed to at home."

When I ate pasta at their house, it was served with fresh vegetables sautéed in olive oil and garlic and with a salad made with homemade vinaigrette dressing and pieces of organic goat cheese on the side.[12] Bjorn, Brie, and I all took turns helping prepare the food and playing with their two children, Gianna and Luka. When it was time to eat, we sat down at the long oak farm table that Bjorn had carefully restored. Brie dimmed the lights and then lit candles on the table. We remained at the table sipping wine and talking long after we were done eating our food.

It is notable that, in groping for ways to explain what differentiated them from others, a number of Viroquans mentioned food, and my observations confirmed that the ways that Viroquans related to food seemed quite different in many respects. Practices having to do with food provided tangible examples of differences that residents (and an ethnographer) could see and name when it came to talking about social distinctions in the town. But what did these variations in practices around food really say about the underlying differences between these groups of people? First, we might begin by saying that the most socially meaningful categories of people in Viroqua seemed to be importantly defined by taste: taste in food (literally), taste in culture, taste for a particular kind of social or political climate, a taste for certain kinds of community making.

Indeed, tastes mattered because they implied ideas about the morality of making community, as was clear when Viroquans talked about where they procured food and why. Many Viroquans felt very strongly about shopping locally. Some shopped locally out of loyalty to particular businesses and owners, and out of a belief that Viroqua as a whole would benefit if more merchants remained open. Sue and Peter Walby, for example, who both grew up in the area and were very involved in their church and a variety of other civic activities, said that they believed deeply, and had tried to teach their children, that one of the most important parts of being a member of the community was shopping locally and paying one's bills on time.

---

12. Bjorn and Brie always had organic feta cheese on hand thanks to Bjorn's friendship with Felix, a local goat farmer who produced his own feta cheese and sold it at food co-ops and farmers markets. Bjorn, a carpenter, had helped Felix build a "goat house on wheels"—a shelter that could be towed along with the goats as they were moved from pasture to pasture throughout the summer. Bjorn, in return, received regular deliveries of Felix's cheese.

Shopping locally, according to this logic, was good because it was good for Viroqua and for the people who lived there—people whom one probably knew personally.

Rather than talking about loyalty to particular local businesses or local business owners, other Viroquans saw shopping locally as a means to combat the negative effects of globalization and corporate consolidation, and to avoid participating in the wasteful throw-away consumer culture of cheap products. People who did most of their food shopping at the Viroqua Food Co-Op often talked about shopping locally as part of larger political and economic logics in which shopping locally was understood as a practice good not only for Viroqua but for communities in general. They believed that if more Americans adopted such a commitment, the world would be a more just place over all. People in this group had taken to heart the slogan "Think Globally, Act Locally." A few even had bumper stickers exhorting others to do the same.

Other Viroquans had different priorities, and not everyone enjoyed a level of economic privilege that would have allowed them to shop according to moral principles. Some shopped for food in town when it was convenient, and made regular trips to discount houses like Sam's Club in La Crosse where they could get better prices. During happy hour at the Legion bar one afternoon, for example, a discussion emerged about where people shopped. "If the local stores aren't going to sell stuff at prices we can afford," said one patron, "I'm not going to go to them just so they can stay in business. I can't. But I won't, either."

Viroquans varied in the degree to which they saw practices like eating and shopping as instrumental means to larger goals. As was the case with Halloween, some Viroquans thought it was important to make consumer choices in light of what those choices meant for larger goals, while others did not see the need for such calculation. For them, shopping was just a necessity, and people who tried to make more of it than that had too much time on their hands, thought too hard, or seriously overestimated their influence on the world. It was this type of difference I mean when I argue, as I do throughout this book, that Viroquans' differing cultures of community were guided in part by different *ethics of agency*. One's ethic of agency is the view one takes of the moral value of individual deliberation and choice. While some Viroquans operated on the assumption that deliberation and individual choice was the basis for any moral action, others thought it more valuable to accept one's situation as part of some "natural" order of things.

Differences in ethics of agency is one of the keys to understanding the moral boundaries (Lamont 1992) that mattered to Viroquans. The degree to which residents shopped locally is a good example of the ways different courses of action followed from different ways of viewing the relative importance of individual choice and the exercise of that choice in the form of action. Patronizing locally owned businesses was important to many Viroquans. For some, shopping locally was a way to exercise a political commitment—doing what one could as an individual to change large structures, such as the world economy. Others, like the Walbys, thought it was important to purchase goods in the community because of their obligation to the town and the particular individuals who owned businesses there. Shopping locally, for these folks, was a way to improve an existing community "rather than . . . transforming a political community by politicizing the private" (Lichterman 1996, 172). Finally, a third orientation to shopping rejected the idea that the choices of an individual consumer could have much influence on the overall functioning of structures as complex and impersonal as the economy, internationally or even locally. According to this ethic, it was more important to focus one's attention on one's personal life and family rather than waste time worrying about forces that were not amenable to individual action.[13]

But Viroquans' varying ethics of agency is not the whole story of the sources of social distinctions that were meaningful to them. As we have already seen, Viroquans who, for example, made deliberate decisions about

---

13. In a similar point to one I make here, journalist David Brooks (2001) argues that the principle distinction between Red and Blue America is "the ego curtain." While the essay in which he argues this point is not based on particularly systematic observations, it puts a finger on something important that played an important part in the difference between the ways Viroquans viewed themselves and their places in the world. Members of Red America, he argues, have few pretensions to having chosen many things in their lives. They live where their families live and take jobs that are available there. "Getting by" is an acceptable goal and sometimes a desirable one in the sense that it won't look like showing off. For Blue America, Brooks argues, the primary motivation is to be a fully actualized individual, to choose everything in one's life for oneself. This might mean choosing to live in a small town, buying groceries at a natural foods store, selecting an alternative school for one's children, or creating a Halloween celebration better than the ones that already exist. Blue Americans want to negotiate a life and lifestyle that they have deliberately chosen. Carving out such a path means deliberately creating improvements or alternatives to conventional ways of doing things, rather than accepting the conventional as the only option.

shopping locally had different logics that guided their deliberations. For some, the goals that guided their choices revolved around questions of what would benefit Viroqua. For others, the focus was more "global." The difference here was in what I call residents' *logic of commitment.* A logic of commitment is a set of ideas about how one is connected and obligated to the communities in one's life, and provides a basis for ordering priorities and evaluating options. Returning to the example of food, Viroquans who saw buying organic, locally grown food ultimately as a contribution to a healthier planet and society tended to shop first at the Viroqua Food Co-op. When it was closed, their second choice was the Jubilee grocery store, because it was locally owned. Their last choice was the Wal-Mart Super-center across the highway from Jubilee. Wal-Mart represented everything this group disliked about contemporary capitalism, sprawl, and material wastefulness. This group's logic of commitment privileged a sense of commitment to abstract social and political ideals.

For Viroquans who cared primarily about the vitality of Viroqua, Jubilee was often a first shopping choice. The store was founded by local residents, and employees owned shares in it through an employee stock-option program. Shopping at Jubilee was a way to keep money in the community for people who needed a convenient place to buy all their groceries, and who worried less about the implications of their food choices as a global concern. The logic of commitment among these Viroquans emphasized a commitment to the particular town in which they lived. According to this logic, shopping at the local Wal-Mart also represented a way to keep local money "local": shopping at Viroqua's Wal-Mart helped protect area residents' jobs there.

Viroquans' ethics of agency and logics of commitment informed the ways that they created communities. Some residents associated community with formal involvement in civic organizations, local government, and church activities. Others preferred spontaneous, informal socializing with kin and friends they had known their whole lives. In the absence of such long-standing ties, new arrivals to the area worked hard to forge a sense of community for themselves from scratch.

Though such preferences may seem trivial, they were not merely expressions of individual priorities. On the contrary, such preferences tended to appear in highly patterned ways. Parents like Mark, who grew up in Viroqua or nearby towns, who enjoyed snowmobiling and stopping in periodically for a beer at the American Legion bar, were quite likely to be parents whose children attended Viroqua's public schools and who bought groceries at the Wal-Mart Supercenter. Parents like Bjorn and Brie, whose children would attend Pleasant Ridge when they got old enough, tended to be people who disdained the mass-produced and shopped for groceries at the Food Co-op. Many of the Viroquans who were like them had only recently arrived in town.

How Americans Make Community Today

I have already given away the short answer to the initial question that motivated this research. The question was: How do Americans make community today?

The answer is: "It depends."

On what it depends helps us understand the basis of the three different social groups in Viroqua. Briefly, the sources of social distinction that really mattered in Viroqua had to do with the ways that Viroquans understood, and practiced, *community*. It was this variety that is the subject of this book. This variety also sheds light on a number of important debates about the possibility for community in modernity as well as debates about what some perceive as persistent cultural divisions among Americans.

Both debates have become matters of concern, not only among scholars, but for all manner of observers who worry whether or not the conditions associated with modern life have deleterious effects on our social, political, and moral well-being. Many of these arguments are familiar ones that, though they have been articulated in a variety of ways over time, have roots in the beginnings of modernity itself. In essence, they are debates about the nature of free will and the nature of obligation, and how human beings can best live a good life. Yet they are more familiar to us in the forms of applied questions about the practical problems of communal and civic life in a culture that prizes individual fulfillment.

A secondary goal of my research was to understand how people go about making a small town together when social, economic, and technological forces have altered many of the conditions that we have associated with small-town life in the past. These concerns about community follow from concerns about disenchantment or meaninglessness in contemporary

American life (Fowler 1991). Many intellectuals complain that we don't know what community is and that we have tried to substitute a whole bunch of other things for it, things such as therapy, "false communities," lifestyle enclaves, consumption—none of which is really a satisfactory substitute. According to such arguments, it's not that community was never a part of American culture. The assumption is that it has just been lost. Through the 1980s and 1990s, critics on both the right and left worried that community was jeopardized by individualism. Traditionally, conservatives thought the remedy was to return to traditional communities that offered moral guidance and provided individuals with anchors in a sea of relativism. On the left, community was treated as means to political empowerment and equality: by participating in public life individuals could improve their ability to see the world from perspectives other than their own and thereby take responsibility for the needs of the less privileged. The arguments in both camps assume that without reliable ways to make community together, we run the risk of compromising our ability to be effective citizens in a democracy. Without social networks that bring us into regular contact with people whose views and experiences are different from our own, without relationships that don't require contractual mediation, we cannot cultivate a sense of our place as citizens who do more than act in our own self-interest.

But Viroquans were thinking of communities in ways different from both of these concepts. They saw community more as a springboard that one might use to take off in any number of directions that were personally fulfilling, rather than as an anchor. I did not find that the conditions of modern, or even of "postmodern," life were obliterating the possibility for having the kind of small-town community Americans say they value so deeply. On the contrary, I found in Viroqua that people created community *using* some of the very features of modern life we generally assume are antithetical to it—features including an emphasis on personal fulfillment and growth and on expressing oneself through material consumption.

While academics and cultural observers on both the political left and right wring their hands about the decline of community, I found that people made community in such a culture *through* consumption (and other apparently rational, individualistic means) that seem antithetical to community as we usually imagine it. In so doing, Viroquans used and reproduced a number of traditional ideas about rural life and community. Despite many years' worth of findings that question the value of the "rural-urban continuum" as a way of making sense of what "community" looks like in different kinds of settings, Viroquans found these categories useful and employed them to organize a sense of identity in their understandings of what it meant to live in a small town and rural setting (Bell 1992). As a result, these categories played an important role in structuring their everyday actions.

For the most part, Viroquans shared a similar sense of what small-town life was, and should be, like. Everyone liked how safe Viroqua felt, how neighborly it was, how easy it was to get things done informally. But not everyone went about enacting community there in exactly the same way. It is around this central point that my analysis differs from both the work in community studies literature, which tends to find that central features of "community" remain constant regardless of time and place, and with the hand-wringing literatures, which lament the decline of community in America. I argue that while *images* of community, particularly the small-town version of it, remain important organizing features of community life, the ways in which people enact community have changed in some fundamental ways. In the first place, the technological and cultural changes that often worry the hand-wringers have undoubtedly changed the ways that people make community today. It makes no sense to argue that community, as Redfield (1955) and others traditionally described it, persists unchanged in small towns or, for that matter, within subcultural groups, as others have argued (Fischer 1977, 1982). However, it is also not the case that these changes are completely a drain on the possibilities for community.

I write here about three distinct orientations to, or styles (Lichterman 1996) of, community making in Viroqua. While I do not claim that these were the only orientations to community within Viroqua, they were the most visible ones. Within the social groups defined by each community-making style, friends and neighbors supported one another, shared gossip, worked together, traded favors, and generally "knew everyone else's business." Between the groups themselves, however, there much less interaction, and individuals in one group often had relatively little specific knowledge of individuals in the other. The differences that divided these three groups were not those that have distinguished groups of small-town residents in the past. These distinctions can be most fruitfully understood by understanding Viroquans' ethics of agency and their logics of commitment.

Regulars, Alternatives, and Main Streeters

I met many residents like Mark and Dave who were both committed to Viroqua as a particular place and who believed that community was something natural that shouldn't require armloads of deliberate effort to maintain. Many of these residents lived in Viroqua because, as one resident's statement typified, "it's home." They were committed to their community by virtue of their attachment to Viroqua as the place in which many of them were born and grew up. Their social networks included family members, former schoolmates, fellow churchgoers, and co-workers, and many individuals in such a person's life were likely to fall into more than one of these categories. Following the vocabulary that many Viroquans used, I call this group the "Regulars." When members of this group called themselves "regular people," they meant that they imagined themselves as sort of a baseline for other residents. They were not interested in standing out, making waves, or drawing attention to themselves.

The Regular ethic of agency discouraged the impulse to make every decision into a matter of personal choice, and indeed rejected such an ethic outright. Just as Mark had rejected the idea that attending the public Halloween celebrations was a requisite for his children's ability to enjoy the holiday, the Regulars rejected the idea that, as one put it, "everything needs to be a big production." That is, one needn't spend life deliberating over every decision—it made more sense to take many things as they came and reduce life's complexity, rather than clutter it up with more decisions than necessary. The less complicated things were, the more one had time for the things that really mattered and were fun, such as spending time with one's family, enjoying a favorite hobby, or simply relaxing when the opportunity presented itself.

A second group of Viroquans was made up of people who had made deliberate choices to live there because they wanted to live in a place where, as one said, "there was more community" than there had been wherever they had lived before. They chose to live there because it offered them a certain kind of "lifestyle" and a place to find people like themselves and *create* community in a way that conformed to ideals they contrasted with their experiences in other places. Because many, though not all, were relatively new to the area, few had family or longtime friends in Viroqua before they moved there. In fact, many sacrificed the opportunity to live in close prox-imity to such people in order to live in Viroqua. Once there, they enacted small-town life to make their experiences in Viroqua conform to the goals they had in moving there—goals that many described in terms of finding a small town where they could live out their social and political ideals with like-minded people. Part of the motivation of this group was to construct and live in institutions that offered literal alternatives to "mainstream" in-stitutions and ways of life. For this reason, and again, taking a cue from the language Viroquans themselves used, I came to call these people the "Alternatives." Living in the country was first an alternative to what they described as the materialistic, fast-paced, rat-racey, amoral, or otherwise unsatisfying life they lived before they arrived. They ended up in Viroqua, not only because they wanted to live in a small, rural town, but because Viroqua offered a number of additional "alternative" institutions that fit their philosophy. Their involvement in these institutions with others who, like themselves, lived primarily through these alternative institutions, pro-vided the mechanism that supported a kind of self-selected segregation based on the desire to live "an alternative lifestyle."

For many of the relative newcomers, including Bjorn and Brie, choos-ing to live in Viroqua was a key building block of their chosen lifestyle. They made deliberate choices to leave suburbs or cities, professional jobs, even important friendship and family ties, in order to begin living the lives they had chosen for themselves. Their interest in alternatives implied some characteristics that set them apart from the area's other residents, and sometimes it implied mechanisms that limited their contact with people outside Alternative social circles.

The Alternative ethos had roots in waves of countercultural movements stretching back at least as far as the Romantics, who emphasized "aestheti-cizing" everyday life, emotional freedom and self-expression, and infor-mality (Featherstone 1991; Brooks 2000). Countercultural movements both produce and consume symbolic goods consistent with their ethics (Feather-stone 1991; Zukin 1982). The dissemination of countercultural ethics then leads to the spread of new cultural practices, including residential patterns. Members tended to be highly mobile, and they value, as part of the proj-ect of aestheticization of everyday life, the opportunity to live in a beautiful place and in institutions that complement their ethics.

Unlike the Regulars, Alternative residents were not bound together by a commitment to Viroqua as a particular place. Because so many were new to the area, the basis of their social ties could not be long-term relationships with neighbors and family members. Instead, they shared a commitment to *an ideal* of small-town and community life that will be described in detail later. Their primary commitment was to an idealized way of life, and Viroqua happened to provide a locale in which they could enact the community they had in mind. The work in which they engaged to bring their ideals to fruition defined this group morally. Hard work and deliberate action in the service of a larger commitment to social goals, mediated by a sense of the importance of self-fulfillment was what made people morally worthy in the eyes of this group's members. The Alternatives saw Viroqua as an instantiation of an ideal small town *they sought out* as part of an overall orientation to the ways they believed they should live their lives. In keeping with their interest in working toward creating a way of living in a small town that met a range of social and political goals, the Alternative people did not always join Regulars in participating in the arenas that had traditionally been important to social life in Viroqua. Instead, they created new institutions: an alternative to the public school, alternatives to existing grocery and clothing stores, even an alternative currency.[14]

A third group of residents shared the Regulars' commitment to Viroqua as a place and also the Alternatives' belief in the moral value of working hard to achieve an ideal kind of community life. This group differed from the Alternatives in that the focus of their improvement efforts was Viroqua itself. This group included primarily middle-class and professional people who were either longtime residents or were new arrivals who had joined the town's existing organizations and institutions. In this group were the city council alders, public school board members, church deacons, historic preservation activists, and Rotary Club and Viroqua Partners members—familiar leaders in American small-town civic life. However, this group's commitment to Viroqua was girded by a sense that if it was to remain a vital town and pleasant place to live, a great deal of work was required to protect it from the economic and demographic forces that led to decline in other small towns.

---

14. The SCRIP program raises funds for the Pleasant Ridge Waldorf School. Individuals purchase SCRIP currency at the school or at Bramble Books bookstore and use it to make purchases at a number of local merchants who have agreed to accept it. The merchants then donate 4–5% of all SCRIP purchases back to the school.

TABLE 1. Summary of Social Groups in Viroqua

	Ethic of Agency	Logic of Commitment
Regulars	Downplays importance of individual deliberation and efficacy	Particular to Viroqua
Alternatives	Emphasizes individual efficacy	Universalistic—primarily to a set of larger social and political goals
Main Streeters	Emphasizes individual efficacy	Particular to Viroqua

There was no obvious label for this group to be drawn from my data. People in this group also tended to think of themselves as "typical Viroquans," and this was especially clear in the comments they made about my research. One, for example, went out of her way to introduce me to a number of people in this segment of the community because she was worried I might be focusing my research too much on the Alternative community. In addition, many expressed surprise that I worked at the American Legion as a bartender. Said one, "Well, that's not exactly the place where *typical* Viroquans hang around." Though scholars have called similar small-town citizens "Men of Main Street" (Pedersen 1992) or "Town Fathers" (Bellah et al. 1986), the contemporary sex composition of this group renders these labels inaccurate. Because the revitalization of Main Street represented the kind of effort members of this group took on the community's behalf, I call them the Main Streeters. Like other Americans in the middle classes, particularly those with higher levels of education, the Alternatives and the Main Streeters both emphasized the importance of self-actualization and self-expression as important moral features of one's life. This belief in the moral value of self-actualization is a symbolic boundary associated with self-defined high-cultural status as opposed to disdain for those they believe are not fully self-actualized (Lamont 1992).

What all Viroquans had in common was a set of *ideas* about the role of a small town in facilitating a particular mode of communal life. All shared some sense that living in a small town gave them privileges that Americans in cities and suburbs did not have. They all believed in the idea that living in a small town gave them access to a valuable way of life, though there were important differences in what they valued about living in Viroqua.

2

The Alternatives

A Kinder, Gentler Counterculture

Brie parked her minivan on the side of the gravel county highway at the end of a row of similarly parked vehicles. Brie, her friend Susan Townsley, and I alighted and trekked past the rest of the parked cars and up a driveway toward a lone house in a field atop a ridge. The January night was frigid and clear. The woman who greeted us at the door was wearing a dark red empire-style dress embellished with embroidered flowers. "Come in," she said. "We're just about to start the ceremony." Stacia, as she introduced herself, was hosting her annual Goddess Party—a gathering for a large group of her female friends.

Stacia's house was not large, but it was thoughtfully constructed with a partially exposed post-and-beam timber framework. The floor plan was open and centered around a woodstove. The only separate room on the first floor was a bathroom that also housed a laundry area. In the bathroom the claw-foot bathtub was painted a deep purple that matched the purple speckles in the bathroom's linoleum floor. The only other division in the first floor was a wall that partially separated the kitchen from the living area. I counted nearly thirty women already gathered in the house. Most had begun forming a circle on the floor of the living and dining areas, while three women in the living room played softly on African drums. On the far wall, a small table held several lit candles, a wide-mouthed mason jar containing stones and water, some small bottles of essential oils, a book, and some bundles of dried plants and herbs.

We deposited the foods and bottles of wine we had brought to share on a small table in the kitchen and joined the circle of women seated on the floor. The women already seated were singing songs that most members of the group seemed to know, but which I did not recognize. After a few of these songs, one about a flowing river, another about a goddess, Stacia held up a decorated stick and asked that we pass it around the circle to each person. As we received the stick, we were supposed to say a few words about what we'd brought for the goddess altar, which I realized must be the table with the candles and other items. I wasn't aware that I needed to bring anything for an altar and was relieved when Brie whispered that neither she nor Susan had brought anything for it either. Susan and Brie seemed to know all of the women in the group. I knew only Susan and Brie, though I recognized several of the others, because I had seen them at the Common Ground coffee shop and at the Food Co-op. I recognized one from the Colonial Laundromat.

Each woman took a turn speaking, and some did tell the group about items that they had placed on the altar. One woman said that she had brought the book on the altar, and that she had chosen it because it was particularly meaningful and had helped her gain a new perspective on her life. Another woman explained that the large mason jar contained an elixir she had made and, reading to us from a page in a paper-bound journal about the different healing and energizing properties of the crystals in the water, asked that we anoint one another with the elixir by dipping a finger into the water and using it to draw a half-moon shape on our neighbor's forehead. Everyone did. A fourth woman said she had supplied the bundle of dried sage and that the herb was used in many Native American rituals, particularly in some having to do with cleansing homes. Another woman talked about the power of feminine energy.

But in addition to these comments, almost every woman used part of her turn to talk about how close she felt to the rest of the group. Many expressed gratitude for the opportunity to get together and enjoy one another's company and be rejuvenated by an evening away from spouses and children.[1] Three mentioned that they had almost decided not to come to the party because of the cold weather, fatigue, or because they did not want to leave children and spouses behind, but they were now very glad that they had come after all. Many said they were grateful for "the community," for the friends they saw as they looked around the room, and for the opportunity to be part of a close group of dynamic women. A slight, elfin woman of about thirty said tearfully, "I'm just so grateful to be a part of this community. The kind of community here is something I searched for for a long, long time but didn't find anywhere else."

She was not the only woman who was moved to tears by the time the ceremony ended, and as the last speaker took her turn, the mood in the room seemed to grow somber. At that moment, someone exclaimed, "Let's party!" and a festive atmosphere was instantly restored. Cuban jazz from the Buena Vista Social Club album filled the room, and the women stood, exchanged hugs, and turned to conversation, to eating the snacks people had brought, to lounging in the hot tub outdoors under the stars, and to dancing. Though some drumming continued, the rest of the party's activities were far more conventional than I expected, given the ceremony with which it began.[2]

Conversations turned primarily to family and children. I seemed to be the only woman in attendance who was not a mother, which turned out to be something of an obstacle in my interactions with the other women. I stood in small groups throughout the evening and introduced myself, and most of the women I met were quick to ask whether or not I had kids and if I had moved to Viroqua because of the Pleasant Ridge Waldorf School.

---

1. When my turn came, Brie suggested that I introduce myself. It seemed an inappropriate time to announce that I was a researcher, so I simply introduced myself, explained that I had moved to town in the fall and that I was looking forward to meeting everyone. I explained my reason for living in Viroqua to a number of people with whom I chatted after the ceremony, however.

2. In addition, Brie had given me a warning me on the way to the party that suggested it might be more bacchanal than it truly was. "Last year at this party," she explained, "I ate some popcorn that had kind of an earthy taste, and it turned out it was ganja popcorn. I got totally stoned without meaning to. If you're not interested in getting stoned, don't be afraid to ask if something you're about to eat is loaded." Though I did catch a marijuana-like scent a couple of times during the party, beer and wine were the strongest substances most of the guests were consuming. It is also possible that the scent came not from marijuana, but from the bundle of dried sage that someone had contributed to the goddess altar.

When I explained that I had not, most politely asked a few questions about my research or about graduate school or about whether or not I had a significant other, but then seemed to run out of things to say and returned to speaking primarily to one another about children.[3] One commented apologetically that I must be bored by all the "kid talk."

Following their lead, I began asking the other guests about their families and how they had come to live in Viroqua. I learned that the women in the room had come to Viroqua from a variety of places, mostly in the upper Midwest, but some from as far away as the West Coast. Though they varied in their details, many of the women's stories were variations on a basic theme. Annie's story was a good example of a number that I heard that night.[4] "I'm a massage therapist, and my husband is an artist and a cabinetmaker," she said. She laughed and added, "Everyone who moves to Viroqua has a wife who's a massage therapist and a husband who is a cabinetmaker!" I asked her if there was enough of a market for her services to make a living in Viroqua, and she said that while there was certainly a market, the challenge was that sometimes people wanted to pay for massages "in chickens, or in installments for, like, the next ten years. I try to be flexible, but chickens don't pay the mortgage."

Annie said that she and her husband had looked for a small town with a school that they liked for their children for a long time. They learned about Viroqua when her husband came to the area to do some work for a client. Now living in a restored farmhouse in the country, they had collected a small menagerie of animals, including a goat, "so the kids can have that as part of the country-living experience." Without prompting from me, she speculated as to whether or not she and her husband would remain in the area permanently, especially after their children finished high school. "I don't know if we'll stay," she said. She could imagine moving

---

3. This is certainly not to suggest that anyone was unfriendly. On the contrary, I think some women were unsure what conversation topics we might have in common. Though it was possible that some may have been wary of talking to me once they understood that I was conducting research, I do not believe this was a significant consideration. Instead, I think the experience was the reverse of the experience professional women say they sometimes have after leaving the workforce to raise children and find that they no longer have much to talk about with former co-workers. Without children of my own, I lacked the most basic connection these women shared.

4. Not this woman's real name. I did not have the opportunity to meet her again to request permission to use her real name.

somewhere warmer, like Arizona, for at least part of the year or maybe back to a bigger city. But for now, living in Viroqua was working out well. The place was serving the purpose it was supposed to: it provided her family with a community in which to give their children a rural upbringing and a type of education they believed was valuable, while also offering a low enough cost of living to allow Annie and her husband to pursue occupations they enjoyed.

The people and events at the Goddess Party exemplified a number of important aspects of being Alternative in Viroqua. Though the party had some New Age overtones, interest in the New Age was certainly not what bound members of the group together. Everyone sitting in the circle was willing to participate in the crystal elixir anointment, for example, but not everyone took it equally seriously. Later in the evening, one woman made a point of drawing a distinction between some of the more New Age women and herself, saying that while she had no problem with it, she "didn't go in for" some of the others' New Age beliefs.[5] In addition, while at first glance the gathering seemed reminiscent of the hippie era, only a handful of the other women wore hippie-style dresses or full skirts. Most were dressed warmly in jeans and sweaters, as was I. Though modest in size, Stacia's house in the countryside was architecturally interesting and not without the amenities most Americans expect in a middle-class home, such as comfortable furniture, indoor plumbing and electricity, and a washer and dryer. In other words, Viroqua's Alternatives were mostly pretty conventional people.

What became clear as I chatted with the other women in attendance was that what held them together was a belief in an ideal of rural community life that living in Viroqua seemed to offer, and a set of complementary ideas about family life, work, politics, and the environment. Though deeply committed to their community of like-minded Viroquans, they were not, as in Annie's case, necessarily committed to Viroqua itself. Alternatives were drawn to Viroqua in large part because of a desire for "community." Just as tourists planning vacations formulate an image of their ideal destination by contrasting that ideal to their everyday experiences

---

5. Other times I heard Alternatives distance themselves from some of their friends' beliefs that they said were "too out there" or "kind of woo-woo."

(Urry 1990; MacCannell 1989), Alternatives sought out a small town that could provide them with the community life that they felt was missing wherever they had lived before. The difference was that Alternatives came to Viroqua to live, not just to visit.

Bill and Susan Townsley were such a couple, and I interviewed them later that winter. After a dinner of curried squash harvested from their own garden, I sat with Susan and Bill in the farmhouse they renovated after moving to Viroqua two years earlier from Evanston, Illinois. Their sons, Charlie, five, and Arlo, three, had gone upstairs after being read bedtime stories, and we settled into chairs in their living room, which was warmed by a woodstove in the corner. When they talked about why they moved to Viroqua, they constructed a narrative similar to that of other Alternatives—a narrative that included some ideas about what community was, and signs that it had been missing in their lives before they moved to Viroqua. Like many Alternatives with whom I spoke, they talked explicitly about leaving the suburbs of Chicago because they wanted to live in a place with "a sense of community." I asked what a sense of community meant to them, and Susan's answer was also very similar to the answer I received from other residents.

> To me, it's people being there for each other and watching out for each other and raising children together. I think those are the main things. People are really willing to share work and help each other when you need it. If we wanted to build a deck on our house this summer, we could make a bunch of phone calls and have a whole crew of people here one day if we wanted to. That kind of stuff. Or when a new family moves into the community, there's ten people already there to help unpack their house and say, hey, you're welcome, it's so nice to have you, we're so glad you're here.

"Was that your experience?" I asked.

"Not ours personally," replied Bill.[6] "Our kids were little, so our kids hadn't enrolled in the school yet. So we weren't really involved in Pleasant Ridge yet. I mean, we certainly visited the school before we moved here

---

6. This kind of assistance when a new family arrives in Viroqua is now part of what the public has learned about Viroqua's Alternative community, thanks to Joseph Hart's (2004) article about living in Viroqua in the *Utne Reader*.

and that was part of our decision, but when we moved out here, we didn't know a soul. So, we didn't have too many phone calls."

"We also didn't get here and move into a house. We went to a rental unit and had, like, a suitcase," Susan added.

"When someone sends enrollment forms to the school, is that how everyone knows a new family is coming?" I asked.

"Kind of," Bill, responded. "The community here is small, Viroqua is small, so news travels. And you get into these smaller and smaller circles, and you know, at Pleasant Ridge, there's only like a hundred and fifty families, it's a pretty small circle, so news spreads pretty quickly."

Susan continued:

Another good example was a couple years ago now, a friend's little boy was in the hospital with pneumonia, so we had their little girl with us, and we went to the [Viroqua Food] Co-op to get something, and someone said, how come [the little girl] is with you, or whatever, and you tell them what's going on. And by that night, there's a whole week's worth of meals lined up for the family. News does travel really fast, and people are always ready to be right there for each other and know that [help] will come around if they need it too.

So far, Viroqua was living up to the Townsleys' hopes. Bill interjected:

It seems like people here appreciate other people. And it doesn't matter if it's at the Pleasant Ridge school, or up here. Our experience up here on [our road] is that our neighbors have been super great. And some of these guys are the busiest guys in the world. [Our neighbor] Mark is milking cows all by himself. He is up at four in the morning, and I've been coming home at midnight and I can hear that he's still milking or still out in his tractor. Twelve-thirty one night I got home, and he was out on his tractor at twelve-thirty and he has to get up at four in the morning to milk. But if I called him up right now and said, "Hey Mark, I got a flat tire" or "Hey, can you help me with something," he'd come right over.

Susan nodded, and Bill continued: "And it's that kind of stuff that's not just people always looking out for themselves. In a community, everyone is willing to do what they need to do to contribute to their family and to spend time with their family, but if someone needs help, people really appreciate it."

Later in our conversation, Susan returned to the topic of neighbors:

I mean, our neighbors on this road could not be more amazing. And when
we moved into the house, [our neighbor] Stan was down one day, and he
said, are you going to do a garden this year? And we were still finishing the
house, and had these two little kids, and trying to move in, and we were like,
well, we'd love to, but we're not sure it's going to happen. And he said, oh,
I'll be down with my plow. And in five minutes he comes down here with
his tractor and his plow and plows out this huge, beautiful garden for us.
It's like, I was sitting there just totally ready to cry. I just couldn't believe it.
That *never* would have happened [in Evanston].

There was this one time [in Evanston] that Bill needed a ride to get his
mom's car—she'd been to the doctor; we gave her a ride, and we needed
to go pick up her car because she needed it in the morning. And Bill must
have made five phone calls, and everyone said, oh, but it's this special show
of *NYPD Blue.*

Bill grimaced, recalling disgustedly:

Yeah, it was the season finale of *NYPD Blue,* and I was like, you've got to
be kidding me! These were *friends* of mine. And I was just like, you guys
just don't get it. And I was so pissed for so long. It's *TV.* How often do I call
and say I'm in a pinch? And they were like, yeah, you're right, but [sighs]
give me a break.

"And they *still* didn't [help]," Susan said, incredulous even years later.

I know if Bill was ever gone, or anything happened, I could call Stan, or I
could call the Langers, and they'd be down here in five seconds, no matter what time of day it was or what they were doing. So it is a time thing—
when we first moved here, it was hilarious, we'd inevitably be sitting down
to dinner and someone would pull up just to say hi.

"That's cause we usually eat around six, six-thirty," Bill laughed. "Everyone else up here eats at four-thirty, five o'clock. They're done [eating]
by the time we're almost done cooking."

Participating in the kind of community they came to Viroqua to find required some adjustment. "So then, we'd try to eat earlier, and sure enough,
they'd be there anyway," said Susan.

But as soon as that truck pulls up, it's like ugh, it's going to be an hour before somebody leaves. But now, it totally feels completely normal and like such a good time. But when we first moved here—I think it takes time to wind down and get in the rhythm of it's okay not to rush. It's okay to see your neighbor and just hang out and connect with each other instead of just being zoom, zoom, zoom, because there's so much to do. And we probably have *more* to do here than we did there. I mean, we're gathering wood and growing a garden, ["and fences, fences, fences" added Bill]. Those are things to do. It's ten times busier, but it doesn't feel like a rat race in the same way.

"And what goes around comes around," said Bill. "I've spent plenty of time helping people build this or that, and I know it's going to come back to me. I don't expect people to pay me or feed me. I don't know. Everyone just pitches in. It's just really nice that way."

What made their lives in Viroqua different from their experiences in Evanston was a combination of the ways that Bill and Susan spent their time and their relationships with their friends and neighbors. The Townsleys not only made connections within the Pleasant Ridge community but also with their neighbors, who were longtime residents. In their rural neighborhood it was not surprising that the Townsleys would be quickly integrated. Small towns generally absorb newcomers easily in small numbers (Salamon 2003). Traditionally, this has been particularly true in farm neighborhoods, where neighbors often have relied on one another to trade labor and equipment.

Farming played an important role in helping the Townsleys get to know their neighbors, even though they came to Viroqua with virtually no farm experience, just a desire to try it. "I didn't even know what a haybine was. I didn't know what was what," Bill laughed when I asked how much he knew about farming before he tried to start haying on his own. Exemplifying the Alternative confidence in the limitless possibilities for individual efficacy, Bill assumed that he could learn farming once he got to Viroqua.

Though he did plenty of his own research, his neighbors had played a central role in his education. In return, what Bill lacked in equipment and knowledge he could return in mechanical skills in fixing equipment. The result was that Bill and the men in the neighborhood traded labor and machinery with one another. Bill spent a great deal of time helping his neighbors fix machines in exchange for their use, though he was gradually acquiring some of his own equipment at auctions. Now, he said, he could "talk hay for hours" with his neighbors. Susan, too, had learned a great deal from the neighbors about gardening, canning, and storing vegetables. "It's February," she said, referring to the squash we had eaten for dinner, "and we're still eating vegetables from our garden. That feels really good."

But what about the community of Alternative people, those that the women at the Goddess Party described? The Townsleys explained that despite their close neighborly relationships with the other families on the hill, the Alternative community was really the center of their social life. There was a qualitative difference between their ties to their neighbors and their friends. If so many people in the Alternative community were relatively new to the area, what was the source of the "community" that everyone kept talking about? Clearly, it was very meaningful to the women at the party, and to Bill and Susan.

Examining the ways that Alternative people carved out their lives in Viroqua tells us two things about contemporary life in America. First, we see evidence of the emergence of a changed mode of countercultural lifestyle that is still motivated by many of the same interests that inspired previous back-to-the-land movements. Second, Alternatives provide an example of the way that some Americans, particularly those of the middle and upper-middle classes (Lamont 1992), believe that they can deliberately deploy certain kinds of cultural resources and strategies to bring their lives in line with an idealized image that combines family, community, and the expression of individual goals. Indeed, they took as a moral imperative the need to enact a lifestyle that fit their values, their sense of themselves as individuals, and their long-term goals.

It was this goal-oriented ethic of agency that brought Alternatives to Viroqua. Their logic of commitment was premised less on a commitment to Viroqua as a particular place than to the long-term goals and values that drew them there. A key difference among Viroquans was between those for whom Viroqua itself provided an anchor and people, like the Alternatives, whose anchor was personal values, or something else.[7] For

---

7. The idea that places have different meanings for different people is not new. Existing research finds that in some cases it is the place itself that is meaningful, while, for others, living in a particular place is a means to some other end. For example, Dobriner's (1963) description of how newly arrived suburbanites and longtime villagers viewed living in the suburb of "Old Town" might just as easily have been written about how the Alternative and Regular communities in Viroqua viewed themselves: "This is the real issue that splits the suburbanite and the villager

Alternatives, Viroqua was an instrument in their pursuit of a life in line with those values or their image of what their lives should be like.

At first glance, it seemed that the Alternatives were caught up in a nostalgic retreat—that they had moved to a small town in hopes of finding the simpler life and community associated with the past in order to escape the dangers and anxieties of the contemporary world. A closer look revealed that, by contrast, their project was more closely aligned with what Lasch (1991) characterizes as a Romantic view of village life. They were not trying to reclaim a way of life that would disconnect them the contemporary world. They hoped that living in a small town surrounded by like-minded people would provide a basis for meaningful engagement in the larger world.

It was not completely surprising to find people like the Alternatives in Viroqua. Viroqua is certainly not the only place people are living out this sort of project (see Brooks 2001, 2004; Kotkin 2001; Halfacree and Boyle 1998). Furthermore, their project is not really a new one, but part of a long American tradition of community making based on moral ideals. Though we tend to think of increased residential mobility as a relatively new phenomenon, the very founding of the United States was premised on small groups of people striking out with others like themselves to carve out communities they believed would match their moral (usually religious) values. Even early colonial settlers did not necessarily stay put in the settlements where they started out. Settlers in seventeenth-century New England "moved from one community to another in rapid succession until they found one that suited them ideologically as well as personally" (Keller 2003, 26). This deliberate self-selection increased the chances that community members held relatively cohesive sets of beliefs and values. This tradition of deliberate community seeking was echoed in the words of Alternatives in Viroqua, as typified by a conversation I had with an Alternative parent over coffee in the Common Ground coffee shop one morning. "We always wanted to live in a small town to raise our kids," she explained. "But so many rural areas are so conservative. We wanted to find one with people we could be friends with."

---

communities apart. For the suburbanites, Old Harbor is another commodity; it is a product that can be rationally consumed; it is a means by which they hope to achieve a complex series of personal goals. For the villagers, on the other hand, Old Harbor is not a means to anything; it is simply an end in itself" (136).

While indicating some continuity with the history of deliberate community making in the United States, this Alternative's focus on "friends" points to an important change as well. The rhetoric of the colonial era, perhaps most famously articulated in John Winthrop's 1630 "City on the Hill" sermon, emphasized the production of model communities that would be beacons of faith and godliness for others to emulate. The moral basis of the community was a set of religious principles ostensibly prior to, and separate from, individuals' ideas about their own needs and desires. By contrast, the project of Alternative community in Viroqua was described, not in terms of some absolute moral or religious framework outside the individual, but in "personalist" (Lichterman 1996) terms that emphasized self-expression and fulfillment. Their commitment to the community was a function of their commitment to an abstract set of goals and values and assumed that the basis of legitimate commitment and action arose from the expression of an authentic self (Taylor 1989; Ricoeur 1992). Like the members of the Green Party in Lichterman's (1996) study of environmental activists, Viroqua's Alternatives were committed to forging a community together on the basis of shared ideals, one of which was their belief in the value of individuals. Unlike the activists in Lichterman's comparison groups, whose environmentalism was based on a commitment to a particular geographic location, the personalist Greens

> committed themselves to activism as highly empowered individuals who took their own efficacy for granted. Being an activist for them meant developing and expressing articulate, individual viewpoints, being able to talk about how Green values worked in one's own life. Green movement groups prized individual effort and recruited new members on the assumption that they would want their own individual voices to resonate strongly in collective projects....Greens with their individualized, portable commitments made their own personhood an important site for political action...they lived personal lives in line with the abstract categories of their politics, without the support of traditional community institutions (Lichterman 1996, 154–5).

The Greens' personalist commitment to activism is analogous to the Alternatives' commitment to community. It was this personalist commitment to a set of broadly progressive ideals rather than to Viroqua itself, that was a principle difference between the Alternatives and other groups in Viroqua.

Much of what I saw in the Alternative community was consistent with accounts of alternative approaches to life and community described in the growing literature that individuals and families are writing about their own experiences (see Ivanko, Kivirist, and McKibben 2009; Heiney 1998, 2002).[8] It is an anecdotally rich literature that gives the reader a good sense of the authors' motivations, the emotional and spiritual dimensions of their experiences, and often a how-to component for those who might wish to pursue a similar way of life. As such, however, these accounts do not emphasize the cultural and historical contexts in which these alternative opportunities and experiences unfold and a sense of what such projects might mean for the possibilities for community making. In the rest of this chapter I examine the historical and cultural circumstances that inform this orientation to community life for the Alternatives. I then examine how the orientation of this group to Viroqua and the ethic of agency they brought with them combined to produce a certain kind of community life.

Back to the Land?

Were Viroqua's Alternatives simply neohippies or back-to-the-landers? Indeed, Viroquans themselves sometimes used these labels to refer to the Alternatives,[9] and some Alternatives said that some of the first members of their group to arrive in the area in the late 1960s were part of the back-to-the-land movement. Were the contemporary Alternatives simply recycling elements of the countercultural movements that have drawn American young people to rural areas in the past?

Viroqua's Alternatives were motivated by the same kinds of impulses that, according to some estimates, drew a million young people into the "back-to-the-land" movement in the 1960s and 1970s (Jacob 1997; Brooks

---

8. In the United States, this literature has roots in the writings of Henry David Thoreau in the nineteenth century, and, in the twentieth century, those of Helen and Scott Nearing (1970).

9. They used these labels in different ways, however. When I heard Regulars use these terms, they were sometimes tinged with disparagement. Alternatives themselves seemed to use them more ironically—sometimes actually chuckling in their use of such words—because they couldn't think of any other shorthand label.

2000). Like the Alternatives I met in Viroqua who talked about their frustration with unsatisfying jobs and a culture they found overly materialistic, most back-to-the-landers of the 1970s were small landholders who lived primarily as couples or nuclear family units. Communal experimental arrangements, however, were more visible and controversial instantiations of the countercultural presence in rural areas (Roberts 1971). Like today's Alternative Viroquans, many back-to-the-landers hoped to live and raise their children in surroundings they considered more wholesome than the urban and suburban communities in which they themselves were raised. As they did fifty years ago, Americans with countercultural goals sought out small towns and rural areas as a way of "returning to their to their metaphorical, rather than their literal, roots" (Jacob 1997, 3).

Despite these similarities, and despite the perceptions of some of Viroqua's Regulars and Main Streeters, most of the area's Alternative residents lived lives that looked far more conventionally middle-class than hippielike. Though they shared many of the same goals as the back-to-the-landers of the 1970s, the Alternatives adopted a style of going back to the land (or, in many cases, back-to-the-small-town) that was distinctly different from the style in which hippies of the 1970s pursued it, and which reflected the changed economic and cultural circumstances in which they sought out a rural area in which to live as part of a larger set of personal and social goals.

A principle difference between Viroqua's Alternatives and their 1970s predecessors was the degree to which each group emphasized self-sufficiency as the goal of living in a rural area (Jacob 1997; Coffin and Lipsey 1981). The 1970s back-to-the-landers came of age on the heels of the Vietnam War and the Watergate scandal and on the cusp of an energy crisis and an economic recession. They were cynical about politics and fearful that the nation's economy would grow worse than it already was (McKibben 2004). Inspired by writers like Helen and Scott Nearing, many 1970s back-to-the-landers were deeply committed to attempting complete self-sufficiency (Agnew 2004). They aspired to live in homes they built from materials available on their own land, to grow their own food, make their own clothes, and distance themselves from the mainstream economy. They hoped that living "off the grid" would not only free them from the precarious and immoral capitalist economy but allow them to lead environmentally responsible and spiritually rewarding lives (Agnew 2004). Though a small proportion did experiment with communal living, most of the 1970s back-to-the-landers were small landholders attempting to carve a livelihood from their land (Jacob 1997).

They found, however, that self-sufficiency was all but impossible—in part because they lacked many of the skills homesteading required (Agnew 2004; Jacob 1997; Whitehurst 1972)—and that the poverty that accompanied distance from the mainstream economy could be more frightening than it was freeing. For some, the pursuit of self-sufficiency turned out to be an isolating experience. Others found living in remote areas too lonely—they missed the cultural and intellectual opportunities they had known in more populous areas. Or the rural school systems did not offer their children opportunities they deemed adequate (Agnew 2004).

Most Alternative Viroquans were not aiming for this type of self-sufficiency. On the contrary, Viroqua's Alternative residents were trying to carve out lives and livelihoods that *balanced* economic needs and realities with broader goals of environmental and social responsibility, while finding self-fulfillment *together* with like-minded people. The Alternatives' more domesticated style of countercultural rural living reflected, in part, a shift in cultural concerns, as well as a changed set of tools for countercultural living in rural areas. These cultural shifts included a shift away from outright hostility toward governments and markets to critical engagement with them, as well as a shift away from a desire to fend for oneself toward a concern about the decline of community and a belief in its capacity to enrich one's life. Finally, the Alternatives had a variety of tools for carving out a countercultural existence that were not available in the 1960s and 1970s, including "green" products and the internet.

Whereas the homesteaders of the 1970s entered adulthood at the beginning of an energy crisis and a significant recession, the Alternatives came of age in a significantly more prosperous period in U.S. history. The prosperity of the 1980s and 1990s was also associated with rampant greed and selfishness, however. Perhaps for this reason, the Alternatives I met in Viroqua were not so intent on divorcing themselves from the market but on living modestly, and, most important, on cultivating community. This is not to say that all, or even most, of the Alternatives in Viroqua partook of the economic boom of the 1990s, growing wealthy and then undergoing a conversion in which they realigned their priorities. On the contrary, most were people who did not need to undergo a radical change in perspective as might be expected from the literature on "downshifters" (Schor 1991). Most described their move to Viroqua as consistent with the goals they had all along. As one Alternative resident put it, they were "save-the-world types," who had worked in fields like social work, teaching, and environmental outreach. Though they may not have been hugely prosperous themselves, most contemporary Alternatives began adulthood in a prosperous time compared to the back-to-the-landers of the 1970s.

For the most part, Alternative Viroquans remained connected to some form of conventional employment, finding novel ways to make a living that were a good fit with their larger goals. A number of Alternatives took steps to ensure that their move to a small community would not result in their family's impoverishment. Susan and Bill, for example, renovated their Evanston home so that its sale would provide them with adequate funds to get started in Viroqua. They delayed their move to save money in preparation. "We wanted to do it right," Bill explained.

When they took up new occupations (once associated with back-to-the-landing), such as organic farming, Alternatives generally took mainstream approaches to it. Organic dairy and produce farmers described their operations using the same highly rational language of business management that the area's conventional farmers used. They balanced the financial realities of entrepreneurship with the less conventional businesses that matched their social and environmental goals. Alternatives in the area owned businesses that included outlets for their own art and crafts; environmentally friendly services, including energy-efficient home products; housecleaning using only environmentally safe cleaners; selling toys for children that encouraged creativity and learning; and straw-bale home construction.

Even if back-to-the-landers of the 1970s had wanted to balance their countercultural goals with more conventional ways of life, the tools at their disposal for doing so were quite limited. The technologies that made telecommuting possible were many years away. Had workplaces offered options like flextime in the 1970s, they would not have been very practical for most people living in rural areas who did not have overnight delivery services, fax machines, and internet capability. Alternatives in Viroqua had access to a variety of tools for remaining connected to mainstream employment. Patti Deutsch, for example, marveled at the overnight shipping services that allowed her to work from home for a company based in California. "It's kind of amazing to think about," she said, "that I can talk to someone in the office in San Diego about a particular file, and then the actual file is in my hands the next day." Without such services, Patti would likely have had to choose between living in Viroqua or working at the job she enjoyed and in which she believed deeply.

Patti worked for a firm that certified organic farms. While her colleagues made the on-site inspections of farms applying for organic certification, Patti reviewed the extensive paperwork farmers submitted. Patti's work arrangements illustrated another important feature of Alternatives' lives that set them apart from the 1970s homesteaders. Rather than distance themselves from the mainstream economy in order to avoid participating in institutions they found distasteful and immoral as the back-to-the-landers had, Alternatives sought jobs that were compatible with their environmental, political, and social values—jobs that were personally meaningful as a result. Patti had been an advocate of sustainable farming for many years. Her job allowed her to earn a salary and to simultaneously contribute to a cause in which she believed.

Viroqua's Alternative community was full of examples of people who had found ways to bring their economic needs in line with their larger goals. Bjorn, for example, not only built furniture, but made his furniture largely from recycled wood and other materials that he salvaged from old buildings. One afternoon I noticed his car outside the Landmark Center where he was renting some shop space at the time, and I stopped in to see what he working on. He was in the midst of finishing a bookcase made from, among other materials, recycled bead board. He explained that one of the things he really liked about the recycled wood was how the new paints and finishes looked when applied over remnants of old paints that often coated reclaimed wood. The uneven and cracked paint beneath the new finish gave the piece a highly textured surface, as if the bookcase had been painted many times over the years, even though it was new. In addition to appreciating the aesthetic qualities of the recycled wood, Bjorn saw the recycling of materials as a stand against "throwaway culture." Like Patti, Bjorn rolled his environmental principles into a livelihood using his artistic skills in a way that allowed him to make a living in Viroqua.

When he and Brie bought an old farmhouse outside town, Bjorn was able to fit the final piece of his life's puzzle together. He turned the garage into a workshop, allowing him to work at home in the country and care for his children at the same time. Pulling into their driveway in warm weather, I often saw the overhead shop door open, Bjorn working inside, while Gianna and Luka played in the yard where Bjorn could see them. Brie hoped to develop a business based in their home as well. Brie had a reputation for baking delicious and beautiful cakes, and she enjoyed entertaining. She hoped she might be able to turn part of their property, an old pole barn, into a rustic, yet elegant, site to rent out for weddings and other events, which she could also cater. Alternatives engaged in an ultimate kind of multitasking—figuring out how to make a living, care for children, and cultivate a meaningful community for themselves all at once. Living in Viroqua allowed them to do it.[10]

It was easier to live a countercultural life in the United States at the turn of the twenty-first century than it was forty years earlier. Alternative people found ways to incorporate practices and products that seemed quite radical to most Americans in the 1970s into their lives in less radical ways, in part because many of these practices had become a part of mainstream culture. Practices like eating organic produce that were dismissed as nonsense by the popular press in the 1970s had become widely acceptable, as evidenced both by the growing share of the agricultural economy it represented and by the degree to which fashion and consumer magazines increasingly covered these practices in a positive light (Croll 2005).

Further, in the 1970s, most people who wanted to eat organic produce had to grow it at home. In Viroqua, it was possible to purchase such produce at any of the three principle grocery stores in town. And the availability of organic produce in stores was not the only way that contemporary markets made countercultural life easier for Alternatives than it had been for the homesteaders of the 1970s. Living in an environmentally responsible manner was an extremely important part of the way many Alternatives talked about their lives and their identities. Many other environmentally friendly strategies used by the back-to-the-landers had been commercialized and were now readily available in the marketplace. The Alternatives saw themselves as "green consumers" who could "have a positive impact

---

10. While building a home from the ground up was a mark of authenticity among the homesteaders of the 1970s, Alternatives tended not to build their own homes but to renovate old ones. If they did build, they mostly did so with commercially available materials, and most incorporated electricity and indoor plumbing. Many incorporated green technologies such as solar panels, and highly efficient water and heating systems, and they tried to recycle materials and appliances rather than sending them to a landfill.

on the environment without significantly compromising [their] way of life" by making careful choices about the products and services they used (Elkington, Hailes, and Makower 1999, 333), whereas their back-to-the-land predecessors might have found "green consumption" a contradiction in terms. None of these material practices, such as buying organic foods rather than producing one's own food, seemed like selling out to the Alternatives, as it might have seemed to the homesteaders of the 1970s. Buying produce at the Food Co-op meant that Alternatives were supporting two types of commercial institutions they believed socially beneficial: the member-owned co-op and the small farms that supplied it.

In addition, Alternatives were often willing to make trade-offs—pragmatic concessions to contemporary circumstances. As one Alternative parent said in explaining why she sometimes allowed her children to eat processed hot dogs, "You just have to pick your battles. You can't always do everything right all of the time. If we're going to be busy doing some good things, like getting the garden ready to plant, and hanging the clothes out to dry instead of just throwing them in the dryer which would be faster, then sometimes we are just going to have to eat hot dogs."

But even these kinds of concessions to speed and convenience could often be accomplished using convenience products that better fit Alternative concerns. By the time I studied Viroqua, the market had responded to consumers who wanted to exercise their social and environmental goals in the marketplace with products that enabled Alternatives to engage in practices that they felt were important, such as eating natural and organic foods (even hot dogs), even when they could not produce the foods themselves. Though the breakfast I ate with Patti Deutsch and her family consisted of whole-wheat waffles and homemade yogurt from their own organic herd's milk, Patti captured the need for consumer compromise nicely when she chuckled that though she and her husband Paul tried to cook most of what they ate from scratch, they had "as many boxes of Amy's frozen spinach and cheese snacks in [their] freezer as anyone."

Patti was referring to Spinach Feta Snacks, "a delicious combination of organic feta cheese, tofu, and baked spinach inside a light tender crust,"[11]

---

11. Amy's Kitchen website, products: snacks: "Spinach Pizza Snack," www.amyskitchen. com/products/category_view.php?prod_category=5 (accessed December 12, 2004). Amy's Kitchen has since discontinued this product.

a product made by the Amy's Kitchen company. Based in Petaluma, California, Amy's Kitchen makes and markets natural and vegetarian convenience foods, and is itself a good example of a large commercial enterprise that grew out of Alternative-type concerns. As the company's website explains, "We didn't set out to become the nation's leading natural frozen food brand. All we wanted to do was create a business that would allow us to earn a living by providing convenient and tasty natural vegetarian meals for people like ourselves, who appreciated good food, but were often too busy to cook 'from scratch.'"[12] Far from attempting to live self-sufficiently, Alternatives were happy to take advantage of such products because they freed them to prioritize their activities, an option the 1970s homesteaders did not have (Agnew 2004), both because of their commitment to self-sufficiency and because such products were not yet widely available.

This is not to say that all of the Alternatives in Viroqua were leading largely conventional lives. There were some intentional communities in Vernon County, at least one of which had roots in the 1970s back-to-the-land movement, and which many people credited as the initial magnet for other Alternative families who began to trickle in during the 1980s. A few Alternatives believed deeply in a variety of ideas associated with the New Age. At a Waldorf School function, for example, I overheard a parent attribute her toddler's dislike of baths to the child's astrological sign. A few Alternative farms went beyond organic production to include the biodynamic agricultural practices developed by Rudolf Steiner, who also developed Waldorf education.[13]

It would not be fair to suggest that everyone in the Alternative crowd had a financially easy time of it. Not everyone was able to make a living in the ways that people like Patti and Bjorn did. Many Alternatives did

---

12. Amy's Kitchen website, About Us, www.amyskitchten.com/about_us/index.php (accessed December 12, 2004).

13. In addition to the Waldorf educational philosophy, Rudolf Steiner developed an approach to agriculture he called "biodynamics." The biodynamic approach was designed to blend scientific methods with a spiritual attitude toward the earth, inspired by Steiner's reverence for the peasants he observed as a child in eastern Austria. Biodynamics emphasizes the "spiritual history" of the earth, the spiritual connections between humans and the cosmos, and it includes very specific instructions on certain agricultural methods designed to "nourish" the earth (Barnes 1997). Some biodynamic practices such as the application of various fertilizing preparations to the soil are not so different from the steps many organic farmers take. Other biodynamic rituals are more mystical and much less conventional.

sacrifice professional jobs for the benefits of living in Viroqua, piecing together livelihoods in service jobs, substitute teaching, and other part-time work. I also knew of Alternative families who supplemented their incomes with public assistance, usually food stamps or WIC (the state's Special Supplemental Nutrition Program for Women, Infants and Children). While I often heard Alternative Viroquans I knew complain about being broke at times, or wish aloud, as Brie did one afternoon as she folded laundry, that she could afford to shop for a pair of jeans that truly fit the way she liked somewhere other than a thrift store, many were able to leverage their educations and cultural capital to piece together a living.[14]

Life As a Rubik's Cube

Carving out an Alternative existence required a great deal of deliberate work and strategizing. Alternatives shared with the 1970s back-to-the-landers a deep belief in their own agency—that they could and were in a sense obligated to make a nearly ideal life in the country work. The difference between them is that the Alternatives did not assume that going back to the land, by itself, was necessarily sufficient for achieving a good life. Living in Viroqua was just one piece of a larger puzzle that included finding acceptable economic opportunities, forming social ties, and meeting the educational needs of their children, that Alternatives had to complete to live the life they sought.

Some of the conversations I heard that best typified the complexity of these decisions were the stories told by those attending an open house informational meeting at Pleasant Ridge Waldorf School. On an early spring evening, twelve parents of mostly preschool-age children gathered at Pleasant Ridge, along with several of the school's faculty and staff members, for a school tour and overview of the Waldorf philosophy and curriculum. While their children played in another classroom supervised by children from the upper grades, the parents and staff members sat in a circle of

---

14. One of the questions Alternatives asked me was what I knew about how their fellow Alternatives made a living. Said one, "We just wonder how people do it. I mean, I know there are a few people with trust funds, but it seems like there are a lot of underemployed [Alternative] people—we just don't understand where they're getting enough money to live."

chairs in the fourth-grade room. Like the school's hallways, the walls of the classroom were covered with students' artwork. A very detailed and realistic chalk drawing of a male mallard duck covered a large portion of one of the classroom's blackboards. The drawing was probably part of a lesson in zoology, a central component of the Waldorf curriculum for grade four. The room contained many natural objects, including branches and dried leaves, and the fourth grade's pet birds chirped throughout the meeting. On the classroom's counter, whole apples and an assortment of herbal teas were laid out for the visiting parents.

Most of the parents were visiting Viroqua for the express purpose of investigating the school and trying to determine whether a move to Viroqua was the right decision for their families. One couple had already taken the plunge and moved to the area and was in the process of renovating an old farmstead. Pleasant Ridge was one of the features that attracted them to Viroqua, and they were attending the information night to meet the families whose children might be starting kindergarten with their eldest son the following fall. Only one of the parents at the meeting had lived in Viroqua for a long period of time. Others came from Milwaukee and communities closer to Madison. Two families came from Minnesota. Initially, all in attendance introduced themselves and said a bit about what brought them to the meeting. Peter Davis was the seventh parent to introduce himself.

> I'm Peter Davis. My wife Renee and I have two daughters, and we're thinking of moving up here to the area.[15] And I think we're pretty sold on Waldorf education. We both grew up in small towns, and I remember my elementary education as being seven hours of drudgery that seemed like it went on for years and years, and I really don't want to subject my daughters to the same sort of thing. And the biggest struggle we're having—we live outside of Madison—is whether or not to sell our house and move up here.

---

15. With the exception of Mary Christensen, all of the names in the section on the open house have been changed. This meeting was my only encounter with most of the families present, and though they knew that I was recording the meeting and why, I did not want to use their real names without checking with them again first. Pseudonyms have been chosen to reflect that in almost all of the married couples at this meeting, husbands and wives had different last names, or hyphenated names that combined both of their last names.

"So," he continued jokingly, "if y'all would just pick up the school and move it to [the town where we currently live]..." He laughed, and the rest of the room laughed with him.

"How about moving the school to Duluth [Minnesota]?" suggested a couple who were visiting from that area and also considering a move to Viroqua. Everyone laughed again.

Then one of the school's staff members spoke up, saying, "We made that move to Viroqua, and we would never go back."

Peter asked the couple who had moved to the area in the last month, "You folks live here in the community?"

Stephanie answered, "We live about twenty miles away, little town called Coon Valley. We have a little hobby farm just outside."

"But we too moved from the metropolis," added Stephanie's husband Todd. There was chuckling in the room, and Peter's wife Renee was next to introduce herself.

> I'm Renee Stanley, and we've been exploring lots of different ideas about how to educate our kids. I mean we started out [thinking] we're going to home school. But our oldest daughter, who is four, *cannot* wait to go to school.... And so we've been looking at all the public schools where we are now. We're very disappointed. And I think that Waldorf education appeals to us for a lot of reasons. I'm a writer, Peter's a musician, and I think that the way that the arts are wended through the Waldorf curriculum is very attractive to us—art isn't something that you go to for half an hour once a week. But as Peter said, the decision to move to Viroqua is really weighty. It's very weighty. Molly is four, so we think at the outside we've got a year, but that's still a really short time to decide to move and uproot our lives. We're here hoping to get a little more information to point us either this way or that way with it. The whole thing's like a Rubik's Cube, trying to fit all the pieces together—where we're going to live, where we're going to work, where we're going to go to school.

A member of the school's staff chimed in, "Ultimately, it's a leap of faith." There were affirming chuckles throughout the group.

"Yeah," sighed Renee in agreement. "Ultimately, yeah."

Renee's image of the Rubik's Cube is telling of the relationship many Alternatives, and particularly those who had recently arrived, had with

Viroqua as a place. The reason for any of these people to move to Viroqua was that doing so might help them get closer to fitting the various pieces of their lives together in a coherent way—so that the needs of each individual family member could be met.

The next person to introduce herself was the school's development co-ordinator. As if to respond to Peter and Renee's concerns, she explained:

> My name's Mary Christensen, and I'm the development coordinator here at the school, which translates into fund-raising and working with the adults in all kinds of ways, but basically supporting the nontuition part of our budget, whatever that is, [and] outreach. My husband and I moved here in 1993 with our six-year-old to attend first grade.[16] We'd been in a Waldorf kindergarten in Berkeley—California—so we've done that too. And that [move to Wisconsin] *was* a big deal—about selling the house, or keeping it for a year, just in case. So I work at the school. I've been here since 1993 and started working here two years later, starting with being on committees and getting involved.
>
> What attracted us to Waldorf education was really the holistic quality of what it would mean for [our daughter's] experience of education, the arts, everything about it, including handwork. My husband is a builder and I'm more the academic, so we needed something we could both sink our teeth into if we were going for private education, because politically, we didn't really feel like that was really what we wanted to do. But we felt that this model offered something truly different, something worth working for, for society as well as our family. That's how I feel about it. Which is why I'm still working here even after [our daughter] graduated last year from eighth grade. She's now at Viroqua High School, just had her first softball game to-night—still a little bit chilly yet.

Several people in the room chuckled, no doubt thinking of the snow that lingered on the ground outside.

Children were an important part of the reason that adults were willing to pick up and move to Viroqua. In the sense that they worked hard

---

16. It is interesting to note the way that Mary, like other Waldorf parents, spoke about her relationship to the school. Rather than saying that they moved to Viroqua so that her daughter could attend the first grade, the way she constructed this sentence and the next one ("we'd been in a Waldorf kindergarten") suggested that, not only her daughter, but she and her husband as well enrolled at the school. This may reflect the deep involvement in children's schooling, and in the school community, cultivated by Waldorf programs in general.

at imparting specific social and cultural skills to their children, the Alternative approach to parenting was generally consistent with what sociologists have found among most middle- and upper-middle-class American families (Lareau 2003). Alternative parenting added layers of intention to middle-class parenting, in that child-rearing strategies were, like other choices, made with larger goals in mind. Alternative parents assumed a connection between the raising of kind, curious, self-aware children with making a contribution to the future of the planet. Transmitting the importance of the individual to their children was an important part of what Alternative parents said about their attraction to the Waldorf school, and the Waldorf philosophy's emphasis on developing the whole child in a setting that cultivated a sense of belonging to a small group was a good cultural fit for Alternative parents' goals.[17]

These larger goals were evident in the ways that Alternative parents implicitly and explicitly criticized mainstream culture, as in the Halloween event described in the first chapter. They were critical of materialism, consumerism, and saw raising children in a small town, and in alternative institutions like a Waldorf school, as part of a project that was not only good for their own families but good for society at large. For the parents at the Pleasant Ridge information night, moving to Viroqua was only one piece of a larger puzzle. The school itself was another. Mary's story exemplified the way many Alternative parents had tried to find an educational option for their children that "fit" both their educational values and the skills they wanted to pass on to their child and to the school community. It also had to be a good fit for their political values and social goals. Alternative parents carefully weighed the trade-offs of moving to Viroqua and choosing a certain kind of education. Mary was not the only parent who struggled with the political implications of sending her child to a private school. Like many social liberals in the United States, she felt strongly about the importance of public schools and worried that by removing her children from them she would be contributing to the decline

---

17. Indeed, the transmission of this set of messages about the importance of the individual and individual growth seemed to be successful, at least in the sense that graduates of Pleasant Ridge constructed their experiences there in the same terms. Julia Hundt, a graduate of Pleasant Ridge and a college student when I met her, said this when I asked her what she valued about having attended a Waldorf school: "You come out a fully formed person, a curious person who is interested in learning about the world and capable of doing things."

of the public school system. In the end, however, she decided that the education her daughter would receive from a Waldorf school would be the best way to help her grow into an adult capable of contributing to society in a positive way.[18]

Mary continued with an observation about the things that drew families to Pleasant Ridge and to Viroqua.

> I think there are many common themes. Both my husband and I grew up in a very rural area in Minnesota, so we wanted that for our children, but we'd lived in the city for twenty years, so we wanted that too—all of it. But what we're finding here is that because there are lots of us here, we can *create community. We have to take initiative. That makes it more real.* So you can find it if you search. There's lots of hard work involved, but there's hard work everywhere.

This creation of community through hard work was a recurring theme that reflected the Alternative ethic of agency. It also reflects what theorists like Melucci (1996) argue is the hallmark of contemporary life: the ability to choose everything for oneself. With so many choices, critics ask, what's to prevent individuals' spinning off into myriad little worlds of their own? One answer is in a conception of community that rests on a personalist commitment that assumes community can be made, and that the very process of *making* community enriches the lives of the individuals in it.

Choosing Viroqua

Alternatives often told me that they selected Viroqua over other small towns because they believed it was a place where they would find people like themselves. Traditionally, sociologists who study community, and particularly the possibilities for community in urban settings, have found that

---

18. Pleasant Ridge is an important part of Viroqua's attraction for Alternative families, but it seems that by itself, it might not have been a sufficient reason for families to move there. More than one parent told me, as Susan Townsend once did, "[Pleasant Ridge] is a good fit for our family right now, but we wouldn't have come [to Viroqua] if Pleasant Ridge was the only [educational] option." The real importance of the school in the growth of the Alternative community is that it signified the presence of an Alternative community in the area, which in turn attracted more Alternatively minded residents.

the "kinds of people" who live in certain locations has been a reason for individuals to *leave* small towns and rural places for urban ones.[19] Most of the newcomers to Viroqua with whom I spoke cited the kinds of people as one of the primary reasons they lived there. Living in a naturally beautiful area that was safe for children was their goal, but as the Alternative quoted earlier put it, they also wanted to find a small town with people they could be friends with, that is, people like themselves. Asked to elaborate on such statements, Alternatives typically characterized such a place as having a critical mass of "liberal" or "progressive" or "open-minded" residents.

How did they know where to find such people? For many, the presence of the Waldorf school was an indication that they would find people like themselves in Viroqua, or at least that Viroqua was not, as one said, the "average small town." Dave Ware and Tamsen Morgan's story about how they came to live near Viroqua exemplified the kind of strategies that Alternatives used to examine the opportunities and constraints before them and to make choices within them to construct the lifestyle they had in mind. After spending a year traveling around the world working on organic farms, they returned to their home in the Twin Cities and began planning their next move. Initially, they looked at real estate in New England, but they found that it was too expensive. They turned their attention to the upper Midwest. Tamsen explained:

> We actually had a checklist. The list included things like "independent bookstores, food co-ops, Quaker meetings—not because we would go— but because we figured that if there were Quakers around, there would be people like us. And we hung up a map and used pins to mark some of these things, and we found this little cluster right around this area.[20]

---

19. Robert E. Park and his Chicago school sociologist colleagues posited that in an urban center, anyone could find a community of like-minded people: "In the long run every individual finds somewhere among the varied manifestations of city life the sort of environment in which he expands and feels at ease; finds, in short, the moral climate in which his peculiar nature obtains the stimulations that bring his innate dispositions to full and free expression" (1967, 41). The result was that social life in cities was importantly centered in any number of widely varied subcultural groups. Fischer's (1982) research in the late 1970s and 1980s found support for this theory in that city dwellers (who were disproportionately young and single) cited "kinds of people here" as the top reason for living where they did, while this reason was cited by fewer than 10% of residents of suburban and semirural places.

20. How had this concentration of Alternative people developed in Viroqua? The answer adds additional depth to our understanding of the social and historical context in which this Alternative community is produced. Part of the answer has to do with affordability and the economic

The Alternatives did not have the same relationship to the town as the Regulars or Main Streeters, insofar as they were there because they wanted to live in *a* small town with certain characteristics, but not necessarily *this* small town. The Alternative people came to Viroqua because they wanted the kind of traditional community associated with small-town life. But that kind of community is premised on the kinds of long-standing ties of kinship and shared history that newcomers do not have. In addition, because the Alternative folks were looking for like-minded people, they were less interested in the kind of traditional ties shared by people thrown together by accidents of birth in particular places and families. As a result, they had to make their own community, and their deep belief in their own efficacy made them confident that they could do so. The ways they enacted community were premised on its very absence. Alternatives assumed that community was something that was "built," as in the commonly used phrase "community building." Everyone shared some ideas about what community should be like, and by behaving according to those ideas about what community should be, the Alternatives performed it together on a daily basis.

The sociological literature on tourism is useful for understanding what the Alternatives are up to, in the sense that it recognizes how places can be made to conform to an audience's expectations (MacCannell 1989; Urry 1990) by creating a product—an experience—for a tourist audience that seems "authentic" to tourists because it meets their expectations of what the place should be like. But the point of the performance of community in Viroqua was not commercial and not for an audience of people passing through. It was for the community of Alternative people itself.

---

changes that have opened up opportunities to put the land and buildings of this area to new uses. As in other locations in and outside the United States, it became possible for countercultural people to appropriate new residential spaces, because these places and the structures in them are in transition as they no longer serve the purpose they once did. Just as the departure of a great number of factories from inner cities made large buildings available for relatively inexpensive loft space in the 1970s (Zukin 1982), in the 1980s and 1990s, the reduction in the number of farms in the Coulee region where Viroqua is located has freed up small farmstead properties at relatively low prices compared to other parts of the country. In rural areas, the shift to a "post-productive" landscape means that land and farmsteads once engaged in agricultural production are now becoming available for other uses (Halfacree and Boyle 1998). The area's hilly topography provided opportunities for people who wanted to own smaller plots of land that would not be of interest to larger farming operations, since it is difficult to grow row crops on it. These smaller plots were available to "hobby farmers," retirees looking for recreational land, and others.

Traditionally, social scientists have questioned the authenticity and quality of such "from scratch" communities, particularly in cases when such communities contain fairly homogeneous members. In an effort to distinguish the kind of interdependence associated with traditional forms of community from the kinds of ties shared by people who share similar leisure activities and tastes in consumer products, Bellah and his group (1985) distinguish a lifestyle enclave from actual "community":[21]

> Whereas a community attempts to be an inclusive whole, celebrating the interdependence of public and private life and of different callings of all, lifestyle is fundamentally segmental and celebrates the narcissism of similarity.... Such enclaves are segmental in two senses. They involve only a segment of each individual, for they concern only private life, especially leisure and consumption. And they are segmental socially in that they include only those with a common lifestyle. (1985, 72)

The Alternatives were deliberately trying to *overcome* the division between public and private life that characterizes lifestyle enclaves. A lifestyle enclave is exactly what they were trying to avoid, though they did expect that their choice of living in Viroqua would free them from ethnic or religious obligations, and it did represent in no small way a matter of individual expression for them (both important elements of a lifestyle enclave). Though they did not use Bellah's language, many of the Alternatives specifically rejected lifestyle enclaves for the same superficiality and shallowness that bothered Bellah and his team. They wanted a community in which the public and private facets of their lives were integrated.

Conventional approaches to community make it hard to see that, to a large extent, all communities have to be constructed purposefully. The Alternatives took as a starting point the tradition of thinking about small towns as sites of community, and they found it when they arrived, not because it was necessarily a site where community would automatically exist for them, but because they went about creating it according to the image of community they had in mind when they arrived. The experience of living

---

21. To be fair, the *Habits of the Heart* team does not paint lifestyle enclaves and communities as mutually exclusive. They argue that "most groups in America today embody an element of community as well as an element of lifestyle enclave" (74).

in Viroqua confirmed their expectation of what they would find there. The existence of "community" became self-fulfilling in this way.

So it was not that the "community" the Alternatives created was somehow false, or a mere simulation of community. It was a particular model of community premised on a specific logic of commitment from its members. As Mary Christensen put it, it was in the "initiative" in the actual working together to produce community that a *real* community—and, by implication, a *better* community for being the result of deliberate action—was actually made. Alternatives went to Viroqua looking for a specific kind of community life. If it wasn't there to begin with, they drew on their ethic of agency—their belief in the moral value of deliberate work in service of a long-term goal—to produce it.

3

THE MAIN STREETERS

The Busiest People in Town

"Is that *all* the butter you're going to use?" the woman serving the pancakes asked me incredulously. I was sitting at the end of a long table in the basement of Good Shepherd Lutheran Church at the annual Fat Tuesday Pancake Supper fund-raiser. The woman, whose attire included an apron and several strands of plastic Mardi Gras beads, was holding two more heavy-looking plates of pancakes destined for other diners, but she was waiting for a response. The pat of butter on my blueberry pancakes seemed pretty generous to me, but I added more. The woman smiled and, apparently satisfied, moved on.

It was not the only time I witnessed butter promotion in Viroqua. To cite another instance, it was the custom among the staff and volunteers (of which I was one) at the Vernon County Historical Society Museum to sit down for coffee and snacks in the building's kitchen at 2:15 each afternoon. Museum visitors, if there were any, were usually invited to join us, especially if they were conducting genealogical research using the museum's people files. One afternoon, a volunteer brought some homemade kringles to share during our coffee break. She had also brought a stick of butter, and she enjoined us to spread some on the top of the kringles.[1] Just then, a museum visitor joined us and made the mistake of asking if we were spreading oleo on our kringles. "Bite your tongue!" the kringle baker exclaimed. "People around here don't milk cows morning and night for you to go eating oleo."

Viroqua's Main Streeters always had an eye open for things they could do to promote and improve the town. They did this in an infinite variety of ways, including extensive volunteerism, holding elected offices, and even in the casual, if relentless, promotion of local products. Some of my fellow historical society volunteers were among the diners and servers at the pancake supper. For five dollars ($3.50 if you bought a ticket in advance from a church member) the supper included a stack of three large pancakes (one's choice of plain, blueberry, or chocolate chip), sausage links or patties, applesauce, fruit juice, and coffee, with ice cream for dessert. The church members worked as a well-oiled machine. Two sat at a table at the entrance collecting money and tickets. Another woman then helped those who had paid find seating at one of the many folding tables set up around the room. Some wiped and re-set places recently vacated by diners. Some took pancake orders and delivered plates to diners. Through a pass-through in the wall, I could see a number of other volunteers cooking and washing dishes. I suspected that the pancake supper, like other fund-raising events I had attended in town, was run largely by the same volunteers year after year.

Garith Steiner, the president of Vernon Memorial Hospital, once told me quite seriously that the way to get things done in Viroqua was "to find the busiest people in town and ask them to help." Many of the town's busiest people seemed to be at the pancake supper. Though I did not know them all by name, I recognized Vernon County Historical Society volunteers, elected county and city officials, Viroqua Area School Board members, Viroqua Partners participants, members of the Retired Teachers Association, the Associates to Restore the Temple Theatre (ARTT) members,[2] Lions,

---

1. Kringle is a leavened Scandinavian pastry. Most recipes for kringle dough already include at least half a cup of butter. There are number of types of kringle. The one found in Viroqua is the Norwegian kringle, which is a lightly sweetened dough baked in small figure-eight shapes.

2. After December 2002, the group's official name changed to Associates of the Restored Temple Theatre, to reflect the completion of the building's restoration.

Rotarians, and Masons, and members of a variety of other organizations. I had seen many of the people in the room in more than one meeting around town. They were, as one Viroquan put it, "the group of people in town who really get involved."

Many of the people at the pancake supper also attended the historical society's Fourth of July Strawberry Shortcake Social the following summer. The historical society held this event yearly at the Sherry-Butt House, one of the historic buildings it owned and operated as a museum. In addition to historical society board members, a number of the society's members had been enlisted to assist with the event. Many individuals, mostly older women, baked the shortcakes at home and delivered them to the house. Others, including myself, assisted on the day of the event. In addition to giving tours of the house, I served lemonade to customers as they came through the strawberry shortcake line. Standing next to me, scooping vanilla ice cream, was Dr. Robert Starr. Despite the hot summer weather, the ice cream was frozen hard and required a great deal of work to scoop from the cardboard tub.

"Gee Doc, looks like you're getting a workout there. Good for your golf swing, I bet!" said one customer as Dr. Starr deposited ice cream atop his bowl of shortcake and strawberries. Two customers later, another warned him, "Better watch out for that repetitive motion disease. Could mess up your golf swing." Eventually I lost count of how many customers commented on the effect that scooping hard-packed ice cream might have on the doctor's golf game. Dr. Starr had recently retired from his work at Vernon Memorial Hospital and his practice at one of the local clinics. He was a familiar presence on the golf course at the local country club and at events like the Strawberry Shortcake Social. When he was not volunteering at such events, he and his wife Janet often attended them, or appeared on the list of event sponsors.

The Starrs were an example of the kind of Main Streeters who, while they were not originally from Viroqua, had dedicated themselves to the town. They had come to the area when Dr. Starr began his job at the local hospital. They had "moved in and joined in" (Cloke et al. 1998), integrating themselves into the local community. People who move in and join in are defined by their expectation that small-town life includes not only basic friendliness and neighborliness but a certain level of involvement in the town's organizations and associations. Viroqua, for the most part, returned the Starrs' apparent affection for the town and accorded them respect. In the mid-1970s, when anthropologist Arnold Strickon asked Viroquans in his survey if there were people in the community they "looked up to," Dr. and Mrs. Starr tied with two members of the local clergy as people most frequently cited.[3]

Unlike the Alternatives who moved in and joined in with others who shared a commitment to "alternative" ways of life, the Starrs and the Steiners joined in with the group I call Main Streeters. Main Streeters shared with the Alternatives an ethic of agency that emphasized the importance of individuals' contributions to the improvement of community life, and individuals' responsibility to make the community—that is, to make Viroqua—a better place. Like the Alternatives, Main Streeters shared a sense that the greatest possible moral failing was apathy. Main Streeters believed that good people worked to improve the town, and they believed that the better the town, the better life would be for everyone who lived there. "Better" meant a variety of things to different Main Streeters. For many it meant a more secure economic future. For others it meant more beautiful and pleasant surroundings to contribute to residents' and visitors' enjoyment of the town (and, by extension, to the town's financial security). For still others, it meant improving the educational or job opportunities for their own, and others', children. Most Main Streeters tended to view all these goals as mutually reinforcing. The words and actions of the Main Streeters recalled Tocqueville's thoughts on "self-interest properly understood" (Tocqueville 2000, 609). Main Streeters' saw their own personal happiness and fortunes as intertwined with the success of the town.

In this chapter I examine the Main Streeters' culture of community. Unlike the Alternatives, Main Streeters' logic of commitment operated through a commitment to Viroqua itself. They were committed to it as a particular community, as opposed to relating to it as an instrument in service of some broad set of universal goals. There was variation in the source of that commitment. For many, the commitment sprang from being raised in the area or having another source of long-standing personal connection to Viroqua as a place. Other Main Streeters were relatively recent arrivals

---

3. Very few of Strickon's respondents actually answered this question. To be clear, I use Dr. Starr as an example here because he was highly visible in the community and certainly respected by many. This is not to suggest that he was necessarily universally liked.

who did not have the same lifelong connection to Viroqua but, who, like the Starrs, had a feeling that being a "part of the community" was something that responsible adults naturally did wherever they lived. Such new Main Streeters essentially adopted Viroqua and committed themselves to the town and its future simply by virtue of moving there.

Community/Family

Carolyn and Odell Solverson are a good example of Main Streeters who had very long ties to Viroqua. Both were raised in Viroqua and had large extended families that were descended from grandparents and great grandparents who immigrated to the area from Norway. When they talked about their lives, they constructed their personal histories in a way that included family and friends whose lives preceded their own. The depth of their unique connections to the area was punctuated by the many photographs they shared with me during our interview—photographs of their families that complemented their stories about their histories in the area. Odell's grandmother had been an avid photographer, and the Solversons had been diligently collecting information about the people in the photos while the family members who remembered them were still alive to provide the information. "I have to show you my favorite picture of [Odell's] grandma," Carolyn said during our interview, as she produced a black-and-white photo of a woman posing on the hood of a car. "Every spring she got a new girdle," Carolyn laughed. "So here she is on her husband's car in her new girdle, her pearls, and her tennis shoes."

"That's probably in the late '50s," said Odell.

"She had her daughter Rosemary, who's the same age as Odell, take the picture, and her husband was just mortified," Carolyn laughed.

Odell grew up on a farm outside Viroqua and studied chiropractic in Davenport, Iowa, after graduating from the University of Wisconsin at La Crosse. When he finished his training, there were already four chiropractors in Viroqua, but Odell was not deterred. "There was no second thought in my mind that I would have my practice here," he explained. "I was born here. I was raised here. This is where my background, my heritage, is. This is where my family is. So it wasn't even a question. This would be where I would end up practicing once I came back again."

Carolyn explored the possibility of living in other parts of the state before deciding to return to Viroqua, and it did not take her long to decide to do so. "When I turned of age," she explained, "I moved to Stevens Point, and Green Bay, and lived there for a while.... I was so homesick for the [Viroqua] area that I moved to La Crosse to be closer to home, and I lasted about three months there [laughing] and I came back to Viroqua.... I missed the smell of the really rich soil and the hills, and the rocks, and all the different-colored trees." She, like other Main Streeters, and Regulars as well, felt particular ties to the town as a physical place.

The Solversons both felt that their primary connection to the community was through their families. Their connection to Viroqua as a place was reinforced by, maybe premised on, even more particular and unique personal connections. It was their familial histories in the town that drew the Solversons into their involvement in community organizations. This was evident in the way that Carolyn saw her own efforts and involvement in the local community arising from a family history of helping others. Though nine of the eleven children in her family all shared a three-bedroom home with their parents when she was a child, she recalled that there were always additional people living in their house. Many Main Streeters described their efforts as a way to "give something back" to the community, and Carolyn's motivation for giving back was inspired by her mother's attempts to combat some of the worst aspects of everyone knowing everyone else's business in Viroqua. "Our mom was always taking in other families, and there were always people—abused women and their kids hiding from their husbands, sleeping on the floor—and she'd be taking care of them. So it was like a shelter almost, at times."

"How did it happen that your house became a refuge for a lot of people?" I asked her.

"My mom was illegitimate when she was born, and her birth father took off and left them.... And she suffered a lot of verbal abuse because of that—in the '20s and '30s, in [the village near Viroqua where they lived], and everybody knew your business. You couldn't keep any secrets at all. And I think that she decided she'd never ever treat anybody that way, and always try to be there to help people if they needed help. And I think we've all kind of adopted that mentality of just, well, if you need help, what can I do to help you? I think I see that in most of my siblings, even in the boys."

Odell described a similar sense of the ways that the long-term social ties in neighborhoods provided safety nets for individuals and families.

> When my mother passed away thirteen years ago, she was working out in the barn and she had a heart attack. I was married and [living] in town at that time, so when my dad called [to tell me about the heart attack], I met him at the hospital. I went back out [to my parents' farm] afterwards with my dad, and here, all the local farmers were on the farm. They were milking cows, they were feeding—it had to have been at least half a dozen or more families. So the cows got milked, the animals got fed, stuff got put away and everything. And all my dad had done was dropped [everything] and ran [to the hospital with my mother]. He didn't tell anybody [about her heart attack], but the word had gotten out.

The Solversons saw themselves not only as people who could be counted on to help but as embedded in networks on which they also knew they could implicitly rely.

For Main Streeters like the Solversons, with long family ties to the area, personal ties bound them not only into family networks and other relationships that were part of their private lives but into public networks. Perhaps because of the size of their extended families and their families' long memories of such experiences with neighbors and friends, the Solversons had a pretty expansive definition of family. When I asked her why she felt it was important to do the volunteer work that she did, Carolyn's answer literally tied family and community together. "I have a really high value on family and community. I just think that's so important. I put a high value on that."

For Carolyn, family and community were part of the same thing. Her "community involvement" sometimes took the form of a nurturing kind of personal involvement with others, like the support she offered to her children's friends, especially those whom she suspected had little support from their own parents. "She hugs everybody," said Odell. "It's so I can smell for alcohol," Carolyn replied. "When my oldest son's friends came over, I always asked had they had anything to eat, and I tried to make them feel welcome." Personal nurturing was the basis of the bonds that drew her into wider kinds of service, as in the Viroqua Partners and the historical society. Individual nurturing and civic engagement, for Carolyn, were mutually reinforcing.

Some Main Streeters had a similar sense of familial attachment to Viroqua without actually having been raised there. Vernie Smith, for example, grew up in Madison, but he had fond memories of spending summer vacations with his grandparents in Viroqua, and moved to Viroqua on his own as a young man. Nancy Rhodes also grew up visiting grandparents in Viroqua. After living in a number of places, including Texas and California, Nancy moved to Viroqua and was able to buy the large Victorian house she had fantasized about owning as a little girl. She ran the home as a bed-and-breakfast.

But it was also possible to develop a Main Street kind of community commitment without actually having any lifelong connections to the area. Garith's wife, Julie Steiner, laughed as she remembered some of the troubles she had when she began her job as news director at WVRQ, the local radio station.

> I can remember them laughing at me with the Norwegian names, not spelling them right. I'd always ask how to pronounce it, but when somebody would see it on a piece of paper, there'd always be a big chuckle because of the way I'd written it didn't match at all. . . . [My colleagues at the station] became my friends, still are my friends even though I don't work there anymore, and coming to town, working at the radio station really gives you an advantage meeting people. Usually they know who you are before you even have a clue who they are. That was nice. I got to know a lot of people in the community right away; it was really easy that way.

"What did people want to know about you?" I asked.

"Just about everything," replied Julie. "Where you're from, who your parents are."

"They check you out pretty good," her husband Garith added. Because both Garith and Julie grew up in Prairie du Chien, about half an hour from Viroqua, it was not hard for Viroquans to vet them through friends of friends. Garith explained:

> There was one lady [named Virginia] who worked at the hospital whose sister was a friend of the family's in Prairie [du Chien], and that's how they got the skivvy on me. So when I got out of college, I came here, didn't know anyone. I was a male nurse, and that was kind of bizarre. I had long

hair, kind of a hippie-looking kind of guy, and they needed to check [me] out, and they did. They did a nice job.... I didn't expect it to the extent that I was scrutinized, but it wasn't that I cared, because I didn't have too much to hide.... I knew if they did check me out, they'd probably find that I came from a pretty decent family and that I behaved myself when I lived there and that I was a pretty good student, and that. Now if they'd checked more in college, they might have found out something else [laughs], but in high school, I was pretty clean. Both of us were.... Once they got the skivvy from Virginia, on me—wow, [the other nurses at the hospital] just completely changed. None of them were ever rude or anything, a lot of them took me under their wing right away and showed me the ropes, but the relationship really improved once Virginia reported back that they had nothing to worry about.

I asked if Garith had ever felt pressure to change things about himself because of such scrutiny, and his answer led immediately to a discussion about how the Steiners felt their commitment to the town had developed over time. "I didn't really feel compelled to any great degree to have to make the change," he said. "And most people accepted me for who I was, not what I looked like or anything. That's why we're still here today."

"Uh-huh," agreed Julie.

Garith continued, "There's an absolute feeling of community, and people aren't judgmental as far as what I found. They really do let you do your thing. *As long as you're in some way contributing to the betterment of the community*—as long as you're doing that, and they know you can do that in many different ways. Even by disagreeing with them you are contributing in some fashion to making things better than they were the day before. And it's been a pretty good run. We've been here since '79."

I asked what that "feeling of absolute community" entailed. Julie answered, "People care about you, and you really find that out when you have a tragedy in your family or something. People here just come out of the woodwork. It's just amazing. And it's not just that—the way people greet you, and things like that."

"*Every* day," Garith interjected.

"Every day. But when you do have something like that happen, it's just amazing, [the] outpouring of support and communication that you have from people."

Garith continued:

The feeling that I have is that there are so many people who are out there who really do try to make it better for the next generation, and when we came here, there were people looking forward. They don't spend a lot of time thinking about where they were but thinking about where we need to be and how we can get there. People, for the most part, have a tendency to try to bring people in, solicit their ideas. There doesn't seem to be as much of a cliquey thing. There are those out there, but people really—because they are all part of the community, and they recognize the value they place on themselves being part of it—they place value on other people being part of it. It is the way, every day, I'm walking down the street and they'll honk or they'll wave or they'll stop to talk to you, and sometimes not even about the bills that we generate at the hospital [laughs]! You know, they really are interested—how's [our daughter] Sarah doing over at college, or how are things with [our younger daughter] Megan. Or you'll get invited to things...just go and have some fun.

Like the Solversons, the Steiners described a public life that was intertwined with their private social lives. Explained Garith:

Just yesterday I got to go pheasant hunting for the first time, and it was just through a community contact. And we had a community discussion amongst four of us who live in the area about what we need next, and what some of the problems are that we're facing and how do we solve those problems. And this was just four guys sitting in a truck getting ready to pheasant hunt, talking about the Viroqua community.... It really is a special kind of thing.

This community is really interested in trying to make things important for the young people here. They have a tendency to really put forth quite a bit of effort, whether it's time, energy, or money, to see that there are things for the youth, and that's great. Whether it's the school, or the programs they offer in the summer with the Park and Rec, it's really great to see. That's one of the reasons that we've stayed here.

Whether they saw their involvement in the community as a function of preserving their heritage or as a way to improve the lives of subsequent generations of residents, Viroqua's Main Streeters perceived their "stake in the place [to be]...intergenerational" (Cloke et al. 1998). Traditionally, small-town residents like these have been professionals who served the community as leaders in local government, in religious and civic organizations, and as benefactors through charitable donations, as well as through direct assistance to needy individuals when necessary. Historically, members of this group remained respected by the rest of the town so long as the intentions appeared to be pure—that is, so long as they were seen as true supporters of the town and its people and not acting solely out of self-interest (Pedersen 1992). This continued to be true in Viroqua in the sense that, as the Steiners pointed out, what mattered most was that one tried to make a positive contribution to the community.

Of course, there was also plenty of self-interest in the Main Streeters' actions. Many Main Streeters said they "got involved" in part because they found it personally fulfilling. Carolyn's involvement was partially about the social connections it offered her. "I really enjoy the women, the other women who are on [the Viroqua Partners] and feel real close to them. I go in and see Ingrid [Mahan] almost every day, and June Pedretti there, so I feel a real connection." Others chalked up their efforts to personal fulfillment too. Said one, "I like to be needed." Said another, "I hate being idle. I need to be busy." Said a fourth Main Streeter, "I feel good when I see that I've accomplished something."[4]

In addition to a personal sense of fulfillment, Main Streeters had other interests at stake too. They were worried about their property values and about the businesses they owned and for which they worked. If the town deteriorated, all of these might suffer. If the town's fortunes took a turn for the worse, the Main Streeters had a great deal to lose. In this sense, they were somewhat like the group Cloke et al. (1998) describe as "local gentry." Fred Nelson, the Dahls, the Felixes, the Krauses, Nancy Rhodes, were all members of families that owned local businesses. Chuck Dahl was Viroqua's mayor for fifteen years, and he and his wife had been active in the Democratic Party at county and state levels. The Krauses were active in many organizations, including the historical society. Nancy Rhodes, Fred Nelson, and Steve Felix played key roles in getting the Main Street revitalization project underway.

---

4. Eliasoph and Lichterman (1999) point out that this description of a personal need or desire to make a contribution is one of the principal cultural options for talking about motivations in the United States.

A substantial number of Main Streeters had professional ties to Vernon Memorial Hospital. The Menns, the Macasaets, the Andrewses, and the Steiners all continued the tradition Dr. Starr was credited with encouraging—the involvement of physicians and hospital employees in the community. The first time I met Gigi Macasaet, we were volunteering at the historical society's table at the Vernon County Fair. Gigi had to use both hands to count up the number of organizations in which she was involved. The list included Toastmasters, the historical society, the hospital auxiliary, and she was just finishing her first term on the city council. Paula Menn taught English at the public high school, and headed the Associates to Restore the Temple Theatre, a nonprofit group that restored the dilapidated 1920's theater on Main Street (a project that required several million dollars). The theater reopened for its first season in 2002. Paula's husband, physician Jeffrey Menn, whose fascination with the traditions of the Old West was apparent in his cowboy-style attire, initiated and oversaw Viroqua's annual Wild West Days festival, which received a statewide award as an outstanding festival in 1999.

There were many other Main Streeters who worked in a variety of jobs, and some who were retired. The Arnetveits, Sharon Stoleson, Bea Small, June Pedretti, Vernie Smith, the Sherries, the Macks, and Thor Thorson were among the energetic people who showed up at apparently endless meetings, basketball games, and school plays. They enjoyed living in a small town in part because, as Gigi Macasaet once put it, they knew they could make a difference there. Similarly, Nancy Rhodes explained, "In a larger city, you run up against bigger interests.... You're just one of a million little grains of sand. In Viroqua, an individual can really have an impact." Members of this group often had wide civic, professional, and personal networks outside the local community, but they were experts at getting things done in Viroqua.

Historically, one of the costs of "being involved" in a small town has been being subjected to the community's scrutiny (Pederson 1992; Lingeman 1980; Blumenthal 1932). Such scrutiny, even when admiring, was not always pleasant. Eighty-four-year-old Helen Felix, for example, said one of the things she disliked most about living in Viroqua was the feeling that she was being watched all the time. As a young woman, Mrs. Felix was probably watched even more than other Viroquans. She arrived in town from the Twin Cities to marry Roland Felix, who was about to take the reins of his family's clothing store.[5] When we shared a table at the annual historical society dinner, Mrs. Felix mentioned her relief that society columns in the local newspaper had decreased in size and importance. Recalling a time when she "felt that anything she did might suddenly appear in print," she recounted the time when she and her husband built a new home. A curious woman asked her what the kitchen would be like. "I don't cook," Mrs. Felix explained to me, "so I didn't care about the kitchen enough to know what it was going to look like. So I said to this lady that there wasn't going to be one." The news that the Roland Felix family's new home would not include a kitchen appeared in the *Broadcaster* the following week.[6]

Jumping Right In

Evidence of Main Streeters' work was everywhere, but the most visible evidence of their work (and their relative success) was in the downtown, two blocks of which were recently added to the National Register of Historic Places. In the early '80s, Viroqua's downtown, like the business districts of other small towns, was ailing. When Wal-Mart opened on the north side of town in 1986, many feared it would spell further deterioration in the downtown (Ukens 1991; Jackson 1992). As the public versions of the narrative go, the owners of several downtown businesses solicited the help of

---

5. Until Steve Felix retired in 2006, Felix's clothing store was located at 102 South Main Street and claimed in its ad in the Yellow Pages to be the "Largest Clothing Store in Vernon County." Felix's carried men's and women's clothing and a selection of accessories like purses, wallets, and handkerchiefs. The shop also rented men's formal wear and sent clothing out for dry cleaning. Started by Steve's grandfather, Max, the store remained open for 101 years.

6. While members of the older generation of Main Streeters described an awareness that their actions, words, and even purchases were part of a spectacle in which the rest of the town had some interest, the younger members of this group did not seem to share such a feeling. If they did feel they were at times scrutinized by others, they did not say so. Assuming a genuine decrease in scrutiny, there might be a number of reasons for it. First, the town was larger than it was when Helen Felix was a young woman. A town that is even slightly larger may afford individuals somewhat more anonymity than a smaller one. Second, the actions and consumption patterns of prominent families in small towns were once an important source of information about places and trends beyond the town. The mass media and increased mobility decreased the need of small-town residents to acquire information about the rest of the world vicariously via the examples of a few families.

a state official whose job it was to provide advice to towns trying to sustain their local economies. The official recommended that the town compete to participate in Wisconsin's Main Street Program, sponsored at the national level by the National Trust for Historic Preservation. Viroqua won, becoming one of the smallest towns in the program. Within two years of winning participation, Viroqua's downtown looked better, some of the businesses initially threatened by Wal-Mart remained open, and, most surprisingly, several new businesses had moved into vacant buildings. An estimated 22.5 new jobs had been created in the downtown area (Ukens 1991). While I lived in Viroqua, an additional downtown project was completed: the reopening of the Temple Theatre.

Like other Main Streeters, Carolyn Solverson articulated the importance of downtown revitalization by invoking the town's history, heritage, and its future simultaneously.

> I just try to get involved and help because I see a lot of validity in what they're doing with the downtown revitalization and how important it really is to keeping our community alive. And I think about as a child, Friday nights were such a huge thing in Viroqua. It was just a huge social event. You didn't go downtown looking like I look now.[7] You combed your hair and you put on clean clothes—your clothes for downtown—and you went as a family. You went shopping. And it was just a huge deal. And then to see, just a few years ago, the downtown was literally dying out. And then all of a sudden, [the] Main Street [Program] came in, and how it's picked everything up, and it was really encouraging, and it's something I really believe in.

Like the Regulars, Main Streeters' commitment to the town as a particular place gave them reasons to be concerned about its historical heritage, though Main Street and Regular understandings of the important elements of this heritage sometimes clashed. Dave Thorson once complained about his heritage being taken away in terms of the informal rules around the use of natural areas for hunting, fishing, and trapping, and a way of life associated with these activities. The attempts to bring more "culture" and "fancy eating places" that Dave (in chapter 1) associated with "city"

---

7. Carolyn was dressed casually in jeans and sneakers.

life were, for him and other Regulars, violations of that rural heritage. For Main Streeters, heritage included not just the natural environment and rural traditions but also the built environment, particularly the buildings in the downtown, the town's history, and an economic identity anchored by locally owned businesses.

Nancy Rhodes was an articulate advocate of the connection between Viroqua's heritage, its older buildings, and its economic future. "You know," she said, "our forefathers didn't build us this environment with cheap products. They built us a quality environment. And we in the last decades have really not given back to that investment they made; we have taken away from it. We have not honored our forefathers in these towns when we don't take care of [our historic buildings]." It was not always easy to convince people of the economic utility of preserving buildings. She continued, "Why should [current owners care to reinvest in older buildings]? If the [rest of the] community is not sufficiently engaged in reinvesting, then why should they? There's nothing in it for them. So it's our responsibility, when we have these projects going, to establish a *culture* where they'd want to reinvest." Honoring the investments made by the town's forefathers and investing in its economic prospects were part of the same project, as Nancy and other Main Streeters saw it.

Nancy applied this reasoning equally to nearly every conceivable object of preservation. Whenever possible, she wanted to maximize the reuse of existing structures, which she saw as markers of authentic history, as in the case of the dilapidated gazebo she rescued when it was removed from the city cemetery. When local veterans' organizations began raising funds to build a veterans memorial, Nancy saw a perfect opportunity to reuse the gazebo. Responses to Nancy's efforts to preserve the gazebo by incorporating it into the new veterans memorial were mixed. On one hand, some of the veterans and some of the other members of the Viroqua Historic Preservation Commission agreed that the new memorial should incorporate the gazebo, which had originally been built in the cemetery as a tribute to veterans. On the other hand, the gazebo was in pretty rough shape and wouldn't necessarily be compatible with the design of the new memorial. One of the people who expressed skepticism about its usefulness was Maynard Vikmyr, a long-time member of, and staff person at, the American Legion hall. Maynard thought that it was going to need too much work to make it worth saving.

The gazebo precipitated a telling incident, however, when Nancy visited the Legion during happy hour to attend a meeting of the Veterans Memorial Committee. She bought a soda from me at the bar, and as she went into the back hall for the meeting, I overheard a patron, who was himself a veteran, saying that "some goddamned people in this town just have a lot of money to throw around and are just out to impress people." I had heard him swear about "those historic preservation people" in the past. He was hostile toward the preservation efforts as they had unfolded in the town, which he attributed to Main Streeters' self-aggrandizement. This was not his sentiment alone. The tension between valuing the work that Main Streeters do and skepticism about their underlying motives appears in existing studies of small-town life (see Blumenthal 1932; Pedersen 1992) and recurred in conversations I had with Regulars in Viroqua throughout my time there. Indeed, when a Regular friend read a draft of this book, his principal comment was that he felt the Main Streeters did what they did "to get their names out there."

Nancy had indeed ruffled many feathers in her preservation efforts, but she was aware of, and undaunted by, the criticism she received. She exemplified the ethic of agency the Main Streeters shared with the Alternatives, which emphasized individual abilities and contributions. Nancy did not consider herself an "outsider," but she knew others saw her that way. She felt she had largely overcome her "newcomer" status through her own hard work. "I don't believe in this thing about, 'Gosh, I've lived here for fifteen years and I'm still and outsider.' I don't believe in that....I believe you are as involved and as accepted as you want to be. And if you open yourself up and get out there, instead of waiting for people to come to you, that's what'll happen. I immediately jumped in and got started in stuff." On the other hand, she thought that not being raised in the community might have been to her advantage by making it easier for her to take risks. "I think I have a benefit that I'm not from here," she explained. "Those people who have lived next door to the same people all their lives probably have more of a fear of [social recrimination] than I do....But, again, it's that courage to stand up for what's right regardless of the [personal] ramifications of it."

Like the Alternatives, Main Streeters believed deeply that individuals could accomplish anything if they worked hard enough, especially if they enlisted the right kinds of help from others. The way to get things done in Viroqua was through personal networks, by getting "the right people to come to the table," and working slowly and strategically to build support for an idea one person at a time. Nancy recalled going from business to business to try to garner support for investigating ways to reinvigorate the downtown. Garith Steiner described the long process of passing a school-spending referendum during his tenure as school board president that was similar to the way he approached running the hospital. The success of any project, he insisted, required working through personal connections and relationships in the community, and building new ones when necessary. In the case of the referendum, he explained, it was a matter of addressing people's questions and finding answers when the advocates of the school addition did not already have them: "I make it a point to be out in the community. I even regularly go out to lunch in the community so I can be grabbed by someone...and that's actually a requirement of all the people that work in the management positions [at the hospital], that they need to be a part of the community in which they live."

I saw examples of this kind of approach to leadership and coalition building often. One particularly vivid example took place during a meeting of a small group of people who hoped to see a bicycle path built through several miles of unused railroad bed. The nucleus of the group included Main Streeters and Alternatives, and almost all of the discussion concerned the individuals who would need to be brought on board to push the project further. Members of the group then volunteered to contact the individuals on the list, one at a time. Some committee members selected names from the list because the individuals were friends or acquaintances. Sometimes, members selected individuals from the list because they believed they had something in common with the individual that would allow them to cultivate some affinity with the person to gain their support.

Even the most optimistic Main Streeters said that it often took some "proof" of success to get skeptics on board a project. But building coalitions across the apparent groups in Viroqua was key, especially when it involved asking people to spend money, as nearly every project did. Said one Main Streeter:

> You've gotta show people it's worth spending their money on. And once you can do that, that's the time you have...kind of a composite group of people who are both newer people in the community and elders. And when you

see there are multiple factions who are working toward the same thing, and they come to you and they say here's what we need to do and here's how we need your help and are you willing to help, by that time you would not say no, because you realize that pretty much everybody, every group out there is covered by this composite group and you kind of go, "Well, yeah, that makes absolute sense to participate in it, and it will add value to the community and being here and bringing other people here."

Getting Things Done Together

In both public and private life, getting things done occurred cooperatively, and interdependence was a big reason that people got involved. Pleased that she and I had been able to provide each other mutual assistance as a result of our contact through ARTT, Paula Menn said, "You helped me, and I was able to help you. Isn't that great? One hand washes the other." Joan Walby echoed this sentiment. Joan was twenty-three years old when I met her. She had returned to Viroqua after graduating from Lawrence University in Appleton, Wisconsin. Through the AmeriCorps volunteer program, Joan was coordinating the America Reads literacy program at the public elementary school. Much of her job entailed recruiting and coordinating volunteers from the community to act as reading buddies for elementary school students. In the short time since returning to her hometown, Joan had become involved in a number of volunteer activities, including coaching the public high school's Odyssey of the Mind team.[8] When I asked her how she happened to be coaching the team, she said that one of the teachers announced that the program needed coaches. "I try to respond positively to requests [like that]," she explained, "so that hopefully, people will respond positively to me when I ask [them to volunteer]."

There were other ways to use personal connections as well. At a meeting of the Downtown Preservation Commission, during which the committee discussed the fate of the rescued gazebo, a lifelong resident said she would be happy to go with Nancy to the next Veterans Memorial Committee meeting and make a plea for incorporating the gazebo. "I'll go and

---

8. Odyssey of the Mind is an international educational program that organizes competitions designed to encourage creative problem-solving skills.

pull some heartstrings," she said. "I can talk about how I used to go to it as a kid and think about my grampa who was a veteran." The way to encourage others to understand the significance of the gazebo was by drawing on personal connections. It was quite likely that members of the Veterans Memorial Committee had known her grandfather themselves.[9]

Coalition building was made easier by the Main Streeters' general willingness to suspend judgment of others, so long as they seemed willing to contribute to the community. Perhaps it was because of this that the Main Streeters were a relatively diverse group. There were as many Main Streeters active in the Temple Theatre restoration project who belonged to the Vernon County Republicans as to the Vernon County Democrats. The members of the Wild West Days committee belonged to different churches and had a wide variety of jobs and positions in the community. The Temple Theatre, Wild West Days festival, and groups like the Viroqua Partners and Main Street Program promoted projects that most Main Streeters could agree would benefit the community. In the moments before one Viroqua Partners meeting began, I heard one member extolling the virtues of stay-at-home mothers and arguing that society was much worse off with so many mothers working. I knew there were other Partners members in the room who disagreed vehemently with this view, but in the context of the Viroqua Partners meeting, it did not matter. Everyone was there to make sure that Viroqua's economy and local businesses thrived. In this sense, the way the Main Streeters got involved in the community largely sidestepped larger social issues, politics, and parties.

This is not to suggest that Main Streeters' projects were never contentious. Newspaper accounts confirmed stories I heard to the effect that, particularly in the case of Main Street's revitalization, the project generated significant, sometimes bitter, debate. In some cases, the personal cost of getting things done could be too high, especially when it led to conflict among residents. As Vernie Smith explained:

> [When] the [Wisconsin State Department of Transportation] widened Main Street, it really split the community into two factions. And there was an effort to get a referendum [opposing the project]. The referendum was

---

9. Ultimately, the gazebo was not incorporated into the Veterans Memorial, which was dedicated on September 11, 2004.

finally approved by the court, and so the city had to hold it. And it failed by about a two to one margin.

[Afterward], the mayor [Larry Fanta] said something to me about how the more important thing is that I can walk down the street and speak to people and have cordial conversations. And I realized that he was absolutely right—that it might be better to let some minor things fall by the wayside. Who cares if we have a wider main street and some of us didn't want it? It might be more important that we're able to put our differences behind us and not let those things separate and divide us. Because those qualities of being able to talk to people and not feel like you're enemies is probably more important to making the character of a place than the appearance of the community. You can have a very pretty place, but if people are at each others' throats, it's probably not worth it.

For Vernie, pushing a controversial project was not worth damaging personal relationships. The "improvement" in a community resulting from his efforts was only valuable if he could still enjoy living there with other residents.

Main Streeters shared the Alternatives' ethic of agency. Their ethic was evident in the typical narrative that many Main Streeters told about overcoming mediocrity and inertia, and coming to a realization that the town was going to require deliberate work to just stay afloat, if not improve. Typifying this kind of narrative was the statement from one Main Streeter who said, "Back in the '70s, downtown business was there, but they were very self-centered—our business *is* here, our business *was* here, our business will always *be* here, so we don't really need anybody. But when Wal-Mart came in, it was a real wake-up call. We had to sink or swim, and we wanted to swim." The arrival of Wal-Mart provided a catalyst that prompted a number of residents to begin to critically examine their own businesses and the downtown in general. According to Main Streeter logic, if other small towns were struggling, it was because they lacked the leadership and spirit that had made it possible for Viroqua to overcome the apathy or mediocrity that prevented individuals and communities from working to improve their circumstances. "That's about what it is," said Nancy Rhodes. "We can live with mediocrity if we choose to, and that's what a lot of these [struggling small] towns are about—mediocrity." Main Streeters believed they had overcome the mediocrity that would have been the death of the downtown.

Main Street parents worked hard to transmit both an ethic of individual achievement and civic responsibility to their children, and to transmit a sense of obligation to Viroqua. Nancy explained that ever since her son was small, she had made a practice of picking up litter with him when they went on walks around town. When her son did this in the company of other children and they asked him why, her son would tell them, "It's my responsibility. It's my town." "Well," she said, "this is all about taking responsibility, one, as individuals within our community, and then being an example to do that. My son [then ten years old] will pick up trash to this day, walking around town."

Despite their extensive involvement in different aspects of the community, Main Streeters did not see their efforts as exceptional. At different times, both Sue Walby and Paula Menn said that they were just regular people, who lived normal, if full, lives. They, like other Main Streeters, did not see their involvement as something that set them apart—it made them, as they saw it, normal average adults. Community involvement was a habit. Main Streeters were in the habit of engaging in what they regularly called "good citizenship." Being a good citizen meant getting involved.[10] Getting involved "could make one a better person in the same way that charitable acts would make one a better person, one who gives service to a pre-existing moral community" (Lichterman 1996, 172). Lichterman's research found that for community-oriented activists, the preexisting moral community was the local community itself, not a set of ideals that could be applied anywhere, as for the Greens in his study. An analogous distinction can be made between the orientation toward community of the Alternatives and the Main Streeters. Main Streeters assumed that the point of community was improving the local community in which they lived, while for Alternatives, community was a goal that intersected with their goals for society as a whole. The Main Streeters' orientation to community was a highly particular one, while the Alternatives' was a more universalistic model.

---

10. This was clear to me in the approbation I often received from Main Streeters, as when Gigi Macasaet told me, "You're such a good citizen. You're involved in everything." It did not occur to her that it was my job as a sociologist to be involved or that having research funds at my disposal made it possible for me to work only part time, leaving me many hours in my day to be "involved."

These differences made for interactions across these two groups that ran the gamut from friendly and cooperative to strained. "I'm the only city council member who comes to these things," Gigi Macasaet sighed, when we ran into each other at the Pleasant Ridge Waldorf School's Holiday Faire fund-raiser. She was proud of her efforts to learn about and connect with the Alternative community. Though it seemed that Gigi was right about her fellow alders, most of the Main Streeters I talked to were at least somewhat sympathetic to, and often appreciative of, the Alternative influx. "I think it's good that they are bringing new ideas in," said one. "And money." Many Main Streeters and Alternatives shared recreational interests, including music, art, and sports such as bicycling.

I heard similar sentiments on the afternoon when Tom Wilson came into the Historical Society Museum. Tom was a member of the Alternative community who owned a business that sold alternative energy products. He was looking for pictures of the large brick Victorian home he had purchased in town. After sitting unoccupied for some time, the house needed significant restoration, and Tom was looking for pictures of the house to see what it looked like when it was first built to guide his work. After he left, one of the volunteers sighed, "He has a lot of work ahead of him." The others agreed, but added that they were grateful someone wanted to restore the house. The house had passed through a number of hands in recent years. Each owner had purchased the house with the intention of restoring it, but ultimately decided it would be too much work or too expensive and sold it. "This fellow seems like he might see the project through," said one. Said another, "Those people are crazy enough to do things like that. God love 'em."

But there was also some ambivalence toward the Alternatives among the Main Streeters.[11] Said one, "I'm not offended by them. I'm not intimidated by them. I see that they have a lot of wonderful qualities, and they're

---

11. And because not everyone made the kind of effort Gigi did, there were some misunderstandings, as in the debate at a city council meeting about whether or not to issue the Pleasant Ridge Waldorf School a license to sell beer and wine at its annual Holiday Faire fund-raiser. The Holiday Faire went on for an entire weekend and included an art fair, silent auctions, and, in the evening, a dance and party for adults. The school wanted permission to sell beer and wine at this part of the fund-raiser alone, but some city council members were dismayed. What kind of school sold alcohol, they wanted to know? It was clear that few city council members had ever attended the Holiday Faire.

just looking for the best in life just like everybody else is. Such intelligent, contributing people! By god, they're all contributing." But later in the same conversation, the same person said that it "kinda twists [me] a little bit" to see a number of Pleasant Ridge parents earning money by substitute teaching in the public schools. "I mean, you come here, and you separate yourselves from us. Our school isn't good enough for you, and yet you'll take money to teach our kids?" Even people who felt somewhat less positive about the Alternatives managed to attribute their less desirable actions to circumstances that made them sympathetic. Said one Main Streeter, "I do find them snobbish. They do stay in their own little community, but maybe they feel that the bigger community would devour 'em if they didn't, so maybe it's just a protective thing."

It was not just the Alternatives of whom some Main Streeters were skeptical. A number were uneasy with the idea that the way to "improve" things was to establish endless alternative institutions. According to the Main Streeters' logic of commitment, it did not make sense to keep establishing alternatives of every kind. Loyalty to the local community dictated working to fix the ones that existed already. One Main Streeter parent expressed this sentiment in talking about withdrawing his children from the local Cornerstone Christian Academy. If he had to do it over again, he said, he would not have sent his children there because he felt the school isolated the kids. "From other kids?" I asked. "From the world," he answered. "How many families do you see that tuck their kids away in the Christian school because public school is so bad? Well, how are we supposed to be a witness to the world if we aren't in the world? We needed take our kids out of the Christian school, put 'em back in public school, and fight for what they needed."

Though few other Main Streeters framed their involvement in terms of religious obligations, this parent's point fit more broadly with a reservation other Main Streeters expressed about the idea that the way to make a community better was to form new institutions that seemed more suitable or desirable at the time rather than remaining loyal to and improving the institutions that already existed. According to their logic of commitment, improving the community meant working *within* existing community institutions rather than abandoning them or setting up new ones that would benefit only some residents, regardless of the form the alternative took (e.g. a Christian school or a Waldorf school). Main Streeters were not uninterested in alternatives, but they preferred to create new options within existing institutions. This was evident in the debate about the closure, for budgetary reasons, of the Liberty Pole Elementary School, a public elementary school still remaining from the country-school era.[12] The small school adopted multiage classrooms and some other innovations in an effort to exist as an alternative to the larger elementary school in town. When the school board decided to close the school to save money, its advocates, many of whom were Main Streeters, protested on the grounds that Liberty Pole provided a "middle ground" between the town's private schools and the conventional public school (Hundt 2004).

Main Street Challenges

One concern about the Main Streeters' approach to community, from the standpoint of scholarly work on community, is that the kind of commitment to public life in the context of a local community may result in a view of the world that blinds individuals to the broader context in which they attempt to improve their own community, resulting in a parochialism that Bellah et al. (1986) call "urban localism." I saw some evidence of this kind of local blinders, when, for example, one Main Streeter talked about why she was happy to do much of her shopping at Wal-Mart. Even though it wasn't locally owned, she said, "It's still local in the sense that it provides jobs to people around here and is a source of tax money. If Viroqua had tried to prevent Wal-Mart from coming, they would have put one somewhere else nearby, and then our residents would be driving to some other community and spending their money there, and that town would be getting the tax revenue that we now get." This view did not take account of the drain that Viroqua's Wal-Mart placed on the economies of nearby towns when their residents drove to Viroqua to shop.[13]

However, Main Streeters were also aware that Viroqua's future was tied to that of other nearby communities. This view came across most vividly in discussions about the possibilities for increasing the area's tourist trade.

---

12. Liberty Pole was one of the many villages within Viroqua Township.

13. Critics of Wal-Mart and similar retailers would also be quick to point out that the firm ignores the impact of low-wage industry on the communities where Wal-Mart's products are made.

It would not be enough to get tourists to come to Viroqua, the thinking went. The whole region would need to develop its tourism potential. Main Streeters also imagined themselves encouraging people in other towns to get involved in improving their own communities. In his role as president of the state medical association, Mark Andrew, another local physician, hoped to encourage community involvement on the part of physicians across Wisconsin. "Part of my other presidential stuff for the Medical Society is actually physician volunteerism.... Because I think that's the old school—we're just going to do our work, serve our patients, and stuff, and we're going to go home and stay out of things. And I don't think that's an acceptable attitude anymore, because physicians have more to offer. They can certainly be out there in the community."

Main Streeters viewed themselves individually and as a group as quite competent overall, but they also recognized that the complexity of the tasks before them sometimes required skills and resources they didn't always have at hand. Much of the data in this chapter came from formal interviews, because Main Streeters were often so busy that the only way I could talk with them outside of meetings and public functions was by arranging appointments for interviews. The Main Streeters I approached for interviews were happy to make time for me. None responded to an interview request with a concern that they might not have any useful information. They were an articulate group. Many were college educated and had experience with public speaking and in dealing with news media in some capacity. Indeed, this group formed the backbone of the Toastmasters. Many had jobs that required significant communication skills. Main Streeters exuded public confidence and competence. Yet despite the perception, especially on the part of Regulars, that they were sanctimonious and self-aggrandizing, I found that many Main Streeters brought a certain level of humility to the work that they did. In meetings, I often heard Main Streeters preface a point with disclaimers about not having all the answers or that they were open to other suggestions. Carolyn Solverson got involved with the Viroqua Partners because of her long-standing ties in the community: people she knew who were already involved asked her to volunteer for a variety of short-term projects.[14] When she was asked to

---

14. Carolyn's story was not unique. Many Main Streeters were recruited into organizations through personal acquaintances, similar to the ways activists are typically recruited into other kinds of activism (see Klandermans 1997; McAdam 1988).

be president, she was not completely sure she had the right skills: "I said [to them], I'll try. You guys are going to have to guide me, tell me what to do."

Especially when the tasks required wading through the complexities of local, county, state, and federal bureaucracies and requirements, the job of even voting in the city council was difficult for Vernie Smith. Vernie described the work of city alders as "stewardship jobs." He saw city council members as caring for the city and making the best decisions they could during their tenure. When their terms were over, the job would be turned over to other stewards. Vernie said that keeping up with the technical information involved in many decisions was a daunting task, and he had voted "no" on a number of items, not because he was sure he opposed them, but because he felt he just didn't have enough information to make a sound decision:

> Sometimes I've voted against things because I've felt we haven't been given all the facts or had enough time—I have probably more "no" votes than anyone on the council in the last several years—and a lot of those decisions are made because I don't have enough information. The committees, when they recommend an item, should be bringing us the information, not assuming that you're just going to rubber-stamp their actions. So maybe I'm stubborn, but I feel very uncomfortable voting for things I don't feel like we've been adequately prepared for. And some of that could be easily changed. Some of those I might vote against anyway. And that's just a structural problem. I don't always have opinions on issues. Sometimes I just don't know...and I should talk to people more.

As with so many other obstacles Main Streeters felt they faced, the solution was to make personal contacts—to talk to people. As a result of some of these concerns, Viroqua, like other towns and small cities across the country, ultimately hired a professional city manager.

Always More Work to Be Done

For Main Streeters, there were always additional improvements that could still be made, and that knowledge was a source of pride and pleasure. When I asked Main Streeters what, if any, changes they would make to the town, they were never short on answers. Some wanted to improve the safety of the area roads for bike riders. Some wanted to make sure that the renovations and improvements in the downtown continued. Some were most concerned about improving the holdings and other resources at the public library. Garith Steiner wished that the public school's drama facilities were better, that instead of the stage in the elementary school cafetorium there were "an actual, more of a larger performance theater connected to the school, so they can actually put on a play.... The one that they have is fabulous—I'm so glad they have it—but it's not conducive to plays with changes of scenery for those things. I'd love to see something advance the arts to another level."

Julie added, "And even the Temple Theatre downtown—the stage isn't quite big enough," referring to its relatively shallow stage and wings. "We've always said if we won the lottery, *that's* where the money would go." Even the Steiners' wildest dreams revolved around making improvements to the community from which many residents, at least those with an interest in performing arts, could benefit.

Like other Main Streeters, Garith talked about the continuous potential for new projects and improvements. The sense that there was always more to be done characterized Main Streeters—there was always another project around the corner. If there were not, it would have been a sign that the community, and they themselves, were slipping into the complacency and mediocrity they dreaded. It was important to keep pressing forward. Said Garith:

> Sometimes, just like the political stuff in the community, in our corporation [the hospital], we don't succeed. But we don't spend a lot of time rehashing it. And we've spent more time figuring out how do we correct it and how do we move forward. A lot of the people in the management part of [the hospital] have finally got it figured out. They always used to ask me, "Why do we always have a list of things to accomplish that is longer than the list of things accomplished?" And I say, "Well, isn't that the way it's supposed to be?"... They always were bummed out because they'd say, "Oh, we have so much to do," and I'd say, "Yeah, isn't it great!"

There was no distinction between the optimism and energy the Main Streeters applied to public life and the way they approached private life.

When the Menns celebrated their twenty-fifth anniversary, they added an enormous evening barn dance to the semiannual cattle drive on their ranch. When Dr. Menn toasted the friends and family he saw as he looked through the crowd that night, he said that in them he saw the people with the energy and dedication to get things done together. "And that's what America is really all about," he concluded to an upwelling of cheering.

In a similar vein, Nancy Rhodes told me, "Life is wonderful. It gives us all kinds of opportunities if you're willing to step up and take 'em. And I have lots more things on my list." She paused before concluding, "Life is great. Truly."

4

The Regulars

Keeping Things Simple

The faces at the bar during happy hour were almost always the same—the only difference from day to day was who took a day off from visiting the Legion. Standing behind the bar, I could usually predict who would sit in which seats: starting on the side of the bar to my right, it was usually Steve and Sandy, Fred and Sheryl, Darlene, Lucy, Vicki, sometimes Diane, "Squeaks" (Jerry), and occasionally Eric, and in the center, any combination of Terry, Tony, the other Tony, Brad and the other Lucy, Brad's sister and mother, Jerry and his wife Vicky, Kim and sometimes his wife Kay, and Arlan. To my left, at the end of the bar closest to the entrance, one could usually find Don, Shirley, and the other Fred. Fred's wife Vivian would sometimes come in later in the evening when she had finished the house-cleaning job with which she supplemented the income from her job cleaning one of the town's medical clinics.

The American Legion was a low, bunkerlike building across the street from Nelson's Agri-Center. About a month after I moved to Viroqua I answered an advertisement in the *Vernon County Broadcaster* that said the

American Legion needed a bartender. Bartending seemed like a job that would bring me in contact with lots of people. The only drawback was that the ad read, "Experience preferred." I had neither bartending experience nor, I realized as I printed out a copy of my résumé, was there anything in my employment history to suggest I had any transferable skills.

When I called the bar, the manager suggested I stop by early that afternoon before the bar opened. It was a bright, sunny fall afternoon, so it took several moments for my eyes to adjust to the darkness when I entered the building. I filled out a standard job application form and proffered my résumé, which the manager said she did not need. She pointed out, somewhat skeptically, that I hadn't listed any local references, but seemed satisfied when I explained that it was only because I was new to town. Luckily, even without an endorsement from anyone in town, the manager was willing to take a chance on me, and I worked part time at the Legion nearly the entire time I lived in Viroqua.

The Legion became my primary source of data on the group of residents I came to call Regulars, Viroquans who had deep connections to the town and who valued informal and spontaneous socializing. The bar was populated primarily by Regulars, most of whom held blue-collar jobs. Though most of this chapter revolves around my observations there, it is important to note that not all Regulars spent time in bars, and that not all were working class. Regulars who did not do their socializing in public places like the Legion (which tended to attract a blue-collar crowd) did so in private settings like homes, so this group was very difficult to meet except through personal connections. While Alternatives and Main Streeters were easy to meet because of their participation in public functions, Regulars who did not feel comfortable in settings like the Legion were much more difficult for a researcher to access.

The Legion was unlike any place I'd ever spent very much time, and it was immediately obvious to everyone that I "wasn't from around." While all the patrons I got to know at the Legion treated me as one of their own from the time I set foot in the bar, there was no question that they thought I was unusual in some respects. For one, I was in my late twenties but had no children. Some patrons thought this was good. On two separate occasions, older men who were themselves grandparents praised me for completing my education before starting a family. Both had daughters who had had children shortly after finishing high school—one in wedlock, and one not.

Both women were now single parents, and one lived at home with her father, who told me, "It's good that you're bettering your own education first. It's too hard to go back once you have kids to take care of."

Some other patrons, mostly women, wondered if there was not something wrong with someone who did not have children by my age. When I replied to one that I just wasn't really ready for a family yet, she informed me, "You'd better get ready. Your grass isn't getting any greener, honey."

I lacked some basic skills, too. I did not know how to play euchre. I did not know any of the many games with dice that patrons played as a way of betting for drinks, so a few times I realized too late that "the bar" had given away drinks on wagers it (that is, I) had not actually lost. Patrons asked me how to pronounce my "funny" last name, which was a departure from the Norwegian last names of many patrons: Thorson, Erikson, Olson, Everson, Gilbertson, Jacobson, Hendrikson, Peterson, Sandwick, Volden, Vikmyr, Bakkestuen, Hanson.[1] During one shift, I looked around the barroom around midnight as I wiped down the bar and realized I was the only person there whose last name was *not* Hanson.[2] In addition to not being "from around" Viroqua or one of the nearby towns, patrons were surprised by how far away I was really from. Early in my tenure at the Legion for example, Tony Bakkestuen, Arvid's brother, who eventually became a close friend and key informant, asked me whether or not I was from "around" Viroqua. I said no, and he said he hadn't thought so. I then asked him where he thought I might be from. "La Farge, maybe?" he answered. La Farge was a town about twenty minutes away.

On another occasion, a customer named Scott peppered me with questions about how I ended up in Viroqua and what I would do after I left, though he knew that I moved to Wisconsin to go to school. Finally, he asked, "Do you not get along with your family, then?"

"I get along with them very well," I answered. "I miss them a lot." The answer must have given him the information he needed to make sense of my situation. "So, you've really put your career before most everything,

---

1. My last name was not unheard of in this area. There were several MacGregors listed in the local phone book, and I was often asked if they were my relatives.

2. This evening was a weeknight, and there were only four customers in the bar at the time. Two of the Hansons were brothers, and the two others were unrelated to any of the other Hansons in the room.

then. I figured there must be some reason if you lived all the way out here, and they were all the way Back East."

That I would voluntarily leave the area where I was raised just to go to school seemed strange to a number of the patrons at the Legion. "So you'll go home when you're done with your school?" patrons sometimes suggested in the recurring conversations we had about what I was doing in school, how long it would take me to finish, and what I would do after that. Consistent with the findings of other researchers, it did not make sense to many of the Regulars I met, many of whom worked in blue-collar jobs, to plan one's life around work options (Leibow 1967). If one's experience with work was that it was not especially satisfying, and one acceptable job was basically interchangeable with another, it made more sense to plan one's life around the things that were satisfying and pleasurable, such as family, friends, and recreation. Unlike many of the Alternatives I knew who were not surprised at all that I moved to town without knowing anyone there,[3] many of the patrons at the Legion found it very puzzling that I would move to a town where I didn't know anyone just to do a school project—especially in Viroqua. A common response went something like, "God . . . and of all the towns you could have picked, you picked this shit hole?"

The first time someone said this, I was quite surprised. No one had said anything so derogatory about Viroqua to me before. Certainly other people had talked about improvements they might make to the town. As we saw in the last chapter, Main Streeters had long lists of improvements they hoped to make. Nevertheless, most of the people I'd met in town to that point had told me how happy they were with Viroqua and recited any number of its virtues for me. So the first few times I heard someone call Viroqua a "shit hole," I was taken aback. The Legion was not a place to look for boosterism.

It made sense that when I did hear comments like this, I heard them in the Legion or one of the other drinking establishments in town. This may have been because alcohol decreased inhibitions against airing the town's "dirty laundry" in front of strangers. Just as likely, however, it was because many of the people I met there were more familiar than some of

---

3. The Alternatives were not surprised I moved to Viroqua without prior social connections to it, but many were surprised that I moved to Viroqua without having children of my own.

the Alternatives and Main Streeters with the area's less-pleasant features. A frequent topic of discussion was the area's lack of "good" jobs. "Good" meant secure, reasonably well paying, and not injurious. As in many other small towns in the Midwest, the consolidation of farming operations over many years had created a large number of adults seeking blue-collar jobs. At the time, Viroqua did have a muffler plant, a fertilizer plant, a plant that made filtration equipment, a cash register label plant, and a few small light-industrial employers.[4] Workers in the market for such jobs sometimes felt squeezed. Many, including Lucy Volden, who owned the house in which I rented an apartment, commuted to La Crosse to work at places like the Trane Company factory. Lucy worked at Trane, which produced industrial air conditioning systems. Other jobs available in town included a variety of service jobs at the hospital, nursing homes, and in the public school system. As in other communities, these jobs were filled primarily by women and tended to be relatively low paying. To the extent that Legion patrons still worked in agriculture, few were farm owners themselves. More were people like Hillary, a young woman who worked a split shift (four to eight o'clock in the morning and evening) milking on a large dairy.

The patrons in the Legion often talked about the job market, particularly as it affected the possibility that their children might remain in town as adults. I heard a number of such conversations early in my time in Viroqua, in the wake of the debate over whether or not a poultry processing plant might relocate to Viroqua. Typical of these conversations was one held by three women at the Legion who were all mothers. I joined the conversation in time to hear one say that the area really needed more jobs to keep children in town. Abby, who worked at the local hospital and whose daughter was about to graduate from high school, added, "I want my kids to stick around too, but…" The three women finished the sentence in unison: "not for jobs at a poultry plant."

The employment squeeze many people felt went hand in hand with a housing squeeze. Property values were rising. As one Legion patron put

---

4. The Howard Johnson fertilizer company closed this branch of its operations in 2005. Some of the town's other manufacturing concerns were later hard hit in the economic downturn of 2008–9. National Cash Register closed its label-making plant in early 2009, leaving eighty-three employees out of work, and Nashville-based Commins Filtration laid off its fifty-three workers in Viroqua a few months later.

it, "You used to take for granted that if you worked full time, you could eventually afford to buy a house. You can't assume that anymore." As in other small towns (Salamon 2003), affordable housing in Viroqua increasingly took the form of trailer homes. While the homes I visited in the city's trailer parks were well cared for, some of the mobile home owners I knew complained about the relative lack of privacy in the trailer parks and about difficulties with noisy neighbors.[5] Others continued renting houses or apartments, and some of the rental units I saw during my time in Viroqua were in rough shape.

The open disparagement of Viroqua in public places like the Legion was a stark contrast to the optimistic planning and praise that I heard in other public places. In their classic study of the small town of Springdale, Arthur Vidich and Joseph Bensman (1968) found:

> In personal conversations with intimate friends, expressions of disenchantment are likely to be heard quite frequently. As the group becomes larger and less intimate, the public ideology becomes a more prominent and forceful focus of attention.... Those individuals and groups who have publicly expressed disenchantment find it difficult both to participate in and to accept the type of rhetoric and exhortation characteristic of public life. As a consequence, the disenchanted withdraw from the public life of the community and, hence, by default leave the field of public and particularly organizational life open to the exponents of the world of illusion. It is for this reason that the public life is dominated by the system of illusion even though many persons do not in an inner way hold to its tenets. (310)

Disenchantment was far more commonly expressed in public by Regulars than by members of the other two groups. Regulars objected to the efforts to change the town by bringing in elements that did not rightfully belong there and who were trying to turn the town into something it was not. But there were also Regulars who had professional jobs or who were

---

5. Some researchers have found that as property values rise in small towns, attracting large numbers of wealthy newcomers, the less-wealthy residents ultimately move out. So far, this does not seem to be happening in Viroqua. Viroqua's economy still includes a mixture of farming, industry, and service employment. According to Salamon (2002, 47), "compared to affluent residential towns, these towns present advantages for blue-collar families, a workforce with a preference for small-town life: the housing is cheaper, the cost of living is lower, and their strong inclination to live near kin can therefore be realized."

self-employed and, as some put it, "did just fine for themselves." As such, it was not possible to chalk up Regulars' negative comments solely to economic disparities. Main Streeters and Alternatives all had good reasons to keep disappointments and disagreements more private—they were the Viroquans who had invested the most in trying to make things good. If things weren't good, it would mean that their efforts had fallen short. For the Alternatives, in particular, to acknowledge significant disappointment with the town would have implied that moving there (or staying there in the case of those who were originally raised in the area) was a poor choice. It would have meant that their careful calculations were incorrect. For Main Streeters, to call the town a shit hole would have been tantamount to admitting that their improvement efforts had been in vain.

Even Regulars who expressed initial support for a public project sometimes became disenchanted when the results did not meet their expectations. For example, one Legion patron complained that she would never again support any ballot measure increasing spending for the public schools. When the patron sitting next to her asked why, she explained that over the previous weekend she had tried to attend a program at the elementary school in which her niece was involved. "The new cafetorium was already full when I got there," she said. "I couldn't even get in." She then said she felt especially angry about the situation because she had voted in favor of the referendum to build the new elementary school with its expanded cafetorium because she understood that part of the rationale for the increased cost was that it would provide increased space and seating for student plays and events that the old building had not provided. "What a rip," she said, and added that she voted to "spend all that extra money," but the benefits she felt she'd been promised by supporting the referendum did not materialize.

Others felt similarly about the resurgence of businesses in the downtown. The revitalization of the downtown was a deeply important sign to the Main Streeters of the success of their efforts, and an equally important sign to the Alternatives that Viroqua was the kind of town in which they wanted to live. The Regulars did not see things this way. Sure, one said, there were new businesses in town, but not ones that "sold stuff any normal person wanted to buy" or could afford. The town's efforts to improve its business district were improvements that catered to others' needs, not the needs of residents like themselves. Perhaps this was the sentiment behind the statement I overheard one evening at the Fraternal Order of the

Eagles, which had a bar similar to the Legion's, that the Common Ground coffee shop and the adjacent refurbished Temple Theatre ought to be burned to the ground.

Sometimes perceived slights were felt more personally. Some Regulars assumed (whether or not it was true) that they were not particularly valued members of the community. This was typified by a conversation I had at the bowling alley one evening after volleyball. On Wednesday evenings during the school year the public school's gym was open to adults wanting to play recreational volleyball. Afterward, many players adjourned to the bowling alley bar for beers. On one evening, a man I did not know explained his view that the kids who got the most game time in high school sports did so because their fathers were "doctors or lawyers or whatever." He named some kids he thought had been shortchanged on the athletic field because their dads had jobs "like driving trucks." This sense that Regular folks like themselves were not particularly valued or respected by the community at large was most poignantly evident in one of the responses to Arnold Strickon's 1975 survey. After the question about people in the community one looked up to, the survey asked whether or not there was anyone in the community that people looked down on. Most respondents did not answer the question. The few who did mostly gave general answers, including "drunks" and "able-bodied people who won't work." But one respondent, an older man whom I knew because he came into the Legion every now and then, had answered this question twenty-five years earlier with the word, "Myself," and then attempted to delete his answer by crossing it out several times.[6]

So where did the Regulars see themselves fitting into the town? In this chapter I examine some of the reasons for the Regulars' feeling devalued by others in town, and occasionally somewhat hostile toward both Main Streeters and Alternatives—reasons that had a great deal to do with unspoken conflicts about what community meant and how to make it. Regulars' ethic of agency led them to reject both the constant choosing and remaking of the Alternatives and the constant push to improve the town embraced by the Main Streeters. Though they shared the Main Streeters' logic of commitment to Viroqua as a particular place, the differences in

---

6. I never discussed this survey with this gentleman out of fear that I might embarrass him.

their ethics of agency placed these groups in a moral conflict in which Regulars rejected Main Streeters as self-aggrandizing and Main Streeters saw Regulars as guilty of the worst sin of all: apathy

Our Shit Hole: The Regular Logic of Commitment

Even though the Regulars I knew talked about Viroqua in a derogatory manner a fair amount of the time, it was clear that they didn't really think of it as a shit hole—at least not all of it, or all of the time. One's depth of knowledge of the area and one's connections to people were a matter of pride. I saw this best in a kind of competitive conversation that sometimes took place in the Legion, in which the interlocutors (who were most often, but not exclusively, men) attempted to demonstrate a superior knowledge of the area. I did not make audio recordings while working in the Legion,[7] and the intricacy of these kinds of conversations included too many details for someone less familiar with the area to recall accurately even minutes after they occurred, so I am prevented from giving a verbatim example of such a conversation.

One example that I recounted in my field notes, however, began as a discussion about the upcoming hunting season. Dave Thorson and one other patron I did not know well began by lamenting that land open to hunters was decreasing. Dave said (as I heard many others say) that when he was growing up, deer hunters could hunt almost anywhere, as long as they respected people's homes and livestock. Now, he said, you had to ask someone before you hunted on their land, and the "tree huggers," who seemed to own more and more of it, were likely to say no.[8]

Dave's partner in the conversation agreed and began to describe some of the places where he had hunted as a young man that were no longer open

---

7. This was not because patrons who frequented the Legion would necessarily have objected, but because I could not find a reliable way to inform each patron entering the bar that a recorder was running. In addition, the layout of the bar area and the room's acoustics were not likely to have lent themselves to comprehensible recordings.

8. It was not just "tree huggers" who prohibited hunting on their land. Seasonal residents from Madison, Chicago, Milwaukee, and the Twin Cities were buying wooded land in the countryside for their own recreational use. They prohibited hunting, not because they were against hunting, but because they were trying to protect their own hunting opportunities.

to hunters. He named specific properties belonging to particular families and included topographical details about which parts of these sites were particularly good for hunting. He recounted some stories about particular hunting trips, recalling the exact portions of streambeds and the sides of particular ridges along which he had driven deer.

After listening to several stories, Dave recounted a few of his own in even greater detail, including not only the names of landowners, but lists of their kin and his connections to them. Dave's stories also included very specific details about the local geography, about the various owners' hands through which particular pieces of property had passed over the years. Yes, he concluded after several stories, he probably knew these hills better than anyone, because he had been spending time in them since he was a child.

The story trading went back and forth for over an hour, and if there was an undercurrent of one-upmanship in the conversation, there was also a reverence for the places they were talking about and for their connections to them. Like the Main Streeters, the Regulars' logic of commitment was based on their connections to Viroqua as a particular place and to the people who lived there. Their "community" was not one that they made from scratch, like that of the Alternatives. Theirs existed before they entered it, and it would remain long after they ceased to be a part of it. The Regular community was not one that was amenable to change by individual effort, like the Main Streeter's community. The Regulars' ethic of agency was premised on the notion that the existence and quality of the community was much too big and too permanent to be fundamentally affected by the actions of individuals. "Community" did not need to be discussed or negotiated or created as it did among the Alternatives, because Regulars felt themselves born into relationships often generations long. Nor did Regulars share Main Streeters' sense that the health of the town's institutions, buildings, and businesses needed constant monitoring and treatment. Any of these might come or go, but community, as the Regulars understood it, was not premised on any of them.

On the contrary, what defined the Regulars was an ethic of agency that rejected the kind of deliberate work on behalf of "community" in both of the other groups. I could not find any incidents in my data in which "the community," as such, was discussed at the Legion or any of the other places, public or private, where I ran into Regular residents. At first this seemed puzzling to me, as discussion about "the community," though it varied in content, seemed such an important part of life in Viroqua. When I examined the data, however, it was clear that this was only the case in the Alternative and Main Street groups.[9] Regulars took the existence and longevity of their community for granted, and therefore they did not *need* to discuss it. Discussing it would have detracted from the most positive aspect of community as the Regulars understood it—the ability to take it for granted and to rely on it without needing to question it. Their community was, first and foremost, a natural occurrence, not something that had to be manufactured, spruced up, or talked up for strangers.

While the Regulars shared with the Main Streeters a highly particularized logic of commitment, the constant push for improvement both by Alternatives and Main Streeters (whom Regulars often tended to lump into one group) was an implicit insult to the way Regulars put "community" into practice. The Regulars felt entitled to call Viroqua a shit hole because it was *their* town. They did not appreciate criticism from people who did not have the same long and intimate relationship with Viroqua that they had themselves, or from people who, despite having lived there their entire lives, always acted as if the town was not good enough for them the way it was. Said one Regular of the observation that so many new (Alternative) residents sent their children to the Waldorf school: "They just got here. How do they even know the [public] schools are that bad?"

Even though the Regulars knew that the Waldorf school was what drew many Alternatives to town in the first place, they still thought of things like private schools as options that only made sense once the existing options had proven inadequate or inappropriate. To the Regulars, both the Alternatives' modus operandi of creating new institutions that were supposed be better than existing ones and the Main Streeters' constant work in the name of civic improvement seemed like out-of-hand rejection of the town, of the Regulars' home, and by extension perhaps, of the Regulars themselves. And, in an important sense, they were. Both the Alternatives and Main Streeters read the Regular ethic of agency as evidence

---

9. I am confident that this difference was not simply a reflection of my depending more on interviews to gather data about Main Streeters than about the other two groups. First, I rarely asked explicit questions about "community" in interviews unless respondents themselves raised it. Second, Main Streeters, and to an even greater extent Alternatives, talked about community extensively outside of interviews as well.

of their "apathy," their lack of caring about their own or the community's circumstances.

It was in these implicit insults to their sense of community as something inevitable and uncontrived that Dave and others felt their "heritage" slipping away. This sense of "heritage" was not just a nostalgic vision of the past but of a past in which they imagined the town and its people were just what they were naturally, nothing more or less. In the world of the Regulars, what made one a good person was simply going about one's business and not trying so hard. It was something like being, as some put it, "real." A good sort of person was someone who was willing to take things—the town and its residents—as they were, without judgment.

Whereas Main Streeters and Alternatives saw work, social life, and political or community goals as intertwined with each other, the Regulars saw them as more discrete arenas. Though some liked their jobs, Regulars tended to see work simply as a necessity. If it happened to provide personal satisfaction, so much the better. Their ethic of agency encouraged Regulars to see work as work, family as family, fun as fun.

Even when Regulars did care about and find satisfaction in the work that they did, they tended not to understand work as connected to other goals. Fred Stephens, for example, worked for the Viroqua Area Rehabilitation Center (VARC), a county agency that assisted people with disabilities in obtaining community-based housing and employment in the small assembly plant it owned. Initially, I was somewhat intimidated by Fred's gruff manner, but I realized over time that he was also a friendly and thoughtful fellow. Fred, like Steve Thompson who often sat next to him at the bar, drove one of the busses that transported VARC clients to work at the plant. Though trying at times, "it's the kind of job that makes you feel good in here," Fred said one afternoon, patting his chest over his heart. But unlike the Steiners, for example, who saw patronizing local businesses as a way to foster the vitality of the hospital where they worked, I saw no evidence that Fred, or most of the other Regulars I knew, made such connections.

Diane Wang liked her job too. She managed the Kwik Trip convenience store and gas station on the south side of town. When I heard her trying to convince Vicki Frederikson to apply for a job there, she described how nice it was to work in a place where she saw so many people she knew coming and going all the time. What Diane valued about her job was that it gave her a way to work and maintain social connections simultaneously. Corporate rules and regulations sometimes made it difficult for her to do her job, but she could live with that. In the unlikely event that an Alternative Viroquan were to take a job at Kwik Trip, he or she might have worried about the nutritional content of the foods sold there or about the social implications of selling lottery tickets. A Main Streeter might have looked for ways to integrate the Kwik Trip's exterior into the town's historic look. Diane didn't worry about either of these sorts of things. Her work allowed her to connect with people she enjoyed as they patronized the establishment.

Whereas Main Streeters who owned businesses or worked on Main Street understood their jobs as playing a role in the overall improvement of the town, I did not see evidence of this in the Regulars. At a meeting of the Viroqua Partners at which tourism development was the topic, one of the principle discussions was how to get people like Diane and the employees she managed to see themselves as people with a role to play in the promotion of the town. After all, one of the first places tourists were likely to stop was one of the town's convenience stores in order to use the restroom or ask for directions. It would be great, meeting participants agreed, if it were possible to train convenience store workers to act as town ambassadors by greeting tourists in a welcoming way and giving them good directions to places they wanted to go. Diane and her other colleagues at the Kwik Trip were certainly friendly, but it was hard to imagine them shifting their images of themselves as workers to include tourism boosting. Ultimately, there was no reason for them to do so. The Kwik Trip would exist whether tourists came to town or not, and the other businesses in town that catered to tourists did not provide much for Regulars. As far as most Regulars were concerned, tourists were fine as long as they did not get in the way of the people who truly belonged there.

Hanging Out in Public

What the Regulars lacked by not having a sense of individual or collective efficacy in public life, they made up for in their sense of entitlement to, and a sense of ownership of, a number of the public places the town had in which to hang out. "Hanging out" as a means of socializing was a good fit with the Regular culture of community: hanging out implied that opportunities for socializing were always available and that individuals could participate or not as they chose. Hanging out entailed no advanced planning or coordination. The Main Streeters had little time for hanging out. It was not that they did not want to hang out, or that they socialized in a particularly formal manner inconsistent with casual hanging out, but because they were so busy that socializing required coordination. Alternatives liked hanging out, and the idea that they could spend more time doing it was part of what attracted them to rural life. But because so many came from places without strong "visiting" traditions, it seemed that many were not yet completely comfortable just dropping in on one another. The other problem the Alternatives faced at the time I studied Viroqua was that they had relatively few public places in which they felt they could do so, especially in the hours after Common Ground closed for the day.[10]

The kind of hanging out in public that was possible for the Regulars followed a traditional kind of hanging out associated with the informality of rural life (Bell 1994). Historically, even private businesses could be appropriated for hanging out, as was clear in a memoir entitled *Seven Miles to Viroqua* by Roy L. Bangsberg (written ca. 1950–70).[11] The pocket-size blue paperback book describes Bangsberg's childhood on a farm outside Viroqua and typical ways that Viroqua's downtown and its businesses served important social functions for people with the kinds of social connections that entitled them to hang out there. When he moved to town to attend high school, Bangsberg found that stores served as places for daily socializing, though apparently mostly for men.

---

10. There was a real thirst among Alternatives, and even among some Main Streeters, for public places for socializing in ways that seemed appropriate to them. When I asked people in interviews if there was anything they would change about Viroqua, eight different people, mostly Main Streeters, mentioned they wanted a replacement for Ricky's restaurant, which had, until it closed, been the only "upscale" dining option in town. When the Viroqua Food Co-op began exploring the possibility of expansion, it surveyed members to determine what the expansion might look like. Overwhelmingly, members' top priority was that a larger establishment should include a seating area and coffee bar. In addition, when Lars Bergan opened the Driftless Café, it served as a gathering spot for Alternatives in the evenings.

11. It is not clear exactly when Bangsberg wrote this memoir. No one I spoke to who knew him was sure what year he wrote the book, and when the *Broadcaster* ran a lengthy feature on it on November 23, 1978 (on the occasion of Bangsberg's death a week earlier), it simply stated that the book had been "published some years ago."

> Every evening after supper [Bangsberg and his friends] gathered at Tom
> Sandwick's clothing store and hung around for a general "bull" session until
> a late hour when Tom finally closed up for the night. Six o'clock closing was
> unknown to Viroqua stores at that time, and Tom Sandwick's was the pop-
> ular hangout. It was principally because of Tom's personality and his youth,
> despite his years, that we ganged up on him. I think he got as much enjoy-
> ment out of it as we did. Marion Qually, his clerk, now at Richland Cen-
> ter, could tell a few stories about those sessions, I am sure. What the endless
> conversation and general "ribbing" was all about, probably doesn't mat-
> ter.... We ducked our cigarettes whenever the door opened, for you never
> could tell who might be coming in, and to be caught smoking... not always
> had pleasant repercussions. But it was all harmless and good-natured and
> for genuine sociability it was a highlight of our after-school diversion in a
> day when pleasures were of your own making. (85–86)

Bangsberg's memoir indicates the role that downtown businesses played
in creating arenas for sociability, and though Sandwick's seems to have
been Bangsberg's primary hang out, his memoir indicated that this shop
was not the only one where young men gathered to socialize. Bangsberg's
friend Martin Gulbrandsen, who eventually became the county's district
attorney, had a part-time job at Stanley Swigger's grocery store on Main
Street, "and here Martin held forth during spare time" (62).

Later in the text, Bangsberg provides a list of some of the regulars at these
"bull sessions," and the names listed suggest that Sandwick's was a gathering place for men only. A search of the Social Security Death Index for the
names of the men mentioned in his account revealed that while some of the
regulars, such as Almon Fortney, were members of Bangsberg's high school
class, Sandwick's was a place that men of a variety of ages gathered. Sandwick himself was fifteen years Bangsberg's senior. Ernest Otteson was four
years older, while Albon Tollefson and Keith Lucas were three years behind Bangsberg. The men and boys who gathered at Sandwick's came from
a mix of country and town families.[12] The memoir suggests that in addition
to "general 'ribbing,'" these kinds of gatherings were forums in which news
was passed around and in which younger boys heard older boys and men
discuss educational, career, and business opportunities.

---

12. Based on information from personal communications with residents and a variety of records at the Vernon County Historical Society.

Most businesses in Viroqua when I was there opened and closed according to their advertised operating hours, and while extended discussions occurred when acquaintances ran into each other in shops; stores did not seem to be the kinds of gathering places they once were after closing time. Businesses that existed primarily to serve food and drinks and provide seating for customers still served this function, particularly the bars (in the bowling alley, the Viking Inn, the Legion, the Eagles Club, and the VFW).[13] There was evidence that certain kinds of retail businesses still acted as gathering places, especially for men. Though I did not see clutches of people socializing for extended periods in any of the clothing stores in Viroqua, I did notice that a couple of the machine, automotive, and tire shops in town were gathering sites after closing time. Shop employees formed the core of these groups, and they were sometimes joined by select friends. These were shops in which retail was only a part of the business. These businesses performed services, and therefore they had facilities and tools that most individuals would not have at home. So the access one might have to such a shop through friends could be quite valuable.

In these shops, work on projects became a reason to gather for socializing after hours. For example, when Jeff Sandwick and some of the other employees of the auto service section of the Heartland Country Co-op in Westby (the next town north of Viroqua) needed to work on someone's personal vehicle, they sometimes did this work in the shop after closing time and provided beer for friends who were willing to help with the project (or at least willing to hang out while the work was being done). I assumed similar gatherings were occurring when I saw the lights on late at night in the garage at Tollefson's repair shop, which was located around the corner from my apartment. Some evenings, when I passed Tollefson's, I saw groups of two to five men of various ages sitting on stools and standing at the counter in the auto parts retail part of the shop, talking in an apparently leisurely way.

Agricultural supply stores have a reputation for providing farmers with a place to "shoot the shit," and they did so. The Heartland Country

---

13. State law limits the degree to which bars can serve as gathering places after closing. Bars and taverns in Wisconsin must close no later than two in the morning, after which only employees clearly engaged in business activities, such as cleaning up and closing out cash registers, may be inside. Bartenders and bar owners can be fined for violating these rules.

Co-op in Westby kept a pot of coffee that customers helped themselves to. It was not uncommon to see a handful of farmers, shop employees, and other acquaintances sitting on the ledge inside the front windows chatting with one another and with the employees at the registers. Indeed, there were rumors that at times this small crowd impeded business by distracting staff and by getting in the way of customers who were trying to make purchases.

The drinking establishments in Viroqua were primarily frequented by Regulars.[14] Technically, there were no drinking establishments in Viroqua: it was, by city ordinance, a dry town that did not issue liquor licenses to taverns or bars. Clubs, such as the Legion, the VFW, and the Eagles, however, could receive licenses, as could some restaurants, such as the Viking Inn and other businesses that wanted to include alcohol sales as part of another business, such as the bowling alley. Like any social space, these places were governed by a variety of informal rules, rituals, and norms. If you knew them, there was a certain ease in the sociability there. It was OK to talk with others, and acceptable not to, though one ran the risk of incurring some flak for being "in a mood." It was fine to play darts, or pool, or fooseball, but it was also fine not to. There were sometimes disagreements about what to watch on the TV, and occasional disagreements about whether the volume of the jukebox was too loud or too soft. One Regular at the Legion said he came there because spending time there felt "like the rec rooms people had in their basements in high school where all the kids went between the end of school and going home for supper," and they did seem that way to me—only they were public commercial establishments.

The public arenas like the Legion where some Regular residents spent leisure time also had a wide variety of ritualized events that greased the wheels of interaction. In the Legion and the other bars in town, for example, there were almost always minor wagers taking place. Much of this gambling was informal, in the sense that patrons and sometimes staff rolled dice or played a hand of cards with nothing more at stake than the price of a drink or a dollar for the juke box. Occasionally, a small group of patrons spontaneously organized a card or dice game with small stakes—usually

---

14. The principle exception to this was the local country club where one could often find some Main Streeters, but this was only open during the golf season.

no more than a dollar or two a game. Games with dice included Horses, Six-Five-Four, and Threes.

Some of these minor wagers were institutionalized, that is, they were officiated by the bar itself. At least three of the bars in Viroqua, for example, ran a Shake of the Day in which patrons, for a dollar, shook several dice and attempted to win prizes that ranged from free drinks or six-packs of beer to the money that had accumulated in the Shake-of-the-Day kitty.[15] At the Legion, the Shake provided patrons with a running topic of conversation. When someone was doing the Shake, those sitting nearby often looked on and commented on how well or poorly things were going. One patron's deciding to Shake often started a chain reaction, as others sitting nearby decided to try their luck also, and the bartender found herself moving from patron to patron down the entire length of the bar, as each took his or her turn, until coming to an empty stool. When the Shake was complete, or while others were Shaking, the conversation often turned to recent Shake events—who won a prize recently, how much money might have accumulated in the kitty, whether or not the results of a particular Shake were indicative of the Shaker's recent luck in general.

These mundane forms of gambling also provided a topic of conversation for regulars and new patrons to share. Often, someone visiting the Legion for the first time might ask if "this place has a Shake of the Day." A visitor and a patron (and the bartender) could then begin a conversation about how the Shake worked at the Legion, comparing it to how it worked in other bars the visitor might frequent. Often such a conversation segued

---

15. A common Shake scheme began each afternoon when a patron or staff member shook one die to determine what the "number of the day" would be. Patrons then said to bartenders, "I'll Shake" or "I guess I'll Shake," and invested a dollar in the hopes of winning. The barkeep placed the dollar in a Shake-of-the-Day kitty. The bartender handed the patron a cup with five dice, which the patron rolled up to three times. After each shake, the patron set aside any dice showing the number of the day, and then rolled the remaining dice. If the patron rolled the dice three times and did not roll any with the day's number, he or she won a free drink. If the patron had four of the five showing the day's number, the prize was a six-pack of the beer. If the patron got all five dice to show the day's number, he or she won all of the money that had accumulated in the kitty since the last win (less some minimum amount that remained in the kitty at all times so that there was something for the next player to win). There were variations on the shake—the number of dice, the number of shakes, the ante, and stakes might vary—and there might be additional ways patrons could win (there were sometimes prizes for rolling straights or other combinations of numbers, for example).

into a broader conversation about the visitor's home and the reason he or she was in Viroqua.

There were numerous other institutionalized opportunities for trivial gambling. During football season, patrons could get in on the weekly football board. Most bars had computerized slot machines. These machines were only legal if used "for entertainment purposes only," that is, if there were no monetary payouts. From time to time, the bar, or the Legion board held raffles, or sold chances on some prize such as a rifle, using pull-tabs purchased from the state lottery commission. The bar also purchased a second kind of pull-tab lottery ticket from the state—small cardboard tickets with five chances each to win cash prizes of varying amounts. The awards were drawn from the money taken in for the purchase of chances. Each batch of 510 tickets included a certain number of winning tickets. Each ticket cost fifty cents, which meant that patrons usually purchased them at least two at a time. More often than not, they proffered a five dollar bill for ten tickets.

One such game offered by the Wisconsin Lottery during the time I worked at the Legion was a pull-tab game called Fast Fifty. Each card cost fifty cents, and the odds of winning a fifty cent prize were quite high: one in five.[16] When patrons won the smallest prizes of fifty cents, they rarely turned in the ticket for two quarters, but instead for another ticket. In fact, when a patron found a fifty-cent winner, she often said that she had "won a free one," as opposed to saying she had won fifty cents. Similarly, many people reinvested two-dollar winners in more tickets. When a patron purchased tickets, if she wasn't busy with other customers, the bartender often stood there while the patron opened them, on the assumption that in a group of at least ten tickets, the patron would win at least one more "free one," and need to be handed the plastic bucket of tickets again. All this happened while others looked on, joking about what good was it to gamble anyway.

Hanging out with the Regulars in private homes was much like hanging out in public places. There was no need to call first before visiting someone—it was usually OK to stop by. If no one was home, sometimes it was even acceptable to go inside the home and wait for him to return.

---

16. The odds for the Fast Fifty game were: $.50, 1:5; $2.00, 1:23; $10.00, 1:255; $25.00, 1:510; and $50.00, 1:510.

If someone was home and watching TV or a movie, no one expected the program to be turned off for the visitor's benefit. There was no elaborate greeting; a visitor could simply make oneself at home on the couch with the homeowner. It was OK with Jeff Sandwick that Tony Bakkestuen and I stopped by his home when no one was there, retrieved the key to his shed from its hiding place, and borrowed his golf clubs. It was acceptable to ask friends for favors, and even though the askee was not always thrilled about having to provide the favor and complained about it, he or she did not question the need to provide it. The assumption was that the favor would be returned eventually or that because of the familial (or other) obligations to the person asking the favor, performing it was unavoidable.

The reader will recall from previous chapters that the Alternatives frequently marveled out loud at this kind of unconditional neighborly exchange. Regulars almost never talked about it at all, because they had the ability to take this system of sociability and favors for granted. It was not the case that relationships, even very long-standing ones, never required negotiations or deliberate working out, it was just that the occasions for negotiations were triggered by elements of those long-standing relationships. In addition, disagreements took place within a network of relationships and a history that virtually guaranteed that they had to be worked out eventually, because there was no way for aggrieved parties to avoid each other indefinitely.

One couple, for example, allowed a friend to store his boat and trailer in their yard and talked in the Legion about how they wanted him to move it elsewhere but were not sure how to bring it up. Two nights later, I heard the couple discussing the issue with the boat's owner, who insisted, several times, that he understood, but nonetheless seemed perturbed. The night after that, I happened to overhear the owner of the boat complaining about the request to another friend in the VFW and wondering aloud where he was going to put it, and about why the couple had asked him to move it in the first place. "It's not like they're doing anything with the space," he complained. It took longer than the couple wanted, but eventually, the boat was removed. Two weeks later, the couple and the boat owner took turns buying each other rounds of beer, and the conflict seemed to be smoothed over. People complained about each other, but with a wide variety of ways to work things out, Regulars did not treat disagreements as crises that required deliberate community building, mediation, or processing.

Regular Deliberation

Though Regulars took pride in their casual and spontaneous approach to social life, the Regular ethic of agency belied a great deal of deliberating that Regulars did just like everyone else. The careful selection of a school for one's children was a hallmark of the Alternative community, but school selection was a matter of choice for Regulars too. Tony, who grew up in Westby, said that if he ever had children he would make sure that he lived within the limits of the Westby Area School District. "No way I'd send my kids to Viroqua," he said. It wasn't a question of the quality of the Viroqua Area Schools. Westby was his school, and if he ever had children, it would be theirs too. Tony's logic of commitment bound his loyalty to the school system in which he grew up.

Another instance of such deliberation about schooling on the part of some Regular parents was an incident at the Bowl-Away Lanes. One evening after Wednesday night volleyball league, some of my fellow volleyball players ran into two other men they knew who appeared to be in their mid-to-late twenties. One said that he and his wife were trying to sell their house. They wanted to move somewhere within the Kickapoo Area School District so that his young children could attend Kickapoo High School when they were old enough. When I asked why he preferred Kickapoo, he said it was because the school was so small there were more extracurricular opportunities for kids. They would not have to try out for sports teams, because everyone who wanted to play made the team automatically. "I went there," he explained, "and I lettered in four sports. I want my kids to have opportunities like that." So deliberation was important, but the difference was in the priorities parents considered in choosing a school—continuing a family connection to a particular place and choosing a school based on the way its size would affect their children's extracurricular opportunities.

Some Regulars did put careers ahead of remaining in the area to live. A good example was my fellow bartender Glenn, who wanted to pursue a career as a professional firefighter. He had served as a volunteer in Viroqua's fire department and had been studying firefighting at the area technical college. He knew that he could never make a living as a firefighter in a small town and was prepared to move "almost anywhere" for a job with a professional force when he completed his associate's degree.

There were also, of course, many events and causes that Regulars were involved in organizing. They did a great deal of organizing through their involvement in clubs like the Legion and the local rod and gun or golf clubs. They organized massive fund-raisers for ill friends that included live entertainment, auctions, and raffles with big-ticket prizes. It was not the case that they never got involved in any public events, but such events were produced for their own sake, not in the interest of improving the town or anything else. Tommy Schrier, for example, put together the Bud Schrier Memorial Golf Tournament in the name of his uncle, who was very much alive and an enthusiastic participant in the tournament itself. Another such event was the lawn tractor–pull contest that took place on the street in front of the Eagles Club in late March.

I knew that organizing the pull was hard work because Gene, one of the principle participants, had been telling me about it for weeks at the Legion. The event was organized under the auspices of American Mini Pullers Inc., a lawn tractor–pull club, and was one of a series of events in the area throughout the spring and summer. The point of the event was to have fun with lawn tractors. Contestants spent the winter souping up the engines of riding mowers to get them to pull more weight—so it was not just a contest of driving skills, but of mechanical ability.

By contrast, when Theresa Washburn described the tractor races that she once organized in her capacity as Main Street project manager, it was clear that while the event was meant to be fun, fun was not its only purpose. She explained:

> The other thing that we did [when I was Main Street manager] that I think is still true now is that we brought back events into the downtown area. We started the farmers market; dismal as it was when we started it, we started it. It's not dismal now. That May Chalk Dust Festival—they don't do that anymore, but we started that. We held tractor races downtown, I don't know if you heard about that. Those were wild. I can't believe we were able to do that. Farm tractors. It was hilarious. Hilarious. Totally illegal, but hilarious. We had guys coming from all over. You had to have an old tractor, only old tractors, and it was a farce almost. But we just kept trying to do things to get people into the downtown.

In the Main Street version of a tractor event, the focus for the event organizers was on promoting the downtown, not on the tractors or racers themselves. Racing the old tractors was not an activity that the event's organizers apparently took seriously in and of itself (though the participants probably took it quite seriously). Gene's lawn tractor pulls were about the tractors and the tractor enthusiasts, and as I learned when I attended more such events in the area through the summer, it was a completely serious business. If there was any additional purpose to the event Gene organized, it was to promote the sport of lawn tractor pulling. It was not hard to imagine why, if Main Streeters treated the hobbies they took seriously as farcical, Regulars did not feel they were especially welcome to "join in" public life.

The way that Regulars got things done in public life, whether it was organizing a tractor pull or a benefit for someone with medical bills, was the same way they got things done as individuals: informally. Regulars' particularistic logic of commitment matched the way they got things done—through informal means using personal networks. They generally preferred to bypass formal ways of doing things when possible. I knew one Regular couple, for example, who purchased a house and waived most of the inspections that were not required by law as part of the sale process in order to save money and to "avoid the hassle." When I sat in on a staff meeting at Viroqua's Century 21–affiliated realty office, it became clear that this was not an idiosyncratic decision but something other Regulars did when they purchased real estate. For the benefit of two new realtors on the staff, owner Adrian Hendrickson reminded everyone that "any buyer should test the water" and that if they refused to do so, they must sign a waiver saying so. To make the point, Theresa Hughes, one of the other experienced realtors in the office, related a story to the realtors at the meeting about a recent transaction in which a buyer refused to have the property's water supply tested. After the sale, the property's well was found to be contaminated by E. coli.

In between the phone calls that constantly interrupted the sales meeting, Adrian reiterated the importance of having buyers sign waivers if they refused to have tests conducted:

> You don't need the liability. You just don't need the liability. Either septic or water, or lead paint. It's just not worth it.... We can't force 'em to [conduct the tests], but we can have 'em sign [waivers] saying we told 'em they should and they elected not to. I don't know why anyone would elect not to. I just don't understand it. You're paying all this money for this place, what's another couple hundred for inspections and tests?

> That's a function of rural real estate. *Locals* will not test anything. They will not do home inspections; they won't test water and septic. People from the city will, 'cause that's the world they're used to. That's why we have these special forms saying sign here saying you don't want to do it, so if you sue us, we're going to hold 'em up and stand behind 'em!

Though he did not advocate it, Adrian understood the "local" impulse to eschew what anyone else would consider standard formal procedure in buying a home. Part of it came from their sense that they understood the area and land so well that they simply did not fear such contamination. As Adrian added, "I guess, I grew up drinking unpasteurized milk....I remember just drinking it out of the bulk tank or out of the can." According to Regular logic, formalized procedures meant to ensure safety were fine for people who didn't know the area or the land or the agricultural product well enough to know what they were doing, or who did not have the rural upbringing that conferred benefits like an immune system capable of combating the "normal" hazards of country life. For many Regulars, and even some Main Streeters, using formal channels or mechanisms to solve problems or get things done was antithetical to their logic of commitment, which bound them as individuals to others in the community. Such formalities were seen only as last resorts when less formal avenues had failed. The use of formal procedures was sometimes seen as adversarial.

The Futility of Politics

The Regulars' world was the one that many people think of when they use the term "Red America"—the segment of the United States that is primarily blue-collar, and politically and socially moderate to conservative, and that listens to country music and watches NASCAR races. In Viroqua, however, I found that Regulars were not necessarily politically or socially conservative. Their politics were all over the proverbial map. While I overheard spirited discussions about politics in Common Ground among Alternatives, for example, their fervor came from a sense of shared outrage, particularly at the Bush administration. While many Regulars supported the invasion of Afghanistan, for example, opinion was split about the invasion of Iraq. Regulars, like Main Streeters, assumed no agreement among themselves about politics and treaded lightly around politics most of the time, but not always. One January evening I was at work at the Legion when the president's State of the Union address aired. There were only two patrons in the bar, R. J. and Mike.[17] R. J. pointed at the TV and said he liked that W. "had balls," more than his father, George Bush Senior. Most of all, he liked how W. "spoke from the heart" rather than "reading off a page." Mike, on the other hand, didn't like Bush at all and said so. According to Mike, Bush was "fucking this country" and only cared about his corporate friends' making money. R. J. conceded the point, agreeing that Bush did seem to be interested in helping his friends who were already rich, but he insisted that the president "showed balls" in his response to events of September 11, 2001, and that was what really mattered when the country was being attacked.

After this exchange, the two men grew silent again for a while, and then Mike spoke up to make a joke that both lightened the mood and drew on a political topic in which everyone found humor. "At least that tie [Bush] is wearing probably wasn't a present from an intern he's screwing!" he laughed, referring to the story that as president, Bill Clinton had given a State of the Union address in a tie given to him by Monica Lewinsky.

"Shit," said R. J., chuckling. The subject of politics was dropped for the rest of the evening. Many of the political discussions at the bar were more substantive. The most frequently debated topic at the time was health care. Everyone seemed to agree that the state of the health-care system was dismal, but opinion at the Legion was divided about how the crisis should be solved. Some patrons thought that it would make the most sense to return to the days when patients paid doctors directly and cut out insurance companies and the government. Others supported a socialized system like Canada's. Still others liked the idea of leaving the system the way it was for the most part, but expanding government safety nets like Medicaid or health-care coverage for children.

For most of the Regulars I knew, politics, national, local, and in-between, seemed relatively distant, but that did not stop many from following political developments. On the days when Eric Vig came into the Legion at happy hour, he always left in time to catch the *News Hour with Jim Lehrer*

---

17. R. J. and Mike are pseudonyms. These men asked me not to use their real names.

and the *Nightly Business Report* on PBS. Fred Amundson kept two TVs on all the time at home and had both turned to different twenty-four-hour cable news channels. He joked that when the little boy who lived next door asked him why he watched two TVs, "I told him it was because I've got a split personality!" Many people read the *La Crosse Tribune* or *USA Today*. Jim Enchringer, a fertilizer plant employee, took some ribbing for the parsimony he demonstrated in his habit of reading the newspaper every afternoon at the public library rather than buying his own copy.

No matter where their ideological sympathies lay, the Regulars shared a sense that actually participating in politics in the form of activism, attending party meetings and the like, was probably a waste of time. The people who engaged in politics were probably out mostly for their own gain, though there were probably a few "good apples" in the political world. Regulars tended to think that the political realm was not one in which individual citizens' actions had much impact. The resulting ethic of agency was summarized nicely by one Regular who I overheard scoffing, "Politics. I can accomplish more in one Saturday afternoon at home than these idiots [the state legislature] can accomplish all together in two years!" In other words, it was more worthwhile to be effective where one could, rather than to waste time in arenas where one could not change things. The Regulars' ethic of agency matched their sense of potential to be effective in political activity. Someone who thought an individual could have any real impact on political life was kidding himself, according to this reasoning. Further, the Regular commitment to the local did not necessarily limit the scope of their attention to or knowledge of politics, but reinforced the suspicion that spending a great deal of time on political activity even at the local level was probably a waste of time.

Community Cultures and the Seeds of Misunderstanding

Mostly, the Regulars ignored the Main Streeters and the Alternatives alike. The activities of the other two groups did not seem terribly relevant to the Regulars most of the time. They did not know much about the Alternatives and considered them to be part of the same group as the Main Streeters. They were curious about the Waldorf school, and often asked me questions about it, as I was often the only person they knew who was somewhat familiar with it. Some Regulars liked the changes in the downtown. I often saw Regular Kay Fossum at the Common Ground coffee shop. She acknowledged that many people she knew refused to go in there.[18] I saw some evidence that Regular residents had some respect for certain aspects of the Alternative institutions. Though she commented that she couldn't afford to shop there, one patron at the Legion said she was glad that the Food Co-op was buying eggs from her neighbor. A second patron sitting next to her added that, these days, it seemed like the government would let big companies put almost anything in food and that he'd consider buying organic food at the co-op too if a loaf of bread didn't cost almost three dollars there.

Similarly, one evening after volleyball league, several players adjourned, as was the custom, to the Bowl-Away Lanes for beers. Jim Radke, a Regular with a white-collar job and a college education, asked if I had been to the Holiday Faire at Pleasant Ridge, the previous weekend, and I said that I had. He had never been, but he'd seen signs for it, he said. Another volleyball player I knew only as Dave spoke up, saying he thought that "the kids over there [at Pleasant Ridge] miss out on a lot of things."

"Like what?" I asked.

"Showering and shaving," said a third volleyball player, at which several people chuckled. The joke was a reference to the less conventional dress and hairstyles of some Youth Initiative High School students.

"No really," Dave continued. "Like sports. I think they really miss out on competitive sports."[19]

Said another volleyball player, "I don't think that Pleasant Ridge can prepare kids to be doctors and lawyers."

Dave added, "But their parents are doctors and lawyers, so those kids are closer to those kinds of people than most kids at public school."

Jim Radke, whose three sons were all recent graduates of Viroqua High School, added, "But one thing they do have over there that I wish we had is parent involvement. They've got a lot more parent involvement." When

18. Kay was also a downtown business owner, however, which may have explained her greater willingness to explore and involve herself in places like Common Ground, which her friends refused to enter.

19. Although the Waldorf schools did not field their own interscholastic sports teams, many students were involved in team sports through the city's Parks and Recreation Department programs and the youth hockey programs at the ice rink.

I interviewed Jim and his wife Donna a number of months later, I learned that they had been deeply involved in the parents' groups that supported sports teams, the band, and other school activities. They had been frustrated by the fact that the same handful of parents usually provided the volunteer time when the school needed it.

It would be easy to criticize Regulars according to the standards of community proffered by most scholars for their apparent withdrawal from public life. One could read their focus on family and recreation for personal satisfaction as the kind of retreat to private life that threatens community (Bellah et al. 1985). But it was the Regulars who still bowled in leagues, belonged to hunting clubs, attended the churches their parents attended, and had extensive, long-standing ties to kin and friends that provided them with the kind of social life that scholars of community believe are valuable. They had all this without having to work nearly as hard at it, or spend nearly as much time talking about it, as the other groups in town. The irony, however, was that their lack of apparent "effort" made their mode of community less worthy in the eyes of the other groups in town.

5

Playing in the Same Sandbox?

What did the existence of these three groups of people and their distinctive styles of community making mean for life in Viroqua? How permeable were these group boundaries? Could members of these groups get along well enough to get things done together if they needed to? In this chapter I examine how Viroquans' tastes for different cultures of community played out in their interactions with one another. In general, these cultures of community did not hamper forming cross-group ties as individuals, but it sometimes made it hard for Viroquans to get things done together as groups.

Of course the boundaries of group membership were somewhat more fuzzy and porous than the preceding chapters probably suggest. Membership was not always so clear-cut, especially for longtime Viroqua residents. Ann Morrison and her husband Jim grew up in Viroqua, left for a time, and returned later. Although they were embedded in Alternative social networks (their children attended Pleasant Ridge and Jim served as its board president), their networks also included Regulars with whom they had grown up and attended school. When they needed someone to help them weld complex trellises for their landscaping business, they turned to their friend Kim, a Regular with a reputation for welding talent.

The same was true of Terry and Christine Noble. Both Terry and Chris grew up in Viroqua and had family ties in the area. When I arrived in Viroqua, Terry was the editor of the *Broadcaster,* a job that brought him into contact with a broad cross section of residents. Chris owned and ran Art Vision, a shop on Main Street, which brought her into contact with many local artisans (many of whom were embedded in the Alternative community), and many of her customers and employees were Alternatives as well. As a business owner, she was also firmly entrenched in the Main Street crowd and was a member of the Viroqua Partners and the Rotary Club.

Relative newcomers also had ties that crossed group boundaries. As a business owner and preservation advocate, Nancy Rhodes was firmly in the Main Street camp. Her son, Dallas, attended Pleasant Ridge, which pulled her into Alternative circles as well. Theresa Washburn arrived in Viroqua to work for the Main Street Program, which brought her in contact initially with Main Streeters, and later with many other Viroquans. She married a man she described as a "local," giving her a foot in the Regular crowd. When I asked her what it was like to have feet in more than one camp in town, she laughed. "It means that you have two groups of people who know everything about you!" she said.

As we have already seen, the Townsleys found themselves quickly and easily integrated into the farming community on the hill where they lived, despite viewing their neighborhood social circle as separate from their network of friends, which included far more Alternative people. A few newcomers with feet in the Alternative camp applied a universalistic logic of commitment in a way that encouraged them to form cross-group relationships. Recall that Dave Ware and Tamsen Morgan systematically sought out a small town that met the criteria they had in mind. No matter where their search took them, they explained, they planned on "putting down roots" once they arrived. They believed that if they wanted to achieve the kind of community they envisioned, they needed to contribute to it by engaging themselves in it. One of the ways they had done this was by making a deliberate effort to get to know their rural neighbors. They knew they and their neighbors had some major differences in worldview. Dave related a story about one of his neighbors railing against the United Nations, claiming that the UN would ultimately be telling everyone how to raise their children, which Dave did not agree with. But rather than see these differences as a reason to disengage from relationships with neighbors, Dave looked to work around them. I asked Dave how he responded to the claim, and he said he simply told the neighbor he thought he was exaggerating and changed the subject. Dave and Tamsen had also developed a special relationship with the elderly woman who had sold them the house in which they lived. Like the Townsleys, however, it seemed that Dave and Tamsen maintained these cross-group relationships in a separate social circle from their "main" circle.

In some cases, I even saw evidence that one's orientation to community making could change over one's life course. Jim and Donna Radke typified couples I knew who became involved in the style of Main Streeters when their children entered school. During this time, the Radkes participated actively in many school events, fund-raisers, and their boys' sporting activities. Now that their sons were grown, they found themselves withdrawing from these efforts, spending time instead in ways more consistent with a Regular orientation: socializing privately with friends and with their adult children and their spouses, or spending quiet time together at their cabin on Potato Lake. They were not the only middle-class couple who described such a trajectory in their community involvement. Said another father of adult children:

> We swore we'd keep going to the [school] basketball games and football games even after our kids graduated, just to keep supporting, you know? Now that our kids aren't in school anymore, we find it is so nice to come home and not have to rush through dinner to get to some game or meeting. We haven't really continued to go to those events the way we thought we would.

When residents did have a foot in more than one camp, it was possible to see how they could reconcile potentially conflicting logics of commitment. When I chatted with Jim Morrison at a graduation (from the public high school) party for the daughter of Dave Thorson, one of the Regulars, he mentioned some disagreement within the Pleasant Ridge community over the school's tuition structure. Since it opened, the school had used a sliding-scale approach to tuition, in which families paid what tuition they could afford based on their income and expenses. Some parents had begun to object to this system, believing that they were bearing an unfair burden of the school's finances. I had heard other Alternative parents who favored the sliding-scale fees justify the system with reference to the broad, universal goals consistent with the way Alternatives viewed their commitments to other things. The Waldorf model of education, they said, should be available to everyone who wanted access to it. Parents who could afford to pay the full tuition should, as their fees helped make the school available to others. Jim supported the sliding-scale system, but referenced the kind of local commitment more consistent with Regulars and Main Streeters. "If you're going to have this school in *my town*," he said, "you better make sure that it's something all the kids who live here can afford."

It is not hard to imagine that these groups might see themselves as competitors, or that they might try to cultivate some sense of exclusivity to keep others out. I did not observe much in the way of overt policing of any group's boundaries; that is, I did not see much behavior that could be construed as deliberate exclusion. Instead, I observed a mixture in all three groups of avoiding, ignoring, and welcoming others. Main Streeters were always happy to welcome on board anyone who wanted to "contribute" to the well-being of the town. Alternatives were pleased when members of "the public" shopped at the Food Co-op or looked into sending their children to Pleasant Ridge. Indeed, they seemed to read such actions as signs that their institutions were winning over new converts to a progressive way of life. In Regulars' gathering spots, I observed mostly neutrality toward newcomers or those in other groups. Anyone was basically welcome in these places, so long as he or she did not try to change the existing atmosphere or activities. Had a few Alternatives, say, become routine patrons at the Legion, I believe they would have been welcomed into the usual crowd over time, though not without some ribbing about their Alternative status. Because everyone endured ribbing in the Legion, however, this would have been more of a sign of acceptance than anything else.[1]

---

1. One Alternative, expressing surprise on learning that I worked at the Legion, described a less-than-pleasant experience the one time she had been inside. She and a friend had gone into the Legion after work in hopes of having a beer and quietly finishing a discussion they had already begun. Once inside the Legion, she said, they were "harassed" by two drunk men sitting nearby. My guess is that this incident had more to do with gender than with group status. It was not uncommon in the Legion for certain men to try to engage any women who happened to be nearby

Viroquans made forays into each others' groups mostly as individuals, as opposed to making coordinated sorties. Despite these connections across groups at the individual or family level, for the most part, Viroquans engaged in what "kindergarten teachers call 'parallel play'...they may not have been in the same groups, but they did play next to each other in the same sand box, and, most importantly, did not throw sand at the other children" (Monti 1999, 114). Developmentally, parallel play is important because it is the first attempt young children make at reconciling private needs and goals with a wider public world in which others sometimes have competing needs and goals. Parallel play is the first step toward collaborative play, in which children actively play together. Monti (1999) applies the parallel-collaborative play metaphor to the ways that people in cities manage to coexist, if not cooperate, with the many fellow residents whom they either do not know or think they may not particularly like.

In this chapter I examine how Viroquans "played together"—both in parallel worlds, and sometimes collaboratively. I also investigate residents' potential to engage in increased collaboration in the future. At first I was quite surprised by the degree to which the groups in Viroqua were able to maintain such distinct parallel worlds. What I was looking at seemed more like what we might expect of cities—the mosaic of social groups described by Robert Park in the 1930s.[2] But when we examine the history of small towns in the United States, we find that they have never been the unified, homogenous villages we might imagine. They have always accommodated "structured diversity" (Varenne 1977) in populations that sometimes got along with one another and sometimes did not. Most of the time, the distinctions that created parallel-playing groups in small towns were the familiar ones: race, religion, ethnic or national origin. In Viroqua, the boundaries that mattered were those defined by differences in logics of commitment and ethics of agency. In addition, some of the mechanisms by which boundaries were maintained had changed over time as well.

---

in conversation, whether the women seemed receptive to their overtures or not. If the Alternatives having a beer in the Legion had been men, it is far more likely that they would have been left alone to have their conversation.

2. A growing body of scholarship on communities argues that despite the traditional images of urban and rural life as diametrically opposed, large cities and small towns have always shared many similarities.

A Brief History of Small-Town Diversity

Existing studies of small towns and the rural communities surrounding them provide numerous examples of the ways single towns often have contained a number of small towns existing almost as parallel universes with circumscribed ways that members intersect with members of other groups. Not surprisingly, the social distinctions on which these groupings were based are those about which social scientists have long been concerned: race, ethnicity (and sociolinguistic groups), religion, and class.[3] The paradigmatic example is probably the segregation of small towns in the Jim Crow South, in which both formal laws and informal sets of cultural practices separated small-town residents socially and spatially on the basis of race. In Dollard's (1957) "Southerntown," blacks and whites attended separate schools and churches and lived in segregated neighborhoods. White and black societies contained analogous class structures, including middle-class professionals, a working class, and a segment of poor residents (though of course whites in every class had significant advantages over all blacks). Each racial community had its own leaders and prominent citizens. Interactions between members of each community within Southerntown were determined by the town's racially based structure. Even when whites and blacks lived in close spatial proximity to one another (as when domestic workers lived in houses behind those of their employers), their relationships continued to be structured by racial categories (Massey and Denton 1998) through both informal and formal (legal) mechanisms. The result was two communities engaged in parallel play, despite their often close residential proximity.

Racial boundaries have not been the only important boundaries structuring small-town communities. In the upper Midwest, including Wisconsin towns just north of Vernon County, historians have described an analogous kind of segregation among whites on the basis of immigrant status, ethnicity, religion, and language (Pedersen 1992; Lingeman 1980). Groups of recent immigrants formed segregated communities within new townships, creating parallel sets of institutions.[4] Within single towns for

---

3. That such socially meaningful categories often occur together in patterned ways is also well documented.

4. Unlike early New England communities, settled by existing groups of people who arrived together and established a town on a specified tract of land, the boundaries of townships in the

example, German Lutherans and Norwegian Lutherans established separate churches and schools, in which they spoke their own languages.[5] Members of extended families often purchased adjoining farm parcels, resulting in spatial ethnic concentrations within single townships. In the days before automobiles and improved roads, the relative difficulty of transportation meant that social distinctions and spatial distinctions reinforced each other. Rural farm neighborhoods required their own general stores, creameries, and mills, so the neighbors one met in such public places were likely to be of similar origins (if not kin). As in the South, each community within the township was likely to have its own parallel set of leaders, more- and less-wealthy families, and networks of mutual assistance. In town, ethnicity also took on spatial dimensions, resulting in small-town ghettos analogous to larger urban ethnic neighborhoods. Towns of just a few hundred had distinct "Bohemiatowns" or "Polishtowns" within their limits.

Even in towns that were more homogenous along racial and ethnic lines, deeply meaningful sets of social distinctions divided residents into groups with logics just as "obvious" and natural to their members as visible distinctions like race or audible distinctions like language. Early New England towns, settled by groups of like-minded religious separatists and often based on egalitarian ideals, for example, contained distinct social groups measured by differences in wealth. As settlement in the Midwest became dense enough to support towns, occupations and diverging economic interests increased the social distance between country and town dwellers over time (Lingeman 1980). In town, wealthier residents (often of Yankee extraction) often built grand homes on one or two streets just off the main commercial thoroughfare, while their domestic workers (often recent immigrants) lived with their families and other laborers, literally, on the "wrong side" of the railroad tracks.

Today, some small towns remain divided along lines of distinction like those described above. Journalist Stephen Bloom (2000) illustrates the ways

---

Midwest and West were often laid out by federal statute prior to any settlement. Promoters and speculators who bought large tracts of land could only realize profits by selling plots to whoever wanted to buy them, so a legal unit like a township was likely to contain settlers of a variety of ethnic backgrounds, as well as adventurous or dissatisfied Yankees.

5. The schools in this case were small country schools that predated sustained attempts at widespread public schooling. These country schools, however, often became the basis of the institutions that became public country schools with instruction in English (Pedersen 1992).

that the religious laws and urban ethos of a group of Lubavitcher Jews who moved to the small town of Postville, Iowa, reinforced their existence in a community highly separate from the rest of the town's population. Sonya Salamon's (2003) study of a number of small towns in Illinois indicates that in many towns, socioeconomic status is still a powerfully segregating source of distinction. Wealthy newcomers who had left "Central City" in search of good schools and small-town surroundings bought large homes in cul-de-sac subdivisions outside the town's older street grid, isolating them spatially and socially from the older, and usually poorer, long-time residents. Similarly, Michael Bell (1994) found that wealthy exurban newcomers to the British village he calls Childerley retained a way of thinking about nature and their relationship to it that circumscribed their relationships to the village's poorer "country people." These "country people" constructed an identity around an ideal of authentic rurality, which newcomers could not claim, thereby staking out an exclusive claim to an important symbolic resource.

Mechanisms of Distinction in Viroqua

Given historical and contemporary evidence of the wide variety of ways that small-town residents draw social distinctions among themselves, and the ways that these distinctions patterned their daily lives and interactions, the existence of Viroqua's apparently parallel towns no longer seemed as surprising as it did when I first arrived there. The question became what kept the play in town primarily parallel. Why wasn't there more collaborative play? And why did collaborative play arise when it did? Viroquans often spoke of the divisions in town in terms of newcomers and old-timers. The problem was that when Viroquans used newcomer/native categories, they usually did not mean literally whether or not someone was raised in the town. They used these labels to imply sources of persistent distinction more analogous to a case like Bloom finds in Postville. There was no expectation in Postville that its newcomers, Hasidic Jews, would ever become indistinguishable from their Iowa-born neighbors. For both the Iowans and Jews in Postville, "Jewish" summarized not only a characteristic of one set of residents but also sets of practices that were the basis for enduring segmentation within the town.[6] In Postville, "Jewish" encapsulated the reasons for this by implying practices like keeping kosher, which prevented Jews from eating suppers in natives' homes.

There are no dietary restrictions preventing Regulars, Main Streeters, or Alternatives from breaking bread together (except perhaps for those few who hew to a strictly vegan diet). Similarly, there were no legal mechanisms for enforcing separation as in the Jim Crow South. While Salamon (2003) and Bradshaw (1993) found that large influxes of newcomers to a small town resulted in social bifurcation, they argue that bifurcation is temporary even when the number of newcomers is quite large. In those cases, old-timers, and the town as they knew it, were subsumed in the massive growth brought by newcomers.

In addition, in the cases studied by Salamon and Bradshaw, there were marked socioeconomic differences between bifurcated groups of newcomers and natives. This was not always the case in Viroqua. There was significant economic variation that cut across groups. All three groups included professionals such as teachers and health-care professionals. In all three groups there were those who found themselves chronically under-employed. In visiting the homes of Viroquans, I encountered families living in housing most Americans would call "substandard" in both the Regular and Alternative groups. The difference was that, in some cases, living without electricity or indoor plumbing was to some extent a matter of choice—sometimes a matter of environmental consciousness, or a way to cut living costs in order to spend less time working and more time on other things, such as creating art. In other cases, substandard housing was a matter of necessity, not a matter of lifestyle.

To the extent that class mattered in shaping social belonging in Viroqua, it tended to operate through the differences in residents' tastes for certain cultures of community. As casual observers like Brooks (2001) have pointed out and social scientists have confirmed, there does tend to be a class dimension in Americans' ethics of agency. Even the Alternatives

---

6. Initially, Bloom says, Postville natives could not understand why Jewish newcomers rebuffed their invitations to participate in neighborly "visiting," whereby newcomers traditionally integrated themselves into small-town communities. The newly arrived Hasidim's image of community was premised on its remaining separate and distinct from mainstream culture.

I knew who lived without indoor plumbing or who relied on WIC to supplement their household budgets tended to come from middle-class family backgrounds.

While it would have been quite possible for longtime residents to use Norwegian heritage to carve out an exclusive kind of social belonging in much the same way that Bell's (1992) "country people" did using their relationship to the authentically rural, I saw no evidence that they did so. It would have been easy to use claims to Norwegian ethnic background as a way to exclude most newcomers from a sense of full belonging in Viroqua. There are perhaps a couple of reasons they did not. One is that for most Viroquans, even those for whom their ethnic heritage was very important, ethnicity was, as sociologist Mary C. Waters (1990) describes, voluntary. It was something an individual, family, or even a community might celebrate at certain times of year, but it wasn't a category they embraced as more meaningful than other social categories. Though vestiges of ethnically based social organizations persisted in the area (particularly in neighboring Westby), their memberships were small and primarily composed of aging men. Perhaps one reason ethnicity was not deployed this way was that so many Viroquans in both Regular and Main Street circles could have laid claim to being "100 percent Norwegian." Their different tastes in ethics of agency seemed to trump any sense of shared ethnic heritage.

Neither was it the case in Viroqua that bifurcation played out geographically, as it did in the mushrooming exurbs described by Salamon (2003), where newcomers lived primarily in new subdivisions outside the city limits of the old town. In the case of such booming exurbs, subdivisions were often designed in such a way that they discouraged interaction among new and longtime residents. Viroqua's few small subdivisions were not populated exclusively (or even primarily) by newcomers. On the contrary, Alternative newcomers were more interested in buying older homes in town or farmsteads in the countryside. When they did build new homes, they tended not to buy lots in subdivisions but in the country, and they tried to build unique homes using various environmentally friendly practices. In talking with Viroquans about their decisions about where to live, the first consideration for members of all three groups was cost. The next consideration was a preference for living in town or in the country. Finally, unless they were building a new home, all residents were constrained by the relatively limited housing stock. For example, a number of the Alternatives who lived in town wanted to live in the neighborhoods east of Highway 14 so that their children could walk to Pleasant Ridge without crossing that busy central artery. This preference might have produced a geographic separation between Alternatives and the other groups in town, but families were not always able to exercise this preference if there was not some suitable housing unit available for sale or rent on that side of Main Street at the time they happened to be looking.

In light of many of the portraits of "declining" small towns in which shrinking populations could no longer support local businesses, and where school districts were increasingly consolidating because of declining enrollments, I was initially surprised that the town could support the variety of businesses, churches, and schools that it did. The number and diversity of these and other establishments was a big part of what made parallel play possible, and ensured that it continued. The parallel nature of play in Viroqua was maintained largely through the choices that residents made about these local institutions. When it came to spending time in public, Regulars mostly eschewed the Common Ground coffee shop in favor of the Blue Diamond Café or Country Kitchen restaurant. Alternatives and many Main Streeters mostly avoided the bars in the local VFW, American Legion, bowling alley, and Eagles Club. I saw few, if any, Alternatives at the Viroqua Country Club, a gathering spot for Main Streeters and a few Regulars. For the most part, Viroqua's Alternatives declined to participate in any of the town's traditional social groups and clubs such as the veterans clubs or the Masons.

On learning that I worked at the Legion, more than one Alternative asked where the Legion was. Despite the building's visibility from Main Street and its proximity to the Pleasant Ridge school, Alternative residents passed the building day after day without having reason to notice it. Only once in the time I worked there did I see any Alternatives come into the Legion. On that evening, three young men, only one of whom I recognized, came in and, after ordering beers, spent the evening playing pool rather than at the bar itself. They had minimal or no contact with any of the Regular patrons while they were in the bar. The Regular customers, for their part, noted the presence of the new patrons, but quickly returned to their own conversations and activities.

Viroquans had become adept at occupying the same sandbox without taking the next step into collaborative play very often. What were the consequences of maintaining primarily parallel play in Viroqua? As Terry Noble once explained to me, the moments when conflicts had arisen in the context of city politics illustrated the extent to which the factions were able to ignore each other most of the time. In one such instance mentioned earlier, some Pleasant Ridge parents applied for a license to sell wine and beer at the school's 2000 Holiday Faire, an annual weekend-long fund-raiser with live music, dancing, and refreshments on Friday night, followed by two days of activities including silent auctions, food sales, and an art fair. Flyers and posters that advertised the event made it clear that Friday evening's dance with live music was for adults only, not a program for children. The Pleasant Ridge parents who appeared before the city's Common Council had missed the official deadline for applying for the license, but pleaded for leniency.[7] Many of the parents organizing the event were participating in it for the first time, and the license was a detail that had escaped their attention until it was too late. The Common Council refused to be flexible. One alderperson growled that he couldn't understand why there should be any alcohol served at a school in the first place.

The episode showed, said Terry, that "[the alderperson] had never even been to the Holiday Faire. He had no idea what it was all about"—even that the part of the event involving alcohol sales was just for adults. Just as most Alternatives had not gotten deeply involved in city politics, many of the city's elected officials, mostly Main Streeters, had not made much of an effort to get to know the new group of residents, whom they ostensibly represented. As we saw in chapter 3, Gigi Macasaet felt she was alone on the council in her effort to reach out to the Alternatives.

Ironically, just moments after I spoke with Gigi at that event, one of the school's staff approached me, and said, "This isn't what you'd expect to find in Viroqua, is it? We're just a little pocket of enlightenment out here in the country." Comments like these demonstrated that for their part, some of the Alternatives held the town's other residents at a distance, at

---

7. A year later, I witnessed an example of such flexibility, when a member of a civic organization missed a similar deadline. The organization was asking for permission to serve beer at an outdoor tailgate party fund-raiser. Not only did he receive permission to do so, the director of the Roads and Transportation Department volunteered to lend some of the city's cones and barriers to cordon off the area where beer could be served. City maintenance workers even dropped off the materials and retrieved them on city time.

least in a collective sense. This was precisely the kind of snobbishness some of the other groups in town suspected of Alternatives.

Possibilities for Collaboration?

Would the gaps among groups shrink or widen over time? My initial data suggested both—that group crossover would continue at the individual level, but that it would not necessarily lead to greater integration over-all, and that especially for the Alternatives, integration might be likely to diminish further, if their group grew in number and became capable of supporting increasing numbers of their own institutions. Subsequent vis-its to Viroqua over the next several years confirmed these initial findings. For example, when I lived in Viroqua, the Alternatives wished for a pub-lic place they could call their own, especially one that would be open in the evenings when Common Ground had closed. By 2006 the Driftless Café had largely met their need for such a place.

Another problem was the relative immovability of stereotypes. There was significant variety among members of all three groups, but because cross-group ties were usually made by individuals, it was easy for mem-bers of each group to imagine that the other groups were more uniform than they were and to paint the others in terms of broad stereotypes, even when they did have personal contact with them. As one Regular said, for example, of an Alternative family that had joined her mainline church, the very fact that the Alternative family had joined her church meant that they were "more normal" than most Alternatives. It would have been hard for her to know this, however, as she had little contact with other Alterna-tive families.

Group stereotypes also persisted because the people who fulfilled them in the most extreme ways in each group were the most visible people to the rest of the town. It was easy for Main Streeters and Regulars alike to cast Alternatives as hippies whose ideas and appearance were "way out there," because their image of Alternatives was largely dictated by the least conventional members of the Alternative crowd—by the rare Alter-native who did wear his or her hair in dreadlocks, for example. Alterna-tives and Main Streeters alike imagined Regulars in terms of the biggest men in the biggest trucks who listened to country music and spent their free time hunting. The Main Streeters whose names tended to show up in the paper repeatedly because they involved themselves in so many activities and causes were the first names Regulars thought of when they complained that Main Streeters' only motivation for doing things was to show off. Stereotypical ideas about what other groups thought of one's own also informed the way groups viewed each other. The Alternatives were pretty sure that they were viewed as weird by longtime residents. Regulars felt that others looked down on them. Main Streeters thought they were sometimes viewed as creating controversy. There was some truth in all of these imaginings, but Viroquans on the whole overestimated the degree to which others in town viewed them negatively. So, for example, though a very small handful of longtime Viroquans viewed Waldorf philosophy as cultlike, many were simply curious about it and most were indifferent.

Under what conditions might Viroquans learn to play more collaboratively? Hobbies and personal interests were an important source of cross-group interaction, at least for individuals. Main Streeter Roger Mack's love of bicycling brought him in contact with a group of avid bicyclists from the Alternative crowd. Bjorn Leonards seemed to be the only Alternative in the Viroqua Men's Chorus (and one of the group's youngest members as well).

There were a few arenas that brought members of different groups together in somewhat larger numbers. One was youth hockey. Through a significant amount of donated time and money, Viroqua maintained its own indoor ice arena and had boys' and girls' hockey programs for children of all ages. In the case of youth hockey, the children and adults in all groups depended on one another. Without the involvement from all three groups, it is unlikely that there would be either enough parent coaches and volunteers or sufficient funding or numbers of children to field teams in each age group year after year (Grasmuck 2006).

One set of overlapping memberships that initially eluded me occurred in churches. When I attended church services in Viroqua, I occasionally saw a family or two that I recognized as members of the Alternative crowd, but overall, it seemed that church attendance among Alternatives was pretty low, though I saw Regulars and Main Streeters in a variety of congregations. When I shared several draft chapters of this book with a group of students taking a class about community and identity at Youth Initiative High School (the Waldorf high school), the students and their teacher, Jacob Hundt, pointed out that I had overlooked churches as points of contact for members of multiple groups. They pointed out that the "couple of families here and a couple of families there" that appeared to me to be low church attendance by Alternatives was actually a fair amount of Alternative church involvement spread out over a large number of churches, both in and around Viroqua.[8]

What, if anything, might inspire greater collaboration across these groups? The desire for cultural opportunities and concern for local businesses (discussed further in part 2) had done much to bring Main Streeters and Alternatives into collaborative relationships. Some Alternatives joined left-leaning Main Streeters in Democratic political activities. What might it take to draw Regulars into collaboration? It might have to be something cataclysmic. The Regular ethic of agency downplayed the ability of individuals to accomplish much in public life, and by extension, discouraged engagement unless the potential benefits of not becoming engaged would make it "worth it."

To engage collaboration from all three groups, it might also have to threaten the qualities that they all valued in Viroqua. Despite their differences in how they approached community making, residents of Viroqua shared some basic ideas about what the outcomes of community making

---

8. Unlike some Main Streeters and Regulars, however, no Alternatives told me that they met most of their close friends through church. There were twenty-one organized churches in Viroqua listed each week in the Vernon County Broadcaster's "Church Notes" section. Typical of communities in the upper Midwest, the largest number of these (eight) were Lutheran congregations that represented the diversity in Lutheran theologies. Good Shepherd Lutheran was the most visible of the Lutheran congregations, with its large building on Main Street. Good Shepherd was affiliated with the Evangelical Lutheran Church of America (ELCA), the largest federation of Lutheran churches in the United States, and one that is relatively theologically liberal. At the other end of the theological spectrum was the smaller English Evangelical Lutheran, a member of the Wisconsin Synod—a federation of very theologically conservative churches. English Lutheran also ran a small primary school. Many of the other Lutheran congregations in the area were not located in town, but in the smaller communities scattered throughout the countryside. Some of these congregations shared pastors.

Viroqua was also home to a Catholic parish and a variety of churches representing a diversity of mainline Protestant and other denominations. These included two United Methodist churches (one in town and one in the country, which shared a pastor), two Baptist congregations, an Assembly of God, a small Latter Days Saints church, a Nazarene church, and an Evangelical and Free congregation that rented worship space in the public elementary school, then the Landmark Center before building its own building. Some Viroquans worshiped outside the immediate area, like in the small Society of Friends meeting in Gays Mills, about half an hour away, or in an Eastern Orthodox community in La Crosse. I also knew Viroquans who said they preferred private spiritual contemplation over participation in organized religious services.

should be, and they shared reasonably similar collective representations of small-town life in general. In many respects, the list of qualities that attract newcomers to Viroqua is very similar to the list of reasons longtime residents remain there. The area's rolling hills, forests, streams, and farmland are an important draw. Members of all three groups talked about the area's safety and the importance of living in a place free of the stresses that come with "fast-paced" urban living. Parents in all groups thought that Viroqua offered a number of benefits when it came to raising children. Perhaps if something were to threaten the health or safety of the town's children, or a natural feature of the area that everyone valued, the entire town could be brought into collaboration.

No such threat presented itself during the time I lived in Viroqua. The only event that might have been somewhat comparable of which I am aware occurred shortly before I moved there, when it became public that a large company was considering placing a poultry-processing plant in Viroqua's industrial park.[9] By the time I arrived in town, the company had ruled out Viroqua as a potential site, so the debate was already moot. But the letters to the editor that appeared in the newspaper during the controversy and the comments I heard about it afterward suggested that there was widespread opposition to the plant among all three groups.

Indeed, it was one of the first topics anyone in Viroqua spoke to me about. On my very first visit to the town, I spoke with two members of the Alternative crowd in a Main Street shop. Some residents of the town, said one, were worried that a poultry plant would attract "transient" Hispanic workers. Her friend was deeply anxious about the plant. She explained:

> I was raised in a liberal family and taught that everyone could get along, so I worry that maybe the reason that I don't want the plant is that deep down I'm worried about people of different races coming here, too. It makes me think about why I left the really diverse place I used to live. It's made me think about what it is I like about living here, and what about it I wouldn't want to change.

---

9. The Viroqua Development Association (VDA) was a non-profit organization that oversaw and promoted the city's industrial park. Like many cities, Viroqua hoped to attract industries as part of its strategy for economic growth. The 115 acre industrial park was located on the north side of town. The VDA worked to recruit new businesses to the park, and the city offered incentives such as tax incremental financing to enhance the organization's efforts.

Letters to the editor in the *Broadcaster* indicated that other Viroquans were also fearful of the population changes that might come with a poultry plant. When I moved there, I heard residents in all three groups discuss this concern explicitly in the context of talking about the relief they felt that the plan had not come to pass. The difference was that I heard more concerns from Main Streeters and Alternatives about the potential environmental impact of a poultry plant and more reservations from Regulars that the plant would not benefit the workers in town who needed better jobs, not more low-paying, distasteful work.[10] For many in all three groups, any benefits of such a plant would not be worth the costs.

At this point, however, the separation of the three groups seems to be serving a useful purpose. As the town faces change, the ability to avoid open and potentially divisive conflicts may provide a mechanism allowing slower, less volcanic adjustment to change. I often wondered, for example, how volatile school board politics might have been had Viroquans not had such a variety of schools from which to choose. What residents may miss with such separation, however, is the ability to understand that they all worry about how change might affect the town they all call home and the powerful potential they have to combine their resources in planning to deal with it.

---

10. Of course, a segment of Main Streeters favored the deal and, as agents of the VDA, were among its brokers.

Part II

Commerce, Consumption, and Community in Viroqua

On one of my first visits to Viroqua, I conducted a small experiment to see how many basic material needs could be met in the three blocks that made up the bulk of its downtown. While I did not have to leave Main Street to find a pound of drywall screws, a toothbrush, or a gallon of milk, I could not find women's underwear.[1] Underwear for men and children, as well as thermal underwear for the whole family, were available downtown, however. With the exception of the underwear, I had choices about where to purchase these basic items without leaving the downtown area. Toothbrushes, for example, were available not only at Dahl Pharmacy, but also at Langhus Pharmacy (across the street from Common Ground), the Dollar Tree, and at the Kwik Trip convenience stores that stood like book ends on either end of the historic downtown section of Main Street. The Viroqua Food Co-op carried environmentally friendly toothbrushes made from recycled plastic.

---

1. I learned later that Felix's clothing store did actually carry women's underwear, but only briefs.

Walking no more than six blocks from my apartment in Viroqua, I rented movies from Box Office Video, bought newspapers and books at Bramble Press, did much of my grocery shopping, went out for breakfasts and lunches, ordered personalized stationery, did my banking, replenished my printer's ink, consigned clothing I no longer wore, bought wedding gifts for friends, and shipped them overnight via Federal Express. Had it been necessary, I could also have purchased insurance, obtained legal counsel or accounting assistance, had my ice skates sharpened or my car repaired, received medical, dental, or psychological care, or bronzed myself on a tanning bed without walking any farther.

Overwhelmingly, residents told me that they shared my sense that one could get pretty much "everything" one needed in Viroqua. Said one Alternative resident, "I can go and buy organic roasted red pepper—I can buy anything here I can get in Madison, *and* I get the safety of a small town." Said a Regular resident, "We get all our clothes here—between Felix's and Mr. G's—groceries, pretty much anything we need. I can't think of the last time we had to go to La Crosse for something."

Such a statement was sometimes followed by a qualification like, "Well, we could use a [the speaker would name a specialty store] here." The blank was filled with a variety of suggestions, often related to the speaker's favorite hobbies or interests. Dave Ware, who played in a local band, wished for a music store that sold a broader selection of recorded music. Junior high teacher and cycling enthusiast Wes Mack wanted a sporting goods shop with bicycling gear. Several individuals suggested a bakery, and a number of others wished that a replacement for Nate's Supper Club would open, to provide a dining option in a building large enough to accommodate big groups of people for special events that was more "upscale" than the halls for rent at the VFW, the Eagles Club, and the American Legion. For the most part, though, I heard little dissatisfaction with the range of Viroqua's goods or services.

When I couldn't find what I needed in one of the businesses in Viroqua's downtown, I got into my car and drove north on Route 14 for two-thirds of a mile. Just this short distance from the downtown shops was a large locally owned grocery store and a Wal-Mart Supercenter. How was it possible that so many of Viroqua's smaller businesses remained open, when Wal-Mart was open twenty-four hours a day just up the road? At a time when other towns' local merchants were closing up shop, Viroqua's downtown was not only holding on but providing opportunities sufficient to attract new business people to the town. In addition, by the summer of 2004, many of the "wishes" residents had expressed when it came to shops had been granted. A bakery had opened on the south end of town, and the Firehouse Restaurant had opened in the building that once housed Nate's. Ravens Cyclery also opened in Main Street Station, a "European-style market" run by the Macasaet family in a renovated building that once housed the Clark/Peterson car dealership.[2]

Viroqua's relative economic security is clear in the handful of locally owned businesses that have remained in continuous operation, some even in the hands of the same families that founded them. Nelson's Agri-Center, a business that started as a general store two generations earlier, celebrated its fiftieth anniversary in 2004. Kathy Dahl, owner of Dahl's Pharmacy, was the great-granddaughter of its original owner. (The pharmacy later closed when a Walgreens opened in town.) Though it had changed hands, the jewelry store owned by three generations of the Lucas family also remained in continuous operation. Steve Felix was the grandson of the founder of Felix's clothing store. His store made the news in the summer of 2004 when, on its way through the town, the motorcade of presidential candidate John Kerry stopped outside Felix's long enough for Steve Felix to hand Kerry a red, white, and blue tie through the window of the campaign bus.[3]

Such local institutions notwithstanding, the businesses in Viroqua's downtown were constantly changing in both major and minor ways, adjusting to changing business conditions, just as small-town businesses have throughout U.S. history (Lingeman 1980; Johansen and Fuguitt 1984). While I lived in Viroqua, businesses opened and closed; were sold to new owners; and made changes in their products, services, and hours of operation. Several businesses closed during the time I lived there, including the Viroqua Home Center and Soda Jo's diner. In both cases, the closing was not the result of insolvency but of retirement. The store fronts they vacated

---

2. Main Street Station is a good example of a Main Streeter's seeing an opportunity to satisfy mutually reinforcing goals of preserving a building, opening a profitable business, and providing indoor public areas for casual socializing.

3. Felix told the *Broadcaster* that if Kerry won the election, he planned to bill the campaign for the tie.

were both filled within months: the Fasciano family opened Bella Luna, an Italian restaurant specializing in New York–style pizza, where Soda Jo's had been, and Second Time Around, one of the town's several consignment shops, expanded into the space that had housed the Home Center.

Though newspaper articles and signs in the windows of the Home Center and Soda Jo's explained the reasons for their closure, I heard more than one patron in the American Legion bar cite the closures as evidence that the town's economy was "tanking" and that no one could stay in business "for himself" anymore.[4] These speculations were reminders of how unusual Viroqua's business community was—as if residents themselves believed that their town would eventually end up like so many small towns in the United States, where few locally owned businesses were left. It was impossible not to be aware of the shadow the Wal-Mart Supercenter up the road cast over these smaller businesses. There were cars in Wal-Mart's parking lot at all times of the day and night. In order for all of Viroqua's businesses, large and small, to remain viable, there had to be shoppers patronizing all of them.

Said *Vernon County Broadcaster* editor Matt Johnson in an essay reporting on area commerce, "There [were] those who might view the revitalization of Viroqua's downtown as a modern-day miracle" (*River Valley Business Report,* July 13, 2004). In the next three chapters I examine the puzzle that Viroqua's business climate presents to sociological evidence and popular debates about the practice of retail and consumption in the United States as they relate to community life. Increasingly, sociologists recognize the centrality of these practices to community life, where once they were treated as peripheral or even detrimental to community relationships. In Viroqua, two modes of capitalism operated side by side: small-town mom-and-pop operations kept running right along with Wal-Mart and, more recently, a second discount retailer called Tractor Supply Company.[5] In many small towns,

---

4. This word choice was interesting, since both of these businesses, and a number of others on Main Street, were owned by women.

5. Based in North Dakota, Tractor Supply Company is a retailer specializing in hardware, farm and pet supplies, outdoor equipment and apparel. According to its website (http://www.mytscstore.com), TSC has 430 stores in thirty states. TSC opened in spring 2004, occupying the empty Wal-Mart building across the street from the Wal-Mart Supercenter. It remains to be seen how TSC will affect businesses like Nelson's. TSC specializes in retailing in rural areas. Their slogan is "The Stuff You Need to Live Out Here."

Wal-Mart and other discount chains have wiped out existing small business (Halebsky 2004; Salamon 2003). I wanted to gain some leverage on the cultural conditions that made it possible for them to coexist in this town.

In so doing, I found that the practices of commerce and consumption in Viroqua reflected and were also shaped by residents' logics of commitment and ethics of agency. Viroquans used commercial transactions and choices to express their assumptions about community making. Examining these activities also provided some clues as to how the three groups in Viroqua got along with each other and their prospects for getting along in the future.

In chapter 6 I examine cooperation among Viroqua's small-business owners. Evidence gathered by historians and in earlier community studies does not necessarily lead us to expect such cooperation. In Viroqua, local merchants adjusted their views of doing business such that they understood their own business as part of a business district, the health of which depended on some coordination. What I have come to call a *language of beneficent enterprise* girded the complex and sustained ways in which Viroqua's local business owners cooperated with one another to keep their small businesses open in the face of competition from Wal-Mart, which made sense given the broader language of community loyalty and achievement that residents used to explain Viroqua's successes over time. This language of beneficent enterprise is a practice consistent with "commercial communalism" (Monti 1999), a mode of community making that has the potential to include a wide variety of people. In this case, it played an important role in drawing Alternatives into civic endeavors together with Main Streeters.

In chapter 7 I interrogate the ways that business is conducted in both small local businesses and large ones like Wal-Mart. Data from Viroqua suggest that the dichotomous small/local versus big/corporate terms in which retailing in the United States is discussed are not sufficient for understanding how business is conducted in a small town today. Though Viroquans themselves used these terms to understand the retail options in their town and to organize their decisions regarding them, I found that small businesses adopted many practices associated with larger, more rationalized retailers, and that the activities in the town's largest, most corporate retailer (Wal-Mart) had some of the same characteristics associated with small businesses.

In chapter 8 I examine the consumption side of Viroqua's business culture. In the last ten years, sociologists have increasingly recognized the need to take consumer culture and practices seriously as they represent such a major focus in Americans' lives and consumer spending accounts for 70 percent of the nation's GDP. I look at residents' taken-for-granted ideas about the relative value of material items and how they used these to understand and organize the practices through which they consumed products. Material excess is often included in the list of trends blamed for the decline of "real" community, but in Viroqua, consumption played an important role in integrating people. "Even when men and women are showing off their investments and purchases...they are engaged in something more important than conspicuous display. They are living out a particular kind of faith" in the communal lives they share with others (Monti 1999, 322). In addition, I found evidence that using material objects to express social status was no longer understood with reference to a single status hierarchy but was a matter of belonging to one of several horizontally arrayed social groups. As such, buying items was no longer a matter of meeting, to the best of one's financial ability, a bar set by a town's middle and upper classes, as earlier community studies indicate it once was. That is, the reference groups by which residents judged their own material satisfaction or achievement had contracted to a small group of social similars. Consuming specific goods and services could cement one's belonging in one of the groups in town by determining one's place in one of at least three *separate* status orders consistent with members' logics of commitment and ethics of agency.

In the conclusion of the book I revisit the implications for our culture as a whole from these findings about community making as it is practiced by the few thousand Americans in Viroqua, Wisconsin.

6

BENEFICENT ENTERPRISE
AND VIROQUAN EXCEPTIONALISM

In their classic study of small-town life in the 1950s, Vidich and Bensman discovered that in the face of increasing competition from larger retailers, the local businessmen of "Springdale, New York," attempted to remain solvent by ratcheting up their individual performances. The way to stay in business, they believed, was to work harder. In so doing, Springdale's small-business owners became fiercely competitive with one another, increasingly unwilling to attempt innovations that seemed at all risky, and increasingly isolated from the community as a whole:

> In their relations with each other, [Springdale's] businessmen are highly suspicious and distrustful. They scrutinize each other's business activities and practices so as to be able constantly to evaluate each other's standing and competition. All this is done with a minimum of social contact; businessmen do not socialize much with each other or with the rest of the community. (Vidich and Bensman 1968, 55)

This response to competition by the local business community produced strain on Springdale's civic life, an additional instance, according to Vidich and Bensman, of the ways in which encroaching mass society was testing the traditional fabric of small-town community. Vidich and Bensman were concerned because of the role local business owners had traditionally been thought to play in small-town community life.

Small-town downtowns and the local residents who conducted business in them were seen as integral to the civic life of small towns. In 1831 Tocqueville argued that merchants and other professionals who owned the small businesses in the communities where they lived themselves formed the backbone of a community's civic life, owing to the personal stake they had in the success of the community. Historically, small-town merchants provided the leadership skills and often the material resources required to solve community problems (Lingeman 1980; Pederson 1992) and, like their counterparts in urban neighborhoods (Jacobs 1992), served as conduits of community news and information. They became directly involved in their customers' lives, extending credit to those who fell on hard times and finding jobs for those who needed work. The ability of small-town business people to provide this kind of communal glue depended on business dealings resting on the personal relationships among the people who were exchanging goods and services. Vidich and Bensman found that the response of local business owners to competition from franchises and chain stores compromised their ability to fulfill these important community functions.[1]

Though I found some evidence that Viroqua's business community may have been similar to Springdale's at one time, Viroqua's business community had adopted a very different kind of response to competition by the time I studied the town. In stark contrast to Springdale's independent merchants, the local business owners in Viroqua were committed to working together for the good of the business climate as a whole, and they were often extremely active members of the community more generally. Small-business owners saw their businesses not just as a means to their own economic security but as part of a larger community of businesses that were

---

1. In general, beyond serving as potential gathering spots, sociologists have not paid generous attention to businesses and commercial life as sites of community making (Monti and Borer 2006).

likely to sink or swim together in the face of competition from Wal-Mart. Said Main Street Program manager Ingrid Mahan, "It took a catalyst like Wal-Mart coming to town for us to fix things." Unlike in Springdale, the effect of increased competition in Viroqua was to encourage a culture of cooperation among small businesses, which included a language of business success that attributed it to the deliberate actions of Viroquans' working collectively and as individuals to shore up the town's economic base out of a commitment to the success of the town as a whole. This language of beneficent enterprise provided a cultural means by which members could construe their individual economic interests and the interests of the business community, and even the town as a whole, as interwoven rather than mutually exclusive. The Main Streeters used this language the most, and it provided a way to draw other people into their projects, especially Alternative business owners. Using many rationalized organizational tools and bureaucratic resources associated with what Vidich and Bensman and other sociologists of their day called "mass society," the Main Street Program and the Viroqua Partners provided a means to respond to the arrival of mass retailers in ways that contributed to, rather than depleted, the town's civic life, and which were completely consistent with the Main Streeters' mode of community making.

The Alternatives' ethic of agency and logic of commitment also made it easy for them to adopt the language of beneficent enterprise. Like the Main Streeters, Alternative business owners believed that their own actions as merchants could have an impact on the quality of the local community, and while their commitment to bettering the community didn't come directly from a commitment to Viroqua, my data suggest that it might ultimately result in deepening their commitment to the town. The Main Streeters were able to use the language of beneficent enterprise to draw Alternative business owners into the Main Street milieu, which opened avenues for cooperation between these two groups and seemed to have the potential to effectively generate more Main Streeting.

Reframing "Self-Interest"

Perhaps the primary example of this phenomenon was the ongoing effort to preserve historic buildings in the downtown. When it came to promoting local business Main Streeters' efforts centered on getting owners to think of their businesses and their properties not only as private enterprises but as public goods as well. One of the ways they did this was by providing support for restoring historic buildings. As Nancy Rhodes said:

> If we people who live in these towns don't understand the economics of maintaining properties, we can think about it this way—if there is a building that's run down, that [commercial] property is unable to pay their taxes because people don't want to walk in there anymore and don't want to shop there, eventually, what's going to happen? The assessed value of that property is going to drop, and that carries other buildings with it. And who is going to pick up those property taxes that the city no longer has? People who live here. *We* have to do it. So there's a built-in incentive, as I see it, for everyone to do this work.

Nancy and I were sitting at the large oak dining table in the Heritage Inn, the large Victorian home she had restored and ran as a bed-and-breakfast. The "work" to which she referred was the work of finding ways to help local business owners make historically appropriate renovations to the buildings they occupied. The renovations of storefronts throughout the downtown represented one of the principle ways that Viroqua's small-business owners had been able to contribute to the town's civic life by cooperating with one another in ways that historical literature on small-town business would not lead us to expect. These renovations resulted from complex and sustained cooperative efforts in the context of participating in formal organizations, including the State of Wisconsin's office of the National Trust for Historic Preservation's Main Street Program.

Nancy compared historic preservation of downtown buildings to other kinds of practices and rules that contribute to a community's "common good" and "quality of life," such as ordinances requiring residents to shovel snow off the sidewalks in front of their homes. She recognized a tension, however, that made the city's participation in the Main Street Program controversial. She said, "I own my own building, and so I understand how [business owners] feel. I don't want people telling me what to do with my building. But fortunately I understand historic preservation, otherwise I'd probably be in trouble too." Scholars are also aware of this tension between the individual and communal in American culture. Bellah and his team worried:

> It is, of course, no easy task to strike a balance between the kind of self-interest implicit in the individualistic search for success and the kind of concern required to gain the joys of community and public involvement. A fundamental problem is that the ideas Americans have traditionally used to give shape and directions to their most generous impulses no longer suffice to give guidance in controlling the destructive consequences of the pursuit of economic success. (1986, 199)

One of the jobs of the Viroqua Partners was to reframe this apparent conflict between self-interest and community concern. For Nancy Rhodes and many of the other local business owners in Viroqua, especially those with shop fronts on Main Street, maintaining buildings was not just about protecting one's inventory from the elements or attracting customers. Prior to entering the Main Street Program, business owners in Viroqua, like those in many towns in the Midwest, had resolved such basic physical-plant issues in ways that were functional and inexpensive, but not especially attractive, such as replacing aging windows with new ones that were much smaller or encasing brick facades in steel sheeting. Getting business owners to improve the look of their stores was a matter of getting them to change their view of their buildings and even of their enterprises: to see their businesses not just as private enterprises but as potential contributions to the public good as well. This way of thinking about structures dovetailed perfectly with the Main Street ethos, and also fit nicely with the Alternative taste for aesthetic pleasure and authenticity.

Where Springdale's local business owners withdrew from civic life in their attempts to compete with franchises and chain stores as individuals, Viroqua's business owners adopted the opposite strategy, finding ways to work collectively to promote their businesses. Viroqua's small-business owners did not see themselves as alone in their struggle to stay in business.

Of course it was not completely true historically that small-town entrepreneurs never engaged in any kind of cooperative activities. Small towns have long borrowed ideas and models for promotion from larger cities (Monti 1999). However, the cooperative efforts of Viroqua's merchants today go far beyond Babbitt-style "boosterism" (Lewis 1950) of the past. While Viroqua's business community still engages in events like "sidewalk sale" days, their cooperative efforts are far more sustained and complex than the term "boosterism" suggests. Viroqua's business community drew on existing organizational models (Clemens and Cook 1999) of nonprofit local development organizations to create two ongoing organizations aimed at coordinating the efforts to promote the vitality of local businesses: the Viroqua Development Association and the Viroqua Partners. While the Partners' focus was primarily on the downtown, the VDA worked on drawing new businesses to the town's industrial park.

Part of the problem for Springdale's business owners was that "working harder" at keeping their own businesses afloat left them little time for anything else. One of the tasks of the Viroqua Partners was to assist business owners by gathering information that owners did not have time to gather themselves. "We would find out what works," said Theresa Washburn, "and be an information dissemination organization. So that you have all this information for business owners so that they can plan. They can't do it on their own; they're small-business owners." Theresa was the first manager of Viroqua's Main Street Program, and these were the sentences she used to describe the job of local development organizations like the Viroqua Partners. The point was to overcome the isolating, nose-to-the-grindstone mentality that prevented merchants like those in Springdale from remaining engaged in the community in the face of competition from chain stores and mail-order houses. The Viroqua Partners tried to provide structural and organizational support so business owners could look beyond their immediate business concerns and remain engaged while competing more effectively.

The Viroqua Partners and the Main Street Program provided the organizational framework that enabled sustained participation in collaborative efforts. The Main Street Program provided Viroqua's businesses with access to organizational resources at the state and federal levels, including consulting for individual businesses, and an organization with the resources to do the work of planning and executing collective promotions—collective solutions to problems that all small businesses faced. One of the major changes that chain stores brought to retail when they first appeared in large numbers was the significant advantage they had over small businesses in their ability to use standard advertising campaigns across a region or across the country, advertising more efficiently and cheaply than local merchants could (Johansen and Fuguitt 1984; Vidich and Bensman 1960). Cooperation among local business owners in Viroqua often took the form of shared promotional events organized by the Viroqua Partners. In addition to the familiar events like sidewalk sale days, the Partners organized and promoted a trade show for school officials and employees showcasing the supplies schools could purchase from local merchants,[2] and published a guidebook for visitors to the area. Viroqua businesses could place free advertisements in the guide, which also included information about the historic and recreational destinations in the area. The guidebook was one of a number of efforts aimed at bringing people into the downtown. Others included the weekly farmers market, and annual events, like Twinklefest, an event that kicked off the Christmas season with a parade, music, and the illumination of the downtown with tiny white lights strung along the tops of all of the downtown buildings.[3]

Securing business owners' participation in this program, however, required the kinds of informal interactions based on personal relationships traditionally associated with small-town community life that the Main Streeters were especially good at. Proponents of the program had to help other business owners overcome some of the fears that plagued Springdale's business owners, including the fear that they would be alone in absorbing the financial risks of making improvements. They also had to be convinced that participating in a collaborative effort, especially one resting on resources provided by a federal agency, would not simply mean that they would be subject to useless restrictions. "We used the small-town gossip rumor mill," said Theresa, to describe how she and the business owners who provided much of the initial support for the program tried to get other businesses to participate and use its resources to make historically appropriate renovations to their buildings. It was important, she thought, that

---

2. Steve Felix explained the origins of this event in one of the workshops that was part of the town's ten-year Main Street review. When a high school teacher forgot to order a number of T-shirts for a school activity in time to get them from a supplier in La Crosse, the teacher called Felix's store in a panic. "Not only could I get them printed in less time, I could get them even cheaper than from La Crosse. We had to let teachers know that they could probably get a lot of the things they needed right here in town."

3. These events certainly attracted people to the downtown. Whether or not these events and the farmers market also brought people into the stores there was an open question.

no one feel forced to make changes to a property. Instead, she used personal interactions to try to convince business owners of the potential benefit to their own businesses and the community as a whole. "We never did any renovations by law. . . . If I found out anyone was going to tear down a building, I would confront them and say, 'You can't! I won't let you.'"

"And did people believe you and go along with you?" I asked her.

"No. A lot of it was the banks [structuring and contributing to revolving funds for low-interest loans for renovating downtown buildings]. What I would do is offer [business owners] services like we gave them free architectural drawings for fixing up their buildings, and we got estimates—I did the footwork for them." In other words, the program put financial and organizational supports in place, so that when Theresa and other leaders in the program lobbied business owners to get involved, it was feasible for them to do so. Main Streeters rallied both informal and formal resources to get things done. Though there was a certain folksiness to their leveraging of informal connections, they were also sophisticated users of bureaucratic organizations and resources.

Early supporters of the program, business owners themselves, then used their personal relationships with one another to encourage participation in the Viroqua Partners and the Main Street Program—that is, to promote the formal organizational solutions to collective problems. Theresa, for example, talked about the centrality of building "one-on-one relationships" with business owners for drawing them into restoration projects. When she heard that a business owner was considering tearing down a building in the downtown, she put the "small-town gossip rumor mill" to work.

> I had this committee. . . . I'd go to this committee and say, "So-and-so is thinking about renovating their building." And I'd show them all the plans, and I'd say, "Now, make sure you spread this rumor. And then, also, go and buy something there and then tell them, 'Oh, I saw the design for your building, it looks great.'"

Fred Nelson, in particular, had a reputation for making such visits to local businesses.

This kind of interbusiness visiting that was used to convince building owners to make historically appropriate renovations to their buildings was still a big part of the downtown culture. I saw many instances of it, even when the lobbying among owners revealed that cooperation among businesses was not perfect. In some of the disagreements that arose in debates over Partners-led projects there were shades of the solitary merchant Vidich and Bensman described, but the stability provided by the organizational structure of the Partners enabled business people whose interests were not always exactly the same to remain engaged with one another rather than withdrawing.

One example was a disagreement about promotional efforts. In theory, any promotion or activity that drew people into the downtown area was good for business in Viroqua as a whole, but business owners vigilantly monitored the degree to which they perceived their cooperation in Partners' projects benefited their own operations. A controversy over the funds for producing a visitors guidebook provided a good example of one instance in which I saw some disagreement over how much such a cooperative project benefited all businesses. Much of the money for publishing the guidebook came from the city's budget, but it was raised through a room tax paid by all hotel guests. The rationale was that a room tax (about $6 per night per room) was an easy way to raise revenue specifically for projects designed to boost tourism. Theoretically, the hotels, motels, and bed-and-breakfasts affected by the tax would also be the primary beneficiaries of the fruits of these assessments. To its supporters, a room tax was an attractive option for raising revenue for this purpose because it did not place any additional burden on the city budget and seemed only a small burden on visitors, who presumably wanted to visit Viroqua for its own sake and would not be deterred from doing so simply because of a nominal room tax (and who were not voters in local elections).

Just a couple of weeks before it closed its doors, I spent the day at the Viroqua Home Center. It was a slow day, and most of the few customers who came in did so because they wanted to sift through the close-out sale bargains. In the late morning, the owner of one of the lodging establishments in town came in to chat with the Home Center's owner and, after some small talk, raised the topic of the city's newly implemented room tax. The room tax, he believed, was an unfair burden on his business, which catered not just to tourists but to business travelers, construction workers, and other laborers who sometimes lodged in Viroqua several weeks in a row to work on a job, returning home on the weekends. For people staying in Viroqua more than a night or two, he said, the tax quickly added up to a significant amount of money. In addition, people lodging for longer periods were not tourists with any particular interest in staying in Viroqua. These patrons were not the captive, short-term customers envisioned when the tax was implemented. He had lost customers who learned about the room tax and then went to look for lodging in Westby to avoid paying it. His business was being harmed, he said, and he didn't think that any return from the investment in the guidebook or other tourist-oriented advertising would cover the losses he was experiencing.[4] The owner of the Home Center mused that maybe the room tax should be amended so that the rate would be reduced for lodgers staying in Viroqua more than some number of consecutive nights.

The objection to the room tax was rooted in one business owner's concern about his own bottom line. However, the conversation was possible at all because of the existing culture of collaboration and the organizations that made collaboration possible. The Partners provided the structural framework in which members could work out differences that arose from their diverging interests and continue working together. This became clear when the guidebook discussion came up again in the spring of 2003 at a Partners two-day meeting led by staff from the state's Main Street Program. The purpose of the meetings was a ten-year program evaluation, to examine how the city was doing ten years after beginning their involvement with the Main Street Program. Jim Engle and Todd Barman, respectively the director and coordinator of the state's Downtown Development Program, toured the downtown and the businesses, met with Partners members and various committees, and just before they departed on the second day of their visit, presented a preliminary version of their report. Barman raised the guidebook as an example of one of the more recent projects begun by the Partners. It was a good idea he said, but he also suggested some improvements to it,[5] and raised the issue of resentment among

---

4. The room tax was somewhat controversial for other reasons as well. In passing the ordinance, the city council did not include clear procedures for assessing the tax. It was unclear to the owners of lodging establishments how and when they were to remit the tax to the city, and this caused some frustration with the city council.

5. The suggestions were mostly aimed at making the guidebook more useful for visitors than it was. For example, he pointed out that the advertising in the book included, not only ads for businesses that tourists would be likely to use, but also for businesses such as insurance companies, that were really only of interest to area residents. Barman suggested dividing the guidebook

lodging-establishment owners who were almost completely subsidizing the guidebook through the room tax. The problem could be addressed in part he thought by charging all businesses for advertising in the guidebook rather than providing the space for free. Businesses that were members of the Partners might get free advertising or be able to advertise in it at a reduced cost, while nonmember businesses would pay more. The idea, he said, was to give member businesses some more benefits for being Partners members and also to spread out the burden of the publishing costs more equitably.

In this case, the formal organizational resources that accrued to Viroqua's business community through its participation in the Main Street Program provided a forum to revisit and rework collaborative efforts in ways that seemed to increase their chances of remaining viable in the long run. Business owners who were not completely happy with the effects of collaborative processes or projects on their own businesses had access to redress beyond informal lobbying or simple withdrawal. In the case of this ten-year review, the resources included access to experienced opinions from outside the community. It provided a backdrop against which business owners could carry on the conversations and contacts that make for a vital civic life while still running their businesses. The formal aspects of cooperation among small businesses went hand in hand with the informal.

It was possible, perhaps likely, that the issue of the room tax was brought to the attention of the state program staff by the same lodging owner who had raised it in the Home Center the year before, but even if his was the only objection, it was not the only evidence I saw of disagreement about how beneficial certain kinds of cooperation would be to particular businesses. Despite the general spirit of cooperation in the interest of promoting all businesses in downtown Viroqua, business owners still kept an eye on the relative returns to their own businesses.

The formal structures provided by the Partners weren't the only avenues for cooperation. Working at the Legion, I saw many instances of casual cooperation among businesses. There were times as an employee that I ran to a neighboring business to ask to trade larger bills for rolls of quarters or bundles of one-dollar bills after bank hours. Sometimes when

---

and including only ads directed at visitors in the front section, while moving all the other ads to a section entitled something like "Considering Moving to Viroqua?".

bartenders ran short of a certain product, a dash would be made to one of the other establishments to purchase more of it.[6] Often, the customer who wanted whatever the bar was out of would provide the courier service. One evening when I was working at the Legion, several workers from the Viking Inn appeared in the door holding large white plastic buckets and looking somewhat sheepish: their ice machine had broken and they needed to "borrow" some ice.

Whether through formal or informal means, business owners had a great deal of contact with one another. Theresa Washburn said she thought that the downtown business people, no matter their duration of residence or social-group membership, ended up working together and interacting because of their common interest in seeing the downtown be as successful as possible. Field data supported her assertion. In addition to some of the formal mechanisms that fostered relationships among many business people and the members of the Viroqua Partners, including the Partners' Shepherding Program, in which Partners members and experienced business people worked with owners of new businesses to offer advice and guidance, mentorlike relationships sprang up informally as well. One example is the story Karen Groves, who managed the Legion bar and restaurant for most of the time I worked there, told me about the period in which she owned her own flower and gift shop in town. "I wouldn't have made it without Fred [Nelson]," she told me one afternoon as we opened up the bar for business. Fred had acted as a tutor, providing advice on everything from bookkeeping strategies to inventory management. These kinds of efforts were also effective in folding Alternatives into Partners' efforts. The Viroqua Partners, made up primarily of Main Streeters, worked to socialize new business owners, often Alternatives, into their way of thinking about doing business in Viroqua. When new businesses opened, they were approached by members of the Partners, who offered advice and assistance, such as help in throwing and publicizing a grand-opening party.

The organizational structures provided by the Partners also encouraged business engagement by businesses other than those on Main Street. Informal economies also have an important role to play in generating community cohesion by promoting interaction among community members

---

6. This practice is actually prohibited by state law.

(see, e.g., Duneier 1999; Venkatesh 2000; Tolbert et. al. 2002). Using the promotional organs they had developed for formal businesses, the Partners promoted a number of events designed to draw residents and visitors into the downtown.

One of these events was the farmers market, at which local producers of everything from vegetables to cheeses to *lefse* came to sell their wares.[7] Though its origins were modest (actually, "dismal" was the word Theresa used to describe its early days), it is now an institution. It provides a routine gathering place for vendors and customers alike. Vendors were primarily members of the Regular and Alternative communities. Amish families from the countryside were also a significant presence. By the time I arrived in Viroqua, the farmers market had been running for about ten years, and it had opened opportunities for a wide variety of entrepreneurs operating in a less-formal economy.

Another such event was the biannual citywide rummage sale. Residents who wished to participate added their names to a list that the Partners published together with a map of the city that showed visitors which homes were holding garage sales that day. It was best not to try to drive a car through town on citywide rummage sale days, even on those when the weather was bad. Main Street was packed with cars, and the sidewalks throughout the downtown teemed with bargain hunters, city maps in hand. During one sale day, I saw a number of Iowa and Minnesota license plates parked along the town's side streets.

Out-of-town visitors were not the only people ambling from sale to sale. "I've already met three families from [the next block] I didn't know," I overheard one sale participant telling her neighbor, who had covered several card tables in her own driveway with small household items and books. The citywide garage sale provided an opportunity for two days each year for any resident to become a merchant whose wares drew others into conversation and the spreading of information. Again, these informal interactions were made possible by the coordination provided by the Viroqua Partners. The Partners provided the structure in which the actions of many individuals in the city could be coordinated, in theory, at least, improving the commercial opportunities for everyone. The event was based

---

7. *Lefse* is a traditional Norwegian flat bread made from potatoes.

on the same logic as the group's other efforts aimed at formal business enterprises.

Technology, Business, and Community

An additional concern raised by Vidich and Bensman, and by numerous others who have studied small-town life and commerce in the past,[8] was the potential harm to public life that might result from the increasing reliance of town populations on automobiles. Automobiles allowed consumers to roam far afield in their searches for the best deals on products they would otherwise have had to buy close to home, and removed them from the social interactions that were part and parcel of the local shopping experience. While the concern today is less about automobiles, contemporary social scientists and commentators remain worried about technological advances and the ability of commercial life to contribute to civic life. Today, however, the technologies of concern are often television and the internet (Putnam 2000). One worry about the internet is its potential to allow individuals to purchase things they need without leaving the private realm of the home, reducing their face-to-face contact with others and, say critics, possibly reducing civic engagement and routine social contact, as well as reducing local tax revenue.

The internet was also a part of Viroqua's economy, but far from having any uniform effect on how Viroquans engaged in business, residents were using it in a wide variety of ways. First, the internet played a role in some of the collaborative efforts of businesses. The Viroqua Partners, the VDA, and the Downtown Preservation Commission all used websites to provide basic information about the town and about its business community. The sites belonging to the Partners and the VDA were particularly geared toward potential investors and business owners. Viroqua also availed itself of websites like www.americantowns.com and www.city-data.com, sites that offered basic information from towns about local employment, real

---

8. The ability of consumers to drive out of town to shop is still a concern, especially in quickly growing towns where strip malls are built outside city limits, drawing people away from downtowns (see Salamon 2003).

estate values, and demographics, and allowed business owners to find this information when searching by geographic areas of the country.

Small-business owners and their employees on and off Main Street used the internet too. In some cases, the internet functioned as a tool by which a number of business people far from Main Street collaborated to promote their businesses collectively. A good example of such an effort is the Wisconsin Alliance of Artists and Craftspeople (www.artcraftwis.org), a site with links to artisans around the state. Many producer-retailers combined virtual storefronts with other kinds of retailing. For example, Susan Johnson, a nationally renowned textile artist, used a website (www.avalanchelooms.com) to display pictures of her own handwoven products and ordering information for them, as well as of the home products and toys she sold in her shop out in the country, which also contained her weaving studio. Kay Fossum used eBay to augment sales in her brick-and-mortar antique shop. Individuals who didn't have their own brick-and-mortar stores combined strategies such as creating websites, selling in stores owned by others, and selling at artisan fairs.

If the internet continues to strengthen business opportunities for artisans in a range of business situations, it may be a major boon for the civic life of communities where such people live, rather than a drain on them. Small towns with higher numbers of self-employed people (whether they employ others or work alone) are associated with higher levels of civic engagement (Tolbert et al. 2002).

While the internet opened up some opportunities to run businesses from Viroqua both on and off of Main Street, I also knew of a case in which a less savvy Viroquan was subject to a scam run by a company that seemed to offer an easy way to start an online business. One evening in the bar as I cleaned the glassware and restocked the coolers, R. J. began by telling me about his ongoing conflict with his teenage step-daughters over their refusal to do a good job with their chores. "I've got macaroni stuck to my socks, and that's *after* the floor has been cleaned," he complained and said he was tired of the girls getting his butter full of toast crumbs. He was also tired of being unemployed. On the brighter side, however, he had a new online business. "Three months ago, I'd never touched a computer, and now I have my own web business," he said. R. J. gave me the URL for his website, on which he said he would be selling camping and other outdoor gear such as tents and sleeping bags.

According to R. J., the website was really easy to set up and "the company" had hundreds of products from which to choose to sell on one's site. When R. J. said this, I immediately became suspicious. After a little online research, I learned that the company hosting his website, Meridian One Technologies, ran television infomercials enticing viewers to start their own online businesses. I found a number of reports on websites that were dedicated to tracking internet scams that indicated that the operation was a scheme in which the hosting company simply acted as a distributor for the products and charged "business owners" like R. J. a minimum of $39 per month to host their sites. Together with other fees, the charges could add up to over $100 per month. A year and a half after R. J. proclaimed that his site was up and running, I was still able to access it on the web. The only message on Meridian One Technology's homepage, however, was that the page was "under construction." The internet seemed most beneficial to Viroquans who produced the goods they sold or who were using the internet to complement a brick-and-mortar store.

The Language of Beneficent Enterprise

The problem for local, independent merchants in Springdale was that as the competition they faced stiffened, their instincts to preserve their own businesses eclipsed the interest they may have had at one time in being full participants in the community as well as business owners. They had no time to be both and, apparently, had no way of thinking about the range of possible responses that would have included even nominal forms of cooperation with one another. What made it possible to do both in Viroqua?

At the age of twenty-seven, after serving in the Peace Corps, Theresa Washburn moved to Viroqua to manage the new, and still fairly controversial, Main Street Program. It was an advantage, she believed, not to be a longtime resident when it came to running the program. Without long ties to other community members, she felt free to say and do what she thought was right without needing to worry about what others might think of her. Theresa was still living in Viroqua when I arrived there twelve years after she had. Theresa had married "a local," and their three-year-old daughter, Naomi, sat nearby on the floor arranging trees and figures on a felt-board as Theresa and I talked one afternoon.

"I really didn't care [about people's opinion of me]," she said. Contrasting herself with lifelong residents like her husband, she continued, "I am still a little more bold, I guess is the word. Maybe just stupid." She laughed.

"Don't say stupid," Naomi chimed in, admonishing her mother.

"Oh, you're right," sighed Theresa, smiling over the edge of the kitchen table at her daughter. "That's not a word we say," she explained, looking at me and rolling her eyes slightly. The members of the business community, she continued, "they take a lot of ownership of this community." Since resigning as Main Street manager, Theresa had done extensive consulting with business leaders in small towns across the Midwest. I asked her if that sense of ownership was common in other communities as well.

She replied, without hesitation:

> No, I don't see that in every community. The more I worked in a lot of different communities in the Midwest, the more I realized there's a uniqueness here that I still can't fully put my finger on. Sometimes it's that power of a few, that beginning. If I looked at it, it would be Steve Felix's dad, Fred Nelson, Duffy Hoffland—he was the bank president and he's our neighbor here [gestures in the direction of the Hoffland house]. They had a real strong feeling—they all began to feel that it was their community, and they began to feel a certain sense of being able to *do* something about it.

Theresa's discussion of this issue was interesting because it typified a way of talking about Viroqua's surprising business success, in which established business people and other community leaders who "cared about the community" took action in ways that benefited the town as a whole, embodying the Main Street ethic of agency that valued and believed in individual contribution and their logic of commitment to Viroqua. This way of talking about the town was applied even to its earliest history:

> You might say that the generous, good-hearted nature of Viroqua's residents was begun way back when in 1852. It was at that time in Viroqua's early history that Moses Decker, the founder of our community, made a critical decision to donate 40 acres of land to the city of Viroqua for a new county seat for Vernon County if Viroqua was chosen in the upcoming vote [on the location of the county seat]. It worked and even today people stop to

shop when they come to do business with the county. Today literally hundreds of folks donate time, talent, energy and treasures in the same giving
spirit. (http://viroqua-wisconsin.com/about/history.asp)

Residents of Viroqua celebrated the collective efforts and beneficent contributions they and their forebears have made in efforts to keep the town
vital. Contemporary residents located their efforts in what they saw as a
long-standing tradition of grappling with change in their community.

The culture of cooperation among local business owners was supported
by the language of beneficent enterprise. This language provided Viroquans with a cultural resource they used to bridge the tension between
business as a matter of self-interest and the place of economic enterprise
in ensuring the vitality of the community as a whole. Business owners and
other active participants in the community talked about the town's economic climate in terms that emphasized that it resulted from the concerted
efforts of dedicated Viroquans. Today, most of the county's retail activity is consolidated in Viroqua, making it the logical destination for area
shoppers—whether they plan on patronizing a national chain or a locally
owned shop.

Of course, Viroqua has accumulated a unique set of structural advantages over surrounding towns, which has resulted in its winning out over
surrounding towns economically. The town's becoming the county seat
gave it a stable base of jobs that, over time, made it a likely choice for the
location of other important institutions such as schools and transportation
hubs. It was quite possible that structural factors of this kind are highly
determinative of the town's economic success, but on a daily basis Viroquans lived, acted, and talked as if their actions were responsible for this
destiny. Using the language of beneficent enterprise, the town's history, including the events through which it acquired some of its structural advantages over other towns in the area, was cast as a series of events in which
dedicated Viroquans had worked over time to ensure the town's stability.
Contemporary efforts on the part of local business owners to remain viable
despite the arrival of Wal-Mart were also framed in this way.

The language of beneficent enterprise framed the town's history as a series of events in which caring and loyal citizens made cumulative contributions to the town as it is today. Much of what is written about the town's
history was a celebration of residents' efforts to improve the community

during periods of change, as seen in the passage included on the Partner's website cited above. Similarly, *Hometown Heritage,* a children's book
written for the town's sesquicentennial celebration in 1996 and published
by the Vernon County Historical Society, concludes by saying that since
the town's first white settlers arrived in 1846, the changes that had happened there had been positive, thanks to continual communal efforts
to meet the challenges that came with it: "The people of Viroqua have
worked to keep our hometown up-to-date and energized....Our hometown gets better and better as time goes by" (19).

These passages are instructive because they illustrate how this language
of beneficent enterprise was used to construct the town's history. The town's
early history was not unique insofar as early white settlers and speculators
forming villages all over the Midwest were aware that agriculture alone
would not be enough to sustain town economies. Historians document stiff
competition among villages to become county seats, to house railroad de-
pots, and to attract public and private institutions. This fierce competition
indicated the awareness, even as towns and counties as we now know them
were just getting their start, that successful small towns, and the businesses
located in them, would be ones located where these other institutions attracted people (Lingeman 1980; Monti 1999; Pederson 1992).

To the extent that attracting these kinds of amenities improved a town's
chances for economic success, Viroqua got an auspicious start. Viroqua became the seat of Vernon County in 1851, even before it was actually incorporated as a village in its own right.[9] As did other town founders during
this period, Viroqua's founder, Moses Decker, launched an aggressive campaign to secure the county seat's location in Viroqua, including a promise
to sell to the county, for a bargain price of $5, forty acres for the court-
house, which he did when Viroqua beat Springville in a runoff a month
later.[10] Though Springville is just three miles from downtown Viroqua, it

---

9. In 1851 the State of Wisconsin approved an election in which the few white settlers in
Vernon County would select their own county seat. Each elector would first vote for any location
he liked. If no location received a majority of votes, a run-off between the top two locations would
be held. Viroqua, still called Deckersville at the time, did not come out on top in the first election, edged out by Springville, a nearby village that received 67 votes to Deckersville's 64 (Vernon
County Heritage 1994). Three other sites were nominated: "John Allen's place" received 41 votes,
the Bad Axe battlefield received 8 votes, and one elector, perhaps with a low opinion of the con-
cept of county governance, voted to locate the county seat in "The River."

10. Viroqua received 152 votes and Springville received 139.

was now little more than a cluster of homes and had been unincorporated. In addition to winning the county seat, Viroqua also became a stop on a railroad line, and the road running north and south through the town ultimately became Wisconsin Highway 14, which continued to be an important throughway between Madison and La Crosse.[11] Decker's ability to secure the county seat in Viroqua certainly raised the value of the rest of the land he owned in what became the city of Viroqua, the forty acres he sold for $5 notwithstanding. The contemporary language of beneficent enterprise retrospectively framed Decker's contribution as an act of generosity but left open other motives he may have had.

Another example of this language was the way that Garith Steiner described the deal struck by the hospital, the city, and the public school district in which the hospital would run the new indoor city swimming pool built at the combined middle school and high school. Initial funds for the pool were donated to the city by the estate of former resident Phil Bigley, who had lost a childhood friend to drowning and wanted to ensure that all of Viroqua's children received swim instruction. The bequest was sufficient to build the pool but not to maintain or run it. After investigating many options, it was arranged that the hospital would take over the management of the pool. Said Garith:

> We [the hospital] won't make much, if any, money on [the pool]. In fact, we'll probably lose money on it in the first few years. But for our business as a hospital, it helps us build relationships with potential clients. Maybe someone who takes a water aerobics class will think of VMH next time they need health-care services. It's also just good for the community. It is good for families—something for parents and kids to do together. Supporting families and kids is as important as anything else.

In addition, Garith pointed out that the hospital's success was good for the community as a whole. It provided jobs and attracted health-care professionals to work and live in the town. He explicitly linked both the economic motives of the hospital and the benefits the hospital could provide to

---

11. At the same time that Highway 14 guarantees a constant flow of traffic through the downtown, which may be good for local business, the high volume of traffic, especially tractor-trailer trucks, at times makes it difficult for pedestrians to cross the street.

the community. The success of the hospital as a viable economic entity and the health of the community were inextricably tied.

As was the case with Moses Decker in the days of Viroqua's founding, these efforts were linked, at least rhetorically, to the efforts of nameable individuals. But the high profile that came with community leadership was not always positive. Despite business leaders' seeing themselves as acting to benefit themselves and the community, the language of beneficent enterprise that business leaders used did not fly with everyone, as we saw when Nancy Rhodes incurred criticism from Legion patrons who suspected business leaders of cloaking self-aggrandizement in a guise of historic preservation. Whether or not they accepted as genuine the language of beneficent enterprise that many business owners used, Viroquans made daily choices about where to do their shopping and with whom they would engage in business transactions.

7

RETAIL MORALITY

"Well, it's not what I would have picked," said the young woman, staring crestfallen at the emerald green bridesmaid's gown that had been ordered for her. "But it's not my wedding."

Maridene Olson, owner of Bonnie's Wedding Center smiled sympathetically, but said only, "Let's get you back and try it on. Did you bring your shoes so we can mark the hem?" As she said this, Maridene gathered up the offending dress and its garment bag, and led the reluctant bridesmaid toward the dressing room. As she walked past the chair she had provided for me to sit in to observe the store, she turned back to the woman and commented that many of the bridesmaids she saw in the store were very special and loyal friends, a tacit acknowledgement that she had registered the woman's disappointment with the dress this bride had chosen for her bridesmaids. The woman chuckled affirmatively as they entered the dressing room area and smiled for the first time since she laid eyes on the gown.

I was watching a master at work. Maridene was able to relax the bridesmaid so that she could perceive Maridene as sympathetic to her discomfort at being required to purchase, and be seen in public, wearing a garment she clearly disliked, without Maridene's betraying any hint of her own opinion of the dress. In addition to supplying the item the customer was purchasing, Maridene ensured a more ephemeral kind of satisfaction to two customers at once: the dismayed bridesmaid in the store, and the bride who had chosen the gown, who would never need to question her selection, at least not because of anything Maridene might say.[1]

As it said on the store's website, "Bonnie's Wedding Center is an independently owned, family owned, service-oriented store." Maridene and her daughter, Melodie Russell, moved to Viroqua from Minnesota to purchase and run Bonnie's, located at 113 South Main Street, in between Bramble Press and Art Visions gift and framing shop. I had been curious about Bonnie's since I moved to Viroqua the month before. The window display contained mannequins clothed in bridal gowns dyed gold, orange, red, and brown and surrounded by faux fall leaves.[2] Whenever I walked past Bonnie's, or watched the shop from the window of the Common Ground coffee shop across the street, it was always doing a brisk business. How could a shop selling such a specialized set of products survive in Viroqua? Even if every Viroqua bridal party purchased all their wedding clothes from the shop, in an average week fewer than two local weddings were announced in the *Broadcaster*,[3] which hardly seemed sufficient to keep an entire bridal shop open.

I ventured into the shop one afternoon and introduced myself to Maridene, who graciously allowed me to observe the business for a day. It was a good time of year to see the store, she said, because it was early October, a time when many weddings were taking place, and when many brides were beginning to plan for spring weddings. When I arrived just

---

1. Maridene's adroit handling of this particular situation was likely the result of its being relatively common. Of four bridesmaids who picked up dresses they had not yet seen (for four separate weddings) on the day I observed the store, each one indicated disappointment or openly disparaged the gown. None of these four bridesmaids was accompanied by a bride who had chosen the gown.

2. Maridene later explained to me that she arranged the window to fit the season, dyeing old dresses that could not be sold in appropriate colors for the time of year, or displaying new dresses with seasonal themes. At Christmastime, for example, in addition to two white bridal gowns, the window mannequins were wearing a variety of special-occasion dresses in black velvet and red-and-green plaid taffeta. In 2008, Bonnie's moved to a new location at 211 South Main Street.

3. Average is over all months in 2001. Engagement announcements were not included in the average.

after the store opened that Saturday morning, I was asked to remove my shoes and leave them at the door, as did the customers who entered. "We have to protect the dresses," explained Maridene. "Shoes bring in dirt from the street—and we do have a lot of farms around here—which gets in the carpet and then on the hems of the dresses." From the folding chair near the back of the store where I spent the day, I could hear and see nearly all of the interactions in the store that busy fall Saturday. Maridene, Melodie, and the two other women who worked in the shop handled brides and bridesmaids; grooms and groomsmen who came in to be fitted for rental tuxedos; and an assortment of accompanying family members and friends of customers in the throes of planning weddings.

The people who entered the shop varied widely in their needs and in the degree to which they seemed happy to be there. Most of the brides who entered the store were either picking up dresses they had already ordered or had appointments to try on dresses for weddings well in the future, but two brides came in to the store wanting to buy dresses off the rack. A few people arrived without appointments. One woman was unhappy with the color a pair of dyed-to-match shoes had turned out. Maridene and the rest of the staff handled all of these interactions with the same kind of aplomb as Maridene had demonstrated in assisting the disappointed bridesmaid. By the end of the day, I was convinced of the shop's description of itself on its website:

> We are committed to *you* and work hard to hone our service skills, stay abreast of wedding trends, provide expertise, professionalism, and value to our brides…we give you peace of mind and leave you truly satisfied with your investment. (www.bonniesweddingcenter.com)

"I think today, people don't really know what customer service is any more," Maridene said in one of the few slow moments in the day. "Especially some of the younger girls—they've only shopped at Wal-Mart or the mall, and they've never had anyone in a store help them find things or try things on before. They are uncomfortable with it, and they say they just want to browse or try things on themselves, but we can't let them do that because we have to protect the dresses."

The staff at Bonnie's tried to manage customer discomfort using a language of indulgence and pampering. The shop's sign in the window read

"We put *you* on a pedestal," which was literally true in the sense that everyone trying on gowns spent a great deal of time standing atop one of two platforms in front of three-sided mirrors near the back of the store. But the staff also used this language to help customers who were not comfortable receiving so much assistance feel more at ease. "This is going to be *your* big day," Melodie told a woman of about nineteen or twenty, who had come to look at wedding dresses with her four-month-old baby and a friend of her own age in tow. "You let *us* do the work. You said you might be interested in some strapless styles—I'll bring several over for you to look at."

Because of the need to protect the expensive inventory, and because the process of ordering gowns and accessories for a wedding requires a certain level of expertise, there is very little that is "self-serve" when it comes to bridal wear. Bridal shop workers rely on their service skills because the ability of bridal shops to deliver their products to customers depends on successfully leading those customers through a lengthy process that only begins with gown selection, and usually includes measuring, ordering, multiple fittings, and alterations (Corrado 2002).

Though Bonnie's Wedding Center relied on customer service perhaps even more extensively than did other businesses on Main Street, it was not the only business in town that emphasized personalized service. Providing highly personalized service in this small shop was also integral, it turned out, to the way that many of the other small, locally owned businesses in Viroqua kept their doors open, but not simply for the obvious reason that customer service was important in any retail business. The personalized service and personal relationships local merchants had with customers were as much a part of their product as their products themselves, because it allowed them to live up to the expectations customers had of them.

I began to understand this when Maridene explained who her customers were. Most of the customers at Bonnie's were not Viroquans, which explained how there could be such a large number of brides in there but not why they came to Viroqua to buy wedding dresses. Maridene estimated that Bonnie's did 80 percent of its business with nonlocal customers.[4] "As

---

4. Chris Larson, the owner of Art Vision, also estimated that a significant proportion of her sales were to nonlocal people, especially in the summer. In the winter, she explained, the people who came in to the store were almost exclusively people she knew. In the summer, she saw mostly unfamiliar faces.

far as the local weddings go," explained Maridene, "we only do the quickie ones—the ones that happen at the last minute." When I asked her why she thought this was the case, she said she believed that when brides-to-be went shopping for gowns, part of the shopping ritual included searching for a gown some distance from one's home. "Our brides [from Viroqua] go and shop in La Crosse or Madison, and brides from La Crosse and La Crescent [Minnesota] come here. I guess shopping for a dress in another town makes it seem more special," she concluded.

In other words, the quality of the shopping *experience* was as important to customers as the actual products the Wedding Center carried. The shop's owners knew this and incorporated it into the way they did business. Living up to what they believed customers expected from a shop in a small town was an important part of doing business at Bonnie's. The uniqueness of the experience in shopping in a small, locally owned shop was seen both by local business owners and by many customers as special compared to mundane shopping experiences in places like, as Maridene put it, "Wal-Mart and the mall." They cultivated this sense of uniqueness because they understood how important it was to live up to customers' expectations of the bridal shopping experience (La Pradelle 2006).

Big Business versus Small Business?

Maridene's use of "Wal-Mart and the mall" as a point of contrast to what she understood her store offered customers echoed a way of thinking about business that I heard from many Viroquans, and which was also consistent with a larger cultural debate about the relative virtues and drawbacks of certain types of retail business in the United States. For many Americans, large-scale versus small-scale retailing has become a serious political and moral issue. "Big" is equated with large inventories, low prices, lower-quality goods, and corporate ownership. Conversely, "small" suggests the tradeoff of broad selection and lower prices for better customer service from local business owners who have a stake in the community.

Viroquans, too, used these categories unproblematically, and in daily life they operated on the assumptions these categories implied. Just as brides from larger towns sought out a special shopping experience at Bonnie's, one Viroquan bride explained that she had not looked for a gown at

Bonnie's because she was sure that "they didn't have anything," that their inventory was too small to offer many choices.[5] But observing the way Viroquans lived and conducted routine business activity, it was hard to see a clear connection between these larger, morally loaded categories and actual practice. No matter how Viroquans felt about big or small retailers, and no matter how mutually exclusive they treated or conceived of them (as having diametrically opposed sets of benefits and drawbacks), these categories were not especially helpful for understanding business in Viroqua. Small businesses in Viroqua relied on many of the same rationalized practices used by large ones to overcome some of the difficulties associated with conducting business on the basis of personal relationships. In addition, larger stores, like the local Wal-Mart, and chains, like McDonalds, had come to serve some of the extracommercial social functions associated with small, locally owned business. While most accounts of retail stores, retailers, and their places in communities of all sizes ultimately come down very squarely in favor of one option or the other, in Viroqua, the benefits and drawbacks associated with both kinds of capitalism were not always easy to tease out.

Why is the debate about the relative merits of big- and small-style capitalism such a charged one in the United States, particularly when it comes to who will get to do most of the retailing in small towns? Part of the answer lies in the centrality of the small-town downtown to our ideas about what makes small-town community meaningful in the first place—an idea reflected in the way that small towns across the country were designed. The most public part of a village or small town was traditionally its central business district—its main street—designed to be the geographic and economic heart of the community. Even when named something else, an American town's main street is easy to find, laid out either perpendicular to a central artery or along a segment of it in the center of a residential area. Downtown shops and offices not only supplied residents with items and services they required but served a number of social functions, such as providing public gathering places.[6]

---

5. Bonnie's Wedding Center carried four lines of bridal gowns, lines that were also carried by retailers in La Crosse and Madison and in shops across the country.

6. Historically, the economic activity of small towns and villages like Viroqua revolved around the needs of agriculture. Village economies grew up around services and facilities that

For many, Wal-Mart has come to represent the biggest of the "big" end of the retail spectrum, and the store has become something of a lightening rod. Debates over where Wal-Mart should be allowed to locate new stores have precipitated emotional and divisive fights in communities across the country (Halebsky 2004). For its detractors, Wal-Mart has come to stand for everything that is problematic about big corporate capitalism and the sprawl-style development encouraged by big-box stores when they are sited on city fringes. Advocates of what we might call "traditional" small-town retail, dominated by small concerns owned by local merchants, argue that the loss of a small town's downtown shops is symptomatic of a community's demise. As storefronts empty and residents must shop elsewhere, they say, towns lose out not just economically but socially. Without businesses to draw residents together in the downtown, the town loses its arena for the routine and natural socializing that makes "small-town stuff" possible.

In addition, critics say, chain stores' rationalized business practices do not allow for the kinds of personal service that small independent merchants once offered, nor do Wal-Mart employees have extensive knowledge about the products the store carries. Such criticisms are reflected in what Viroqua's small-business owners say in public about the ways they have tried to compete with Wal-Mart. As for interpersonal contact and sociability, say critics, the best the likes of Wal-Mart can come to cultivating these is a superficial version of it in the form of paid "greeters" who stand by the door to welcome customers. When Viroqua's local business owners talked publicly about how they have managed to stay in business despite the presence of Wal-Mart, they invariably drew on these taken-for-granted ways of talking about big-versus-small retail.

Advocates of small retail equate locally based retailing, not only with personalized customer service and the ability to generate a sense of community cohesion, but also with social responsibility. Critics point out that large discounters sell goods made cheaply in sweatshop conditions and reduce overhead to keep prices down in a variety of ways that have their

---

farmers required for storing and marketing their products, and around retail and service establishments required by farmers and village residents (Brunner 1928; Brunner and Kolb 1933). As retail centers, small towns served as a link between rural areas and larger urban centers (Brunner 1928; Johansen and Fuguitt 1984; Lingeman 1980).

own negative consequences, including keeping employees' wages artificially low and providing few employees with benefits such as health insurance (Dube and Jacobs 2004). The money made by small merchants, their advocates say, is recirculated in the community, while money made by chain stores is sent away to corporate headquarters, further draining rural economies that in many cases are already fragile. In addition, say critics, large corporately controlled stores feel little obligation to the communities in which they build.

On the other hand, supporters of franchises and discount merchants in small cities and rural areas argue that critics' ideas of traditional retail rely on faulty, unrealistically nostalgic images of it. Typifying this view was an opinion piece in the *New York Times* that, while acknowledging that "the chains do take businesses from neighborhood stores and the like," argued:

> It is a mistake to elevate the sale of pipe elbows and duct tape to the level of a sacrament. There are some things that big stores do better. There is also the dirty little secret that some local stores have never lived up to their image, instead providing a unique combination of high prices and poor service sustained only by the local monopolies that they enjoyed before the advent of the chains. (Askt 2001)

This view of small-town economies argues that far from providing a sound model for retail, the kinds of small, locally owned operations associated with the traditional small-community downtown was never an effective or sustainable way of doing business. Small businesses in small towns fold because they simply cannot compete with more efficient competitors like Wal-Mart. It is impossible to be efficient and competitive if the basis of business transactions is personal relationships.

Proponents of the larger chain stores say that rural consumers in particular benefit from the expansion of chains like Wal-Mart, because they offer alternatives to the limited inventories and higher prices of locally owned stores. Even the author of a book subtitled *How to Defend Your Main Street against Chain Stores and Why it Matters* (Mitchell 2000) admits that "corporate retailers have brought innovation to some sectors. Bigness does command certain competitive retail and service providers to streamline operations, improve service, stay open longer, trim prices, and expand product lines" (11).

The ways that business was actually conducted in Viroqua illuminated a number of complexities that are glossed by the current terms of the big-retail versus small-retail debate. One problem with the big-versus-small debate is the ahistorical terms in which it is usually conducted. Though "big" business is often seen as the source of most of the current challenges to small-town businesses, many of the struggles small-town businesses face are not new ones. It has always been hard to keep a business open in a small town (Lingeman 1980). In addition, small businesses have always faced evolving challenges and sought ways to adapt themselves to those challenges. Small-town businesses, and ways of doing business, have always evolved along with the communities and economies of which they are a part: "part of a larger integrated system of centers offering goods and services of varying scale and specialty in response to both market demand and location relative to competing centers" (Johansen and Fuguitt 1984, 107).

Nevertheless, these oppositional images of big and small retail persist. Why? In part, these categories, though not reflecting what happens inside many business transactions in Viroqua, provided a useful cultural resource that residents used to make sense of themselves, their commercial relationships with others, and their daily practices. They provided a logic that residents could use to make decisions about those practices as both sellers and buyers that reflected the differences among Viroquans' logics of commitment and ethics of agency.

The kind of personalized service valorized by proponents of small businesses is closely related to Blumenthal's conception of "small-town stuff," in which all the interactions, and in this case transactions, in a small town are facilitated by the detailed knowledge that all residents have of one another. The result is a social milieu characterized by high levels of personalization and informality. At the most personalized end of the business spectrum, the informal economy was alive and well in Viroqua. A fair amount of business was still conducted very informally in Viroqua, both among individuals who are well known to one another, and even among individuals who are not.

I watched numerous transactions take place at the Legion, for example. In many cases, transactions did not even involve monetary exchanges. Over beers, patrons who knew each other made arrangements to exchange everything from car parts to remodeling assistance to firewood and baby-sitting. Sometimes money was involved in these informal transactions, as when I overheard a patron I did not know strike a bargain with Kim Fossum, a skilled welder, about doing a small welding job for him over the weekend. Close to Christmastime, the Legion's manager, Karen Groves, brought in a sample of her homemade jalapeno jelly that she hoped others might buy from her as gifts.

We often assume that these kinds of informal transactions depend on the participants' having personal ties to one another—both because of the information needed by both parties to initiate the transaction and because of the degree to which personal ties provide a means for leveraging social pressure to ensure that both parties fulfill their ends of an agreement. In Viroqua, the informality of much commercial life extended beyond transactions between acquaintances, as I learned when I went about trying to rent an apartment. After looking at several apartments,[7] I decided to rent one at 322½ Independence Street, on the second floor of a brick Victorian owned by Lucy Volden, who lived downstairs. Two days after seeing the apartment, I called Lucy to tell her I had decided to take the apartment. She said she was happy to rent it to a single person, because having more than one person upstairs increased the noise downstairs. Lucy worked the second shift at the Trane Company in La Crosse. She returned home around 3 a.m. and needed to be able to sleep well into the late morning. She did want the names of a couple of references, and I promised to mail her several names along with a check for my first month's rent right away. I suggested that when she received my information and check, she could mail me a lease, which I could sign and return to her.

"Oh...a lease?" she asked. "I've never used one, because...well, I just haven't." I was surprised that she did not want to formalize our agreement, if for no other reason than to guarantee follow-through on my part. Consistent with many Regulars' reluctance to formalize many kinds of agreements, she explained that it was equally in her interest not to have tenants sign leases. Perhaps sensing my puzzlement, she volunteered, "Sometimes, I get people I want to boot out right away, and you can't do that if they have a lease." After I hung up the phone I realized that Lucy and I had never even exchanged last names. I felt very awkward at the idea of calling Lucy back to ask her last name, so in order to mail her my references and check,

---

7. For an extended discussion of how I chose a place to live in Viroqua, please see the methodological appendix.

I used the reverse look-up function of an online telephone directory to find it. These kinds of exchanges were certainly not restricted to Regulars—I just had the most opportunities to see it among members of this group.

In the formal economy, there was plenty of small-town stuff baked into the business transactions in Viroqua's downtown, as might be expected. Small-town stuff took mundane forms, as in merchants' abilities to anticipate the needs of regular customers. I developed pride in being able to serve most of the Legion's regular customers their usual drinks without their having to ask. I knew which customers sat in which seats, and which ones would need ashtrays placed nearby. Not to remember a regular patron's usual order could be construed as a slight, causing a comment like, "How many times have I been in here, and you still don't know what I want?" or "Jeez, I guess I'm not very memorable."

I heard many stories about local merchants' willingness to track down special products or provide special services for customers. The most dramatic example came from a couple whose son found himself in legal trouble during a trip abroad several years earlier. Though his parents felt torn between their concern for their son's safety in a foreign prison and a sense that he was old enough to have to sleep in the proverbial bed he'd made for himself, they decided they had better bail him out. To do so, they needed access to their bank account, but, as it was Saturday, the bank was closed until Monday. Unsure what else to do, they called the president of their locally owned bank. The president met the couple at the bank on Sunday morning and helped them withdraw the funds they needed. "Where else could that happen but in a small town?" the mother of the imprisoned son asked. "Do you think you could get anyone to open a *bank* for you on a *Sunday* in a *city*? No way!"[8]

It was not only customers who benefited from the kinds of personal knowledge that came with repeated interpersonal contact in places of business. The people behind the counters were the beneficiaries of small-town stuff too. One Wednesday night, the adult volleyball league in which I sometimes participated adjourned after two hours of play at the high school gym to the bar in the Bowl-Away Lanes, Viroqua's bowling alley. In the context of a discussion about how much everyone in town knew

8. Notable here is that the comparison she drew was between a bank in a small town and one located in a city, not between a locally owned bank and a branch of a national chain.

everyone else's business, Mary, who tended bar there, told me that she was once pulled over for speeding on the busy Route 14 on her way to work. By the time she arrived at the Bowl-Away, the patrons had already taken up a collection to pay for her ticket.[9]

The detailed knowledge of regular patrons and personalized service that such knowledge allowed is part of our image of traditional small-town retail, but they were not the only places where I observed such service. I saw similar examples of detailed knowledge about customers' needs elsewhere, even in the context of the highly bureaucratized retail setting of the post office. Indeed, post offices have long been valued for their ability to serve as community gathering places. One afternoon, I stood in line at the post office window behind an elderly couple: a man and a woman who could have been husband and wife, but could just as easily been brother and sister. As they stepped to the counter, the man took from his pocket a check that had already been made out. He explained to the young woman behind the counter that the woman with him needed five books of stamps. The postal clerk asked what kind of stamps she would like, addressing the woman herself. The older woman seemed unable to respond verbally— though she nodded her head, smiled brightly, and made a series of "sh" sounds.[10] "She wants pretty stamps," the man explained to the clerk.

By this time, a second postal worker, a burly man with a beard who was much older than the first clerk, had stepped up to the counter with several books of stamps in hand and arrayed them on the counter in front of the elderly woman. She smiled broadly and continued nodding her head, while the younger clerk took a small step to the side so the older clerk, and not she, was standing in the center of the service window. The older clerk said, "We're out of the flower stamps." The woman gestured to several books she seemed to like, including the latest "Love" stamps, a series of stamps commemorating Lucille Ball, a book of stamps that depicted drawings of an orange and an apple on alternating stamps. While the woman made her selections, the older clerk stepped away from the window again,

---

9. I asked Mary how the patrons found out about her ticket before she arrived. She said she was not sure, but believed that a patron had seen her car on Highway 14 while she was pulled over and told the rest of the crowd at the bar when he arrived ahead of her. It was also possible, she said, that someone had heard about her being stopped on a scanner.

10. I wondered to myself if the woman might have suffered a stroke, or if perhaps she was a victim of Parkinson's disease.

and when the selection process was complete, the elderly man asked the younger clerk for "one of those nice bags to put them in." Just at this moment, the older clerk appeared again in the service window and handed through a glassine bag, into which the man deposited the stamps, before escorting the woman out the side door. Clearly, the older clerk had served the elderly pair enough times to be able to precisely anticipate their needs, and the younger clerk read the situation quickly as one in which her older colleague had more expertise than she did, and stepped aside.

The kind of small-town stuff that we expect of small-town business was pervasive in chain retailers as well. Just as Heidi, who cooked breakfast at the Blue Diamond Café, knew how just about everyone who had ever eaten breakfast there liked their eggs cooked, the morning shift workers at McDonalds knew what their regular breakfast patrons would order. There were clerks at Wal-Mart who saw certain patrons heading for the checkout and anticipated the kind of cigarettes they would want to buy. Personal knowledge shared between patrons and staff did not drop away in such settings, because such places were still staffed by people likely to be one's neighbors or friends or members of one's extended family.

The Personal and the Rational

At the beginning of the chapter, we saw an example of one of the many ways that Viroqua's local merchants cultivated personalized service and small-town stuff in an effort to generate business. In the terms that the small-versus-big retail debate is usually conducted, the personalized is the domain of the small retailer. Larger ones increase efficiency by standardizing their inventories and services, and conducting transactions according to a set of rationalized practices. We might expect to find that transactions are regulated by store policy in a place like Wal-Mart, but Viroqua's small businesses also avail themselves of many of the rationalized practices associated with larger businesses. These rationalized practices insulated small businesses, to some extent, from some of the risks associated with doing business in a small town.

To return to the example of the bridal shop, as much as the staff at Bonnie's counted on the promise of personalized service to draw customers to the store, the store's service was not so personalized that making sales depended completely on personal relationships. Bonnie's relied on written policies to make sure that customers held up their end of business deals and paid for merchandise.[11] When, for example, the young mother I observed in the store found a wedding gown she wanted to order, she was then led to the counter, where Melodie spent nearly twenty minutes detailing the store's policies about required deposits, the number of months prior to the wedding by which orders had to be placed, and the cost of alterations. The will to provide customer service did not trump store policy, as I saw when a woman came into the store carrying a bridesmaid's dress that had already been altered. She had not purchased the store's service plan that included all necessary alterations and had decided to wear a pair of shoes other than the pair she had been wearing when the hem was marked. Since she had been charged for the first hemming, she wanted to know if the new alteration could be free. While we might expect a small merchant to go out of her way to accommodate a customer in order to keep the customer's business, Melodie simply told her, "I'm sorry, we can't do that" and referred to the store policy stating that there were charges for all alterations except when customers purchased the service plan, which covered all alterations for a flat fee.[12]

In other words, cultivating the service associated with small businesses did not mean that small businesses or the manner in which they conducted transactions were completely idiosyncratic or unpredictable. While the contemporary big-versus-small discourse about businesses in the United States makes it sound like the threats to small-town businesses are new and immediate, historical evidence makes it clear that staying in business in a small town has never been easy for a number of reasons having to do largely with the drawbacks associated with being too personal. While the rise of rationalized business practices and technologies has made large chains like Wal-Mart possible and competition stiff for small businesses, small businesses also availed themselves of many of the same practices and

---

11. This would be especially important to a business such as Bonnie's, which relied so heavily on out-of-town customers, who could not be held accountable by local social networks and pressures.

12. The nature of the bridal industry probably decreases the shop's incentive to make special exceptions such as this. While neighboring businesses on Main Street hoped to cultivate repeat customers who would make many purchases over a long period of time, bridal retailers cannot count on repeat business and must make larger sales to customers, who, assuming they stay married, will not need the services of a bridal shop in the future.

technologies, though on a smaller scale. In this sense, keeping a small business in Viroqua open was no longer simply a matter of being good at being small. It was also a matter of making use of practices that the terms of the big-versus-small debate might suggest are the sole purview of big business. This becomes evident when we examine the historical evidence about how hard it has always been to keep a small business open in a small town.

Though competition from Wal-Mart definitely made staying in business a challenge in Viroqua, some changes in the way retailers did business made it easier for small retailers to stay in business than in the past. Improvements in transportation technologies made it easier for small businesses to have products that customers needed on hand at all times. While small businesses did not, of course, own fleets of tractor-trailer trucks, they had access to the services of reliable transportation companies like the U.S. Postal Service, UPS, and FedEx ground service. In addition to receiving shipments of products from their suppliers with which they stocked their shelves, some small businesses, such as Art Vision, made use of shipping services to extend their market beyond the local area, both by publishing and mailing a small catalog several times each year and by offering shipping services to customers who placed orders from the shop's website.

Many (if not all) small-business owners had adopted many rationalized practices that helped overcome some of the difficulties that plagued small-town businesses in the past. At one time, few merchants of small businesses had training in or familiarity with skills such as formal accounting practices (Lingeman 1980). By the time I arrived, the vast majority of Viroqua's small retailers used electronic cash registers and/or computerized systems for tracking transactions and inventory. Many used accounting software; some had part- or full-time professional accountants or bookkeepers. Most accepted not only cash and checks but also debit and credit cards.

The extension of consumer credit was an example of one change in U.S. retailing that illustrated a way that even small-scale merchants had access to some of the tools once available only to large ones. At one time, local merchants operated largely at the mercy of credit systems based on personal ties. Today, few local retail businesses extend credit to individuals, though businesses hold accounts with one another. Individuals who wish to open a credit account at a local business that did offer it are no longer approved as a matter of course, or on the basis of personal relationships, but are subject to credit checks. Checking credit reports as a matter of routine made the extension of credit an impersonal matter and insulated merchants from the vicious cycle that reliance on credit caused in the past, in which merchants were often put out of business as a result of the combination of bad accounts and the high prices they had to charge in an effort to make up for them (Blumenthal 1932; Lingeman 1980).

The store credit system that was so large a part of doing business in small towns for so long was not necessary as it once was. For one thing, the incomes of small-town and rural residents tended to be more regular than in the past. Farmers and early factory and mine workers made the bulk of their income during harvest or production seasons (Lingeman 1980; Blumenthal 1932). The ability to buy basic supplies and groceries on credit was essential if a rural family, especially a farm family, was to survive to its next pay season. Today, fewer of Viroqua's residents depend solely on seasonal work for their income. Like most farm families in the United States, most of Vernon County's farm families have at least one adult working off the farm, providing farm households with more regular income throughout the year. While I did meet a few trade and construction workers who expected to be laid off for part of each year, federal unemployment benefits provided these workers with some income to tide them over in the (usually winter) months when they were not working.

Consumer credit was still a part of doing business in Viroqua, the difference was that individual consumers used credit cards. Financing for the purchase of larger items like cars, farm implements, or snowmobiles was extended through programs offered by the manufacturers of the products, banks, or other lending agencies, not by the retailers themselves. Customers still made purchases on credit, just not on credit extended by local merchants, which enabled merchants to make sales to customers who needed to finance their purchases without incurring the risk of providing the credit themselves. As a result, merchants were no longer responsible for as much collection of debt as they once were, and they were usually paid for the amount of the purchase at the time that it was made by the intermediary extending the credit.

Sometimes, merchants still had difficulty receiving payment for sales they had made. In one year's worth of Viroqua Police court reports,[13] which appeared monthly in the newspaper, 14 percent of the citations issued

---

13. Not a consecutive calendar year: twelve months of reports were selected randomly from two years' worth of issues of the *Broadcaster*.

TABLE 2. Summary of Worthless Check Citations over Twelve Months

Retailer	Number of citations issued	Median bounced check (nearest $)	Total bad checks for 12 months (nearest $)
Wal-Mart	27	65	3282
Jubilee Foods	14	67	1039
Culver's Frozen Custard	7	18	120
Equipment/hardware (NAPA, Nelson's, Effinger's)	7	67	543
Entertainment (Bowl-Away, Vernon Square Cinema, Eagles Club)	5	69	591
Clothing stores (Center Stage, Felix's)	4	50	401
Dollar Discount Store	3	22	161
Dahl Pharmacy	3	44	113
City of Viroqua	2	–	162
Veterinarians (Dr. Piper, Rising Sun Animal Wellness)	2	–	179
Cheese Corner	1	–	8
Total	75	54	6599

by the city police department were for the writing of worthless checks. In twelve months, sixty individuals were cited for bouncing seventy-five checks at a variety of local establishments.[14] Certainly, many more than seventy-five checks were bounced in Viroqua businesses during this period, but they were resolved before resulting in police citations.

Most businesses attempted to collect on bad checks by contacting the individual who wrote it first, either by phone or by certified letter if necessary. At the Legion, for example, managers first phoned individuals whose checks had bounced to make payment arrangements, and involved the police only if the individual could not be reached or if they refused to settle up. According to an assistant manager I talked to by phone, the accounting department at Viroqua's Wal-Mart followed the same procedure. Both large and small retailers had the same recourse when a customer wrote a bad check.

The striking thing about this summary of citations is that the amounts of money owed to the largest stores for bad checks were so much higher

---

14. During this same twelve months, there were no reports of store break-ins, robberies, and only two citations issued for shoplifting, so bad checks seemed to be the principle crime problem for local businesses.

than for all other stores, though the median amount of the bad checks written was not necessarily higher. In other words, the significant difference between the total dollar amount of bad checks written at Wal-Mart during this period and the outstanding amounts at other businesses is not the result of a few customers' making large purchases at Wal-Mart with bad checks but of a higher volume of bad checks for relatively small purchases.[15]

The amounts owed to locally owned businesses on bad checks were generally quite small, and small-scale merchants used the same procedures to collect on bad checks that Wal-Mart did. "Bad check" customers' debts were not enough to cause stores to collapse the way that "bad pay" customers' outstanding credit did in the old days, and bad checks provided an example of one case in which locally owned businesses actually had an advantage over chain stores when it came to customers' deployment of their understandings of large and small retailers. The fact that relatively few bad checks written to locally owned businesses made it to the citation stage suggested that there was more social pressure to rectify a bad check at a business whose owner one knew (or who was likely to know people one knew) than at a business owned by a large, anonymous chain. No one wanted word of something as embarrassing as a bad check to get around.

In addition, many Viroquans expressed a sense of obligation to patronize locally owned businesses. Given the evidence of this kind of loyalty, it made sense to think that someone in financial straits would try to settle up with local businesses before settling up with Wal-Mart, on the logic that a store as big as Wal-Mart could afford the loss more than a small business. I asked four different residents about my interpretation of this information, and all agreed that there was significant social pressure to make good on checks written to local residents. They also confirmed my guess that some residents thought that a large company like Wal-Mart didn't "need" to be paid as urgently as local merchants did.

---

15. Though there was no way to verify it with certainty, it seemed that the discrepancy was also not simply the result of the higher volume of sales at Wal-Mart. The assistant manager with whom I spoke estimated that as much as 50% of the bad checks they received were not resolved, resulting in a citation. The two other local business owners with whom I spoke about this issue estimated that a much smaller percentage of bad checks, as small as 10%, ended up requiring citation.

Some other observations on worthless check citations: citations were issued equally to men and women. Women receiving citations for worthless checks were, on average, younger than men cited (about twenty-seven and thirty years old, respectively).

In reality, doing business was a mixture of small-town informality and rationalized policy. Customers and merchants in Viroqua could appeal to either set of "rules"—either the rules of doing business on the basis of personal contact or of formal store policy—to try to get the answers or deals that suited them. Much of the small-town stuff in local business life took the form of minor exceptions to official rules. When Karen Groves took over as the manager of the Legion bar, for example, she instituted a rule that we could not accept checks numbered under 700, after what seemed to be a rash of bad-check cashing in the winter of 2002. She posted a large sign next to the cash registers to remind us bartenders of the new rule. It was not long, however, before I found reasons to make exceptions to the rule: once for a fellow employee, once for a regular "good pay" (Blumenthal 1932) customer who had switched banks and therefore had a new set of checks numbering only in the 500s, and once for the daughter of a fellow Legion employee. In each case, exceptions were made for individuals on the basis of personal connections and history, and in anticipation that the business's relationship with the customer would continue in the future. It was also easy to make exceptions in these cases because each individual was in a position such that their connection to the bar was one in which significant informal social pressure was brought to bear on them to cash only good checks (and in which, as in the cases of the employee and the child of another employee, there was every reason to believe that the bar could easily recover the cost of any check that might happen to be overdrawn).

At the same time, having formal rules in place in the Legion also made it easier for me to say no to customers who made requests with which I, as an employee, could not or did not want to comply. Sometimes these were Legion policies. For example, Wisconsin law allowed people under twenty-one to be served alcohol in a bar in the company of their parents or legal guardians, but placed the burden of verifying the relationship between a minor and an adult claiming to be his or her parent on the server. The Legion had its own policy that people under twenty-one were simply not allowed in the bar after nine p.m., which allowed me to avoid controversy on several occasions when people I did not know claimed to be the parents of a minor and asked that the minor be served. On both of the busy weekend nights this happened, I leaned on the Legion's policy—and pointed to the magic marker sign on the wall that stated it—that club rules prevented me from serving the minor at all, as the minor was no longer allowed in the bar.

Patrons could also make selective use of the formal policies and roles at the bar when it suited them. For example, one regular patron asked every so often to take home a bottle of peppermint schnapps and pay for it later in the week, when he received his paycheck. Especially as a new employee, I said I could not accommodate this request, and the patron politely said he understood and didn't want me to do anything if I thought I might get in trouble for it. He was sincere, I believe, in not wanting to put me in a difficult position, and in saying this he also explicitly acknowledged the potential consequences of my bending the rules for him.

Later, however, he asked to borrow the phone and called the manager at home and made the same request. The manager agreed (for many of the reasons listed above for bending the rules), and she then told me over the phone that I could go ahead and let the customer take the bottle and pay for it later. By appealing to the formal employment structure and asking my superior, the customer was able to get the rules bent for him, but also avoided putting me in a bind, by placing the responsibility for the rule-bending with someone who had the formal authority to bend the rules.

Another option might have been for the customer to simply try to badger me into bending the rules, as sometimes happened in the bar, especially when patrons had already had a few beers. Such an approach would have frustrated me, and I would not have been able to change my mind without appearing to "play favorites" or losing face and any semblance of authority with the other customers, even if I had wanted to.[16] Badgering would also have been a risky strategy for a customer to choose in the sense that he or she might have become vulnerable to the bartender's neglect for the rest of the evening, or to rebuke by other customers for being pushy. By finessing the formal hierarchy of the bar, the customer was able to get what he wanted without running these risks.

---

16. In these kinds of situations, customers often came to my aid, telling a pushy patron to lay off or give it up. On other occasions, however, customers allied with each other and tried to convince the bartender that an exception to the rule was necessary or was routinely made for others or granted by other bartenders, and that it would therefore be unfair not to make it in the case at hand.

Shopping in Private

While small retailers have adopted some of the rationalized practices associated with larger retailers, Wal-Mart continues to offer something that smaller businesses cannot: more privacy. For all of the social benefits associated with small-town stuff and locally owned businesses, a downside can be that, as one Viroquan put it, "if you stop off to pick some things up after work, by the time you get [to a destination where you meet other people you know], they already know what you bought and how much you paid for it." While the personal knowledge entailed in small-town stuff may indeed have enabled merchants to provide services to customers they otherwise could not, it also meant that people one knew also knew everything one purchased.

In the past, the only ways to purchase merchandise from someone one did not know personally was to make one's purchases in another community, or to order items by mail. Mary, the bartender at the Bowl-Away Lanes, said that some embarrassment about making certain kinds of purchases persisted. Mary lived in Westby and said there were still a few, mostly elderly, people from Westby who were members of Lutheran churches with more ascetic traditions and sometimes traveled to the bowling alley in Viroqua to purchase an occasional bottle of liquor to take home. "Whenever they come in and I'm here, they always say, 'You're always here!' because the whole reason they come here is so that they don't have to buy [liquor] from someone they know, and then they come here and it's just someone else they know from [Westby]."

Because of its size, its multiple check-out lanes, which allowed customers some latitude in choosing whether or not to be checked out by an acquaintance or by a cashier they did not know, Wal-Mart offered a little relief from the social intensity of the mom-and-pop retail experience. Shopping at Wal-Mart required none of the local knowledge or appreciation that buying from local merchants sometimes entailed. Though there was certainly no guarantee of privacy at Wal-Mart, the mere size of the store enabled shoppers to maneuver around each other in ways impossible in a shop with just a few aisles. I had a few "near miss" encounters in Wal-Mart in which I felt myself feeling relieved that the store was large enough to allow customers to avoid each other when they so chose. In one instance, I spotted at the opposite end of a long aisle the woman who was managing the Legion when I began working there but who had been fired shortly thereafter because she was suspected of embezzlement. I had not seen her since the day she learned she was fired, and I studied something on the store shelf in front of me, bracing myself for an awkward conversation with her. When I looked up the aisle again, however, I saw she had turned her cart in the opposite direction and disappeared around the end of the aisle. Though I had no way to confirm it, I suspected that she was eager to avoid conversing with me. Relieved, I went in the opposite direction from the direction I'd seen her go.

Wal-Mart's presence helped make Viroqua a shopping destination for residents from surrounding communities, which contributed to the overall economic success of the town. In addition, it provided a venue where residents could acquire the goods local merchants did not carry, and it remained open at times when local merchants were closed. Wal-Mart also offered an option for residents who felt uncomfortable shopping in locally owned businesses either because they lacked knowledge required to shop there, or because the store's prices were too high. Simply by virtue of being a physically large place and being open at all times, Wal-Mart was able to co-opt some of the ability to provide social opportunities usually associated with small downtown shops, at least in the big-versus-small debate as it is usually framed. This was especially clear in the ways Viroquans made use of the variety of opportunities for consumption in Viroqua.

Like many of the stores in the downtown area, Wal-Mart did provide a site where residents ran into people they knew and engaged in a variety of sociable exchanges—ranging from basic pleasantries to extended conversations in the middle of the store's aisles. On one occasion, for example, I observed a meeting of two acquaintances in the car-and-tool section of Wal-Mart. Both were men in their thirties who were similarly dressed in jeans and insulated plaid shirts. One was accompanied by a woman who, it became clear later, was his wife. After greeting each other, the man shopping alone asked the other if he had been able to find work yet. No, the second man explained. He had been looking and had been hopeful that a job opportunity he heard about through his brother-in-law might work out, but it had not. The men then discussed the difficulties of being laid off, including the loss of health insurance. "But you're covered by hers, right?" asked the first, addressing the woman, who nodded and said something I couldn't hear.

The second man then agreed that he was lucky his wife had a job that provided insurance for the whole family. The first man then said that he was enjoying his current construction job. His boss was "a good guy" and the pay was good. His boss was interested in expanding his contracting business, and it looked like the company had work lined up steadily for some time into the future, much of it in Iowa. He had given the unemployed man's name to his boss and said that his boss had indicated that he would be hiring more workers soon. They talked for a few more minutes and parted with a handshake. The exchange lasted nearly ten minutes.

Though the primary activity in Wal-Mart is certainly not conversation, of all the business places where I saw people gathering informally, it was one of the most accessible to and accommodating of everyone. Viroqua's Wal-Mart was probably the place where one had the greatest chance of running into people one knew and people outside one's own social circles, because whether they wanted to or not, most Viroquans had to shop at Wal-Mart sometimes. It was also open twenty-four hours a day. The only other establishment open twenty-four hours (with the exception of the hospital emergency room) was the north-side Kwik Trip convenience store.

At the opposite end of accessibility and inclusiveness was the experience of shopping at the Viroqua Food Co-op. For the Alternatives, the Viroqua Food Co-op provided an important meeting place. While I did not see evidence there of the after-hours socializing I saw among Regulars in some of the town's automotive shops, the co-op was a place where Alternative people expected to run into people they knew. In its small building, it was not at all uncommon to find that an entire aisle obstructed by two or three acquaintances chatting there. Often, someone wanting to look at items on the shelves in that aisle would have to wait for the chatters to rearrange themselves to allow the shopper to pass. On more than one occasion, I observed that someone in the group of chatting people would notice that other patrons needed to get by and would make a comment like "we really are blocking traffic, aren't we?," and the group might move to the small open area near the front door, or outside the building in nice weather, to continue the conversation. The Food Co-op also was a center for passing information in another way—more than almost any other business in town, its bulletin boards were always full of flyers, business cards, posters, and announcements. Whenever I was in the co-op, there was almost always someone perusing the board.[17]

So the co-op was an important gathering place for Alternatives, but it did not always feel especially inclusive to others. Several Viroquans who were not frequent Food Co-op shoppers said they experienced discomfort on the rare occasions when they had entered the store to, as one put it, "see what it was all about." The size of the space had a great deal to do with the production of this discomfort, as someone new to the co-op could not browse with any degree of privacy, because aisles were often jammed with shoppers. One shopper reported that the only time she had been in the Food Co-op, she had not felt comfortable with the idea of browsing in an aisle where two people in the middle of a conversation would have had to move in order for her to get by.

In addition, shopping at the co-op required a certain amount of practical knowledge. One Main Streeter told me that she had ventured into the Food Co-op one morning because she was curious about it and because she enjoyed drinking a wide variety of coffees and had heard that the co-op had a large selection. When she found that the co-op coffees had to be purchased from bulk dispensers, she became discouraged because she did not know how to use the dispensers or what container to put the loose beans in. Discouraged from buying coffee, she bought a bag of corn chips "because everyone can see you're in there and it would have been embarrassing to walk out without buying anything," but she had never returned.[18] It was true that people turned to look at you when you entered the Food Co-op. Viroqua was a small town, after all, and when the door of any establishment opened, everyone inside wanted to know who had arrived.[19]

---

17. The board was also incredibly useful to a researcher.

18. I had a similar experience the first time I entered the Food Co-op, on one of my first visits to Viroqua. Though I was quite familiar with food co-ops and comfortable being in such a place, the small size of the store meant that in this one it was impossible for everyone inside to be unaware of my presence, and even though I had intended to simply look around and maybe chat with anyone who was there, instead I felt scrutinized and awkward. Instead of taking my time to investigate the co-op that day, I quickly selected a couple of snack items, paid for them, and left.

19. This was also true at the Legion and other bars, especially because in all of these places most bar patrons had a direct view of the entrance. It took time to become a "regular" at any such place and to overcome the kind of awkwardness that comes with entering an unfamiliar social situation.

There was an irony, however, in that the Food Co-op, which was created, owned, and run by members of the local community, would seem to be a shopping venue with great potential to function incidentally as a gathering place for Viroquans. This was not the case. Wal-Mart did a better job of this for larger numbers of townsfolk. This was no doubt partly because of the co-op's small space, which made it impossible to browse there with any privacy, and in part because of its more limited hours of operation. Wal-Mart's design, hours, and pricing practices grew out of a tradition of merchandising that emerged in the late 1800s and aimed to meet the needs of *all* shoppers in a single store (Zukin 2004; Leach 1993).[20] In contrast to department stores emerging around the same time that catered to members of the upper classes, variety and five-and-dime stores sold things that all shoppers needed and that most shoppers could afford. Higher-end items in variety stores were displayed on shelves right next to cheap ones. They were stores where all shoppers felt they belonged, even though some shoppers had the resources to purchase more goods than others (Zukin 2004).

Wal-Mart, and other large discount chains that began emerging in the 1960s, continued to offer shoppers the experience of "freedom and control" (Zukin 2004, 80). They sell nationally advertised, brand-name goods that appeal to middle-income shoppers and are simultaneously affordable to lower-income shoppers. Shopping in these stores requires no special knowledge, and no one needs to wonder if he or she might feel out of place inside. Discrete video cameras, rather than other patrons, monitor shoppers unobtrusively, maintaining the illusion that they are not being scrutinized. For all these reasons, shopping at Wal-Mart has a more inclusive feel than shopping at the Food Co-op. As Zukin (2004) argues, the

---

20. Though many of the local retailers have extended their operating hours beyond nine and five, few open before nine, and most are still closed by seven. Almost all are now open for at least some portion of the weekend, many for most of it. Shopping locally still depends somewhat on having a reasonably flexible daytime schedule (which is maybe why more of the Alternative folks can do it).

When Darlene needed a new battery for her watch, she had to go to Wal-Mart, because it was the only store that was open before she had to be at work at VARC at 7:30. But even Wal-Mart could not completely meet her needs at that hour, as there was no employee assigned to the jewelry counter that early, and therefore no one who could replace her watch's battery. To solve the problem, she bought a watch for seven dollars on the spot. Some of the other regulars at the bar that afternoon commented that it was probably cheaper to buy a new watch than a new battery anyway.

experience of shopping at Wal-Mart "tends to minimize social class distinctions and nurtures the illusion that shopping is the same for everyone"
(69). For the uninitiated, shopping at the Food Co-op highlighted one's
lack of knowledge and belonging.

I heard Alternative Viroquans who routinely shopped at the co-op wonder aloud why more members of "the public" didn't shop there. Though
the co-op expanded its hours and was working toward moving into a
larger building, changes that might help increase its accessibility, it did not
seem that it would necessarily move in the direction of being a place where
"the public" would feel comfortable shopping. The prospect of moving
the market into a larger space was a key agenda item at the co-op's annual
membership meeting in 2003. While there seemed to be broad support for
expansion, a number of members and board members expressed concern
about whether it was financially feasible.

One question was how the Food Co-op's current inventory might be expanded to draw in more business to cover the costs of occupying a larger
building. The co-op manager answered decisively that if the co-op were
to expand its inventory, it would move in the direction of carrying high-
end "gourmet" foods. "We won't be carrying Crest toothpaste," she said.
"That's not what we're about. There are plenty of places where people can
by that stuff already." True to the mission of providing an alternative to
mainstream shopping venues, the co-op did not see itself carrying products
that "the public" could buy elsewhere.

Of course, Wal-Mart would not be able to open such large stores, stay
open such long hours, or offer such low prices were it not for the back-
ing of its enormous parent corporation and its vast resources. Advocates of
small-scale, locally owned business are quick to point out that the apparent
egalitarianism of Wal-Mart is an illusion. Wal-Mart pays its workers noto-
riously low wages, provides few benefits, and has been repeatedly accused
of practices like shaving hours and overtime from employees' time cards.
Its suppliers depend on producing goods in foreign labor markets with
even lower wages and poorer working conditions. The conditions that
made the Wal-Mart experience what it was depended on conditions that
critics say exacerbate the unequal distribution of wealth on a global scale.

In many ways, the difference between the experience of shopping at the
Food Co-op and Wal-Mart are emblematic of the real bases of social distinction and distance in Viroqua. It didn't matter that the *goals* of the co-op

were extremely egalitarian in the sense that it tried to promote economic equality through practices such as selling fair-traded and locally grown products and by giving consumers a say in the running of the store as member-owners. For Regular and even many Main Streeter shoppers, the Food Co-op experience just didn't feel at all egalitarian. To the uninitiated, it felt snooty and exclusive, and people who didn't shop there or had tried and hadn't returned told me they felt like co-op shoppers looked down their noses at them for shopping elsewhere (especially at Wal-Mart).

In 2005, when it celebrated its tenth anniversary, the Viroqua Food Co-operative opened a new store in a brand-new building on Main Street. The new store has wider aisles and a seating area where shoppers can sit with a cup of coffee or eat a sandwich from the deli. The building's vaulted ceiling and many windows add to the openness of the space. The size of the building alleviates some of the sense of scrutiny one felt in the smaller, old building, and I knew a number of curious Viroquans (especially Regulars) who used the opportunity of its opening to visit the co-op for the first time. It stands as something of a monument to some residents' efforts to combat corporately-owned, standardized chain stores with a unique store owned by its members. Ironically, in the lot immediately adjacent to the expanded Food Co-op, a Walgreen's drugstore opened in 2006. Walgreen's arrival precipitated the closure of the locally-owned Dahl and Langhus pharmacies.[21] No doubt Viroqua's retail landscape and its mixture of big and small retailers will continue to shift, but Viroquans seem committed to retaining a variety of locally-owned concerns.

---

21. Walgreen's arrival generated a good deal of controversy. The Viroqua Partners were ultimately unable to take a collective position on the store, as it brought the two facets of the group's mission, attracting new businesses and retaining existing businesses, into conflict. In addition, under the city's existing policies, the store qualified for tax-incremental financing, and many in town thought that a chain store should not receive any municipal assistance—that such policies should benefit only locally owned businesses.

8

CONSUMPTION AND BELONGING
IN VIROQUA

Depending on whom one asked, my 1994 Volkswagen Golf was either a hot item or a joke. According to Alternatives in Viroqua, my car was highly desirable. Several Alternative acquaintances commented on what a nice car it was and what "great shape" it was in for its age. Strangers commented on it too. One afternoon, I stopped at the Landmark Center to use the gym. I parked across the street from the main entrance to the Pleasant Ridge Waldorf School and saw a woman in her late thirties or early forties exiting the school with a young boy. The woman called after me as I walked past them. She wanted to know if I'd bought my car used and, if so, where I'd found it. "We've been looking for one," she explained, but the used VWs she had found were either too new and too expensive, or too old and in poor repair.[1]

---

1. On each of these occasions that my car was admired, I carefully explained that I only bought it because I had gotten a good deal on it.

The same car, however, was the butt of gentle joking at the American Legion, where domestic cars, trucks, and SUVs were strongly preferred over foreign cars (and over small hatchbacks in particular). One afternoon when I was still quite new to the job, several patrons were discussing cars and someone asked what kind of car I drove. "A VW Golf," I told him.

"I'm sorry," he replied with mock earnestness.

"Why?" a second patron asked me skeptically. I said I'd gotten a good deal on it, it got good mileage, it always started no matter how cold it was, and it was fast.[2] "Yeah," the first customer replied, conceding that "those German cars" were supposed to run a long time. There were numerous other occasions on which my "little foreign car" was mocked. Cars that rated serious attention and admiration in the Legion were vehicles such as Jeep Grand Cherokees (of which two used ones were purchased by regular Legion patrons during my time there) and new or nearly new trucks.

Just as it has in many of the community studies of the past, consumption emerged as a central theme in Viroqua. In many settings, patterns of consumption—one's own or others'—were common topics of conversation. In analyzing my field data, I found that there were lots of interactions in which the topic of buying things—having bought things, someone one knew buying things, wishing to buy things, where to buy things, getting a good deal on things, or getting something for free—figured prominently.[3] Talking about consumption was an important form of recreation.

Consistent with broader cultural images of small-town and rural life, Viroquans themselves imagined that living in a small town and a rural area insulated them from what they perceived to be the excessive materialism of Americans who live in suburban and urban areas. Regulars, Main Streeters, and Alternatives drew specific discursive links between small-town community and lifestyles that made it easier to focus one's attention on "more important things" than possessions, such as relationships with family and friends. Newcomers in all three social groups talked about

---

2. I justified owning this car using what Sharon Zukin (2004) identifies as the rational language of consumption that Americans often use to make sense of themselves as active and empowered agents. I replied in a very similar manner when my car received compliments.

3. Most of these conversations do not take place directly in front of the purchaser. If the purchaser of something new arrived on the scene, there might be discussion about "I see you have a new——," and the purchaser would usually respond in a way that downplayed the significance of the purchase.

moving to Viroqua as a way to consume less—both because the cost of living was relatively low and because there was less pressure to keep up with the proverbial Joneses. The latter was especially important to parents.

At the same time, however, Viroquans differed little in their consumption from other Americans, in the sense that they viewed purchases as rational, saw purchasing as an exercise of agency, and used material items as markers of status and social-group membership (Zukin 2004). Traditionally, scholars who have studied community have assumed that material consumption drained community life. When individuals' focus shifted from public life to private fulfillment in the form of material gain, they argued, community was diminished. In this chapter, I argue that the ways that group membership is marked by material items has changed somewhat since earlier community studies. Consumption is no longer about achieving a place in a status hierarchy in the way that it was found to be in earlier studies. Instead, it is about integrating oneself in the social group in which one feels the most comfortable, in accordance with one's orientation to community making. Material consumption plays an important integrative role (Garcia Canclini 2001; Monti 1999; Cloke, Phillips, and Thrift 1998) in community making in Viroqua.

Avoiding Consumption?

There is an old New England rhyme that goes: "Use it up, wear it out, make it do, or do without." The adage encapsulates some of our stereotypes about rural thrift. This cultural link between rural life and a rejection of materialism was reflected in Viroquans' beliefs and practices and is part of a larger set of cultural ideals—a cultural sense that there is a wholesomeness, even a nobility, in making do, in being self-sufficient, and in the idea that the best things in life are free. And even though (or maybe because) most Americans no longer live in small towns or rural places, we imagine that if there is any place in America where the best things in life are still free, it is probably in small towns and rural areas.[4]

---

4. A recent instantiation of this kind of collective representation is the excitement generated by the "Quilts from Gee's Bend" exhibit that opened at the Whitney Museum in 2003 and traveled to museums around the country. That these quilts are appearing in some of the country's most

This facet of our collective representation of small-town life is clear in graphic artist Lou Beach's revision of Grant Wood's *American Gothic,* which appears on the cover of Juliet Schor's *The Overspent American.* As depicted by Wood, the painting's subjects certainly look like people who might "use it up, wear it out, make it do, or do without." But in Beach's image, they are thoroughly accessorized with cell phones and fancy sunglasses. The irony in this appropriation of Wood's image is immediately obvious—it seems instantly wrong to us that these plain folks should have replaced their pitchfork, a tool of necessity, with such items.

One of the sources of our "make it do" image of small towns comes from the fact that, traditionally, small towns have been places where there was relatively little to buy. Historians (e.g., Lingeman 1980) point out that until the advent of large-scale national trucking, small-town retailers had great difficulty getting shipments of new stock, and in the days when staying in business depended on extending credit even to people who were unlikely to pay their bills, they often didn't have enough cash on hand to order new goods. This was no longer the case in Viroqua. There were plenty of goods to buy in town, in La Crosse, and, when necessary, online or by mail; but the image of small towns as materially isolated continues to be perpetuated by causal observers of small-town and rural life (e.g., Brooks 2001).

There were two principle means by which residents believed small-town life dampened the materialism that they believed to be rampant elsewhere. Many Viroquans still shared the values of thrift and self-sufficiency associated with rural life in general, and the social networks and intimate knowledge many residents had of one another allowed them to procure many things they needed outside the formal economy. There was evidence of the make-do mentality in that there were four clothing resale shops and several shops that sold used furnishings. There were also two "dollar" stores and a close-out discounter on the north edge of town. Second, I saw a great deal of evidence that it was, as several Viroquans put it, "just not acceptable to flaunt your wealth."

---

prestigious museums of modern art is interesting in and of itself, but it is relevant here because one of the things almost all the media coverage of this exhibit makes explicit reference to is that these quilts, these works of art produced by poor, rural African-American women, were made to be functional. The quilts that are hanging on the walls before viewers have lain on children's beds, and they were made as quilts traditionally were—of scraps. They were products of necessity, and all the more aesthetically valuable for it.

For a number of Viroquans, living in a small town was still a way to cut down on consumption and avoid materialism. In fact, a number of new-comers in all three groups mentioned that one of the draws of living in a small town was that such a place would provide an escape from the "materi-alism" they experienced elsewhere. Bjorn and Brie referenced the excessive materialism of the suburban community where they lived briefly after they moved back to the Midwest from San Francisco. It wasn't a community they particularly enjoyed. "I couldn't wait to get out of there," Bjorn told me. "It's like, the only hobby people have there is shopping. It's just gross."

Main Streeter Nancy Rhodes had similar reasons for leaving a home and successful business in Orange County, California:

> I actually found out that I wasn't fitting in real well with the lifestyle in which I was living. I mean, the area where I was living, the least expensive house was about $350,000, and I owned a couple pieces of property, but they weren't in the area that I lived in. I was renting a great little house in a won-derful community, but where [the residents'] aspirations were not to drive the Mercedes, because they already had that, but to buy a Rolls-Royce. And there was a Rolls-Royce dealer about a half a mile from where I lived. So you know, it was a lifestyle that was much too much materialistic for me. I like nice things, but I also don't live for them.

Regulars too were concerned about getting away from areas where people were "materialistic," and this was especially true of parents. One Regular, who had recently relocated to the area with her husband and eleven-year-old son, mentioned that in addition to wanting to get away from the congestion of Milwaukee's suburbs, she thought living in Viroqua would provide several advantages for her son. One was increased safety. "Believe it or not," she said, "there are gangs [in the suburban commu-nity where we lived]." She continued, "And it's not good for kids because so many of the other kids have so much stuff, and our son was starting to want that stuff too. New sneakers every other week. We couldn't keep up with all that, and we didn't want him to think that just having stuff is so great. We have family back here, and we thought this was a good place to get him away from all that."

Jim and Donna Radke, who had lived in Viroqua for over twenty years, also made a connection between raising children and avoiding materialism.

Their comments typified a sentiment I heard from a number of Viroquans that living in a small town provides some insulation from values that emphasize material possessions and allows them to devote more time to family. The Radkes were solidly middle-class, possibly upper-middle class, Regulars. Jim worked as a conservation officer in the county's USDA office, and Donna worked for many years as an office assistant for an optometrist in town. Their three sons were grown and they had two grandchildren. I asked Jim and Donna if they thought that being raised in Viroqua gave their children a good "jumping-off point."

Donna replied, "I think it was. I mean, I feel like they got a good education, and they grew up in a nice town, where they felt comfortable and secure and…"

"You know, I'd have to think about that, Lyn," Jim intervened. "Maybe it's two different issues. Growing up here is just a nice spot to grow up in, a nice place to be kind of like a family group, you know, and what's that Barney show—you know, with the kid and the fish? *Mayberry*! That's what I'm thinking of!"

"Oh!" laughed Donna. "I was thinking of the purple Barney, the dinosaur."

Jim continued:

> You know, it's kind of a nice spot. I don't know if Viroqua's doing that much extra good of a job of helping kids go out and meet the challenge of being nuclear scientists any more than any other place would do. I don't think we've got that advantage over it. It's just a darned good spot to have a family together. And I think to have those family values, because the families that people get into [as adults], their families are going to be the same way. I can just see it with [our] two kids that have families right now. They've got the family relationship, you know, and the feelings, and you know, the habits that go into it.

I asked him to be more specific. He said:

> Well, like the oldest one, him and his wife like to do the things that we do, like get together for a family meal. You make yourself comfortable in a home and invite friends in, have a good time and party, you know. They've established some values that I think we tried to have with our kids.

Donna added:

Doing things with your family. But doing your own thing too, I think. I guess that's something we always wanted them to feel—like they could be themselves, an individual besides.

Money has never been an important thing to us, and we tried to make that issue with the boys too, even though they're going to go through stages in their lives where they're impressed by the big city, or impressed by fancy cars, or a job that sounds just too good to be true. But we tried to impress on them that [money] wasn't the most important thing. Make yourself happy. And I think they were able to do that. Maybe they would have gotten that anywhere they lived, just because that's the way we feel, I don't know. Cause, you probably know if you lived around a big city, or just being in Madison, that there's a little bit of that keeping up with the Joneses that you don't get as much of here as you do...

Jim interjected, "Without a doubt. When we go down to visit relatives in Illinois..."

"Oh, gosh, yeah," said Donna, shaking her head.

Jim continued:

I mean, I love my relatives, but you really see it. Like, people may or may not be making money, but they're all driving huge SUVs, the biggest houses they can, some of 'em can't afford furniture because they're trying to have the outward appearance. Really so common there. In Viroqua, I've always said, it's antisocial to flaunt your wealth. Some of the richer people in this town, you wouldn't know it, because it's not socially acceptable to go out and flaunt your wealth. And it's funny to see some of the new people move in, especially from places like Illinois. They haven't learned that lesson yet. And they come here, and they're sometimes almost shunned.

Donna concluded, "So that probably made it easier to get that across to the kids, living in this area. That's just the way it is."

"Yeah, it's sad," Jim said, reflecting on this for a moment. He then offered his own Bourdieuian analysis. "Maybe it's just because we couldn't afford to keep up with the Joneses anyway—maybe it's just sour grapes!" he laughed. In an exaggerated character voice that perhaps he has developed reading stories to his grandchildren, he said, "I didn't want those grapes anyway!"

All three of us were laughing when Donna said in a more serious tone, "Yeah, it does sound like sour grapes, I guess. But it's true with us. I don't know, I guess I'm just not so interested."

In the analysis provided by the Radkes and other Viroquans, decreased "materialism" helped families to teach children what they believed was really important. While these data suggested nothing about the way parents living in other kinds of communities viewed the values they communicated to children regarding material possessions, what was interesting in Viroqua was the consistency with which residents in all three groups talked about small-town community life as particularly suited to avoiding raising overly materialistic children. The idea that living in a small town provided a buffer against the excesses of consumerism in other places was another aspect of the collective representation of small-town life all Viroquans shared. Like other researchers (Bonner 1997), I found that Viroquans believed that life in a small town, and the rural life that accompanied it, was uniquely equipped to communicate these lessons. The lessons did not always take right away. Parents still lamented their children's choices when it came to taste and consumption. One Alternative parent said that despite all her hard work to instill thrift and a respect for quality in her children, all her preteen daughters wanted to wear was "cheap junk from Wal-Mart."

How to Talk about Consumption in Viroqua

Even though many Viroquans said that what they enjoyed about living in a small town was that they avoided the more materialistic attitudes in the wider culture, it was also true that everyone bought things and often wanted to buy nonessential items. Another theme in existing literature on small-town life is the degree to which residents' buying habits are, or are believed to be, subject to community scrutiny. For Main Streeters, especially those who grew up in Viroqua or in a place like it, the immediacy of material comparisons had a different effect. Professionals and business owners in particular were under a great deal of pressure not to "flaunt" their wealth, not to "throw their money around." As the wife of the owner of one of the town's pharmacies explained, "How would it look to the little old ladies who come in to the store and have to spend most of their monthly income on their prescriptions to see us driving around in big fancy cars?"

Because "flaunting one's wealth" was unacceptable, some residents attempted to disguise purchases to avoid scrutiny. Theresa Washburn explained how she and her husband Bob approached renovations they made to their home—which, from the road, appeared to be a modest, one-story bungalow. At first, the renovations were subject to a great deal of comment.

> When we redid this house, I mean, every single person, people we didn't even know, would come up and say, "Oh, what are you building on that part of it?" We live on [Highway] 56—you can see what a public road it is. And Bob, he just said, "Oh great, here I go." And when we did this, he, being a local thought, "I'll make the front [of the house] look exactly the same, and then the back will change," and lots of people don't know how much we really did.

What they did to their home is pretty dramatic. Across the back of the house, Bob built a sunroom and a broad Spanish-style terrace over a large garage and workshop. Similarly, Theresa told the following story about her in-laws, both business owners, and the lengths to which they went to downplay new acquisitions: "Bob's family is from here. His dad owned a business, and his mom owned a business. If they did well and, let's say, they'd buy a new car, they'd buy exactly the same car, in the exact same color, because that way some people would miss that you had enough money to buy a new car."

Even children could be sensitive to the imperative to avoid the appearance of flaunting one's wealth. A resident who once owned a travel agency in town told an illuminating story about her son, whom she took on a trip to Hungary when he was in junior high school. When they returned from the trip, he told his friends they had simply been in Milwaukee, she said, because "he knew it would seem like bragging if he told them where he really went."

When it is impossible to simply hide a purchase, residents used a variety of discursive strategies to downplay it. Because so many conversations around town revolved around acquisitions, Viroquans employed these discursive moves all the time. Such moves were not unique to Viroquans.

Zukin (2004) argues that the rational discourses that Americans use to explain their consumption to themselves and others is a key feature of our consumer culture, and we see evidence of them even in fiction. Indeed, they appear frequently in some of the most popular contemporary stories about small-town life—such as in Garrison Keillor's tales about Lake Wobegon, Minnesota.

One of the available discursive disclaimers is a necessity disclaimer, in which one justifies purchases on the basis of practical need, discursively rejecting taste, aesthetics, exclusivity, or luxury as bases for consumption of an item. The first person in Lake Wobegon to own an air-conditioner, for example, was obliged to explain that she bought it for her daughter, who suffered from allergies (though she ran it all summer, even when her daughter was not visiting).

The necessity disclaimer was frequently used in Viroquan stories about the demise of some item that required replacing, and was usually reported in the context of a sad narrative about the inconvenience of the item's death and the difficulty of replacing it. A typical invocation of the necessity disclaimer was a story one of the frequent patrons at the Legion told about his lawn mower, which "quit" right in the middle of his mowing his lawn on "the only day this week" he had "any free time" to mow. As a result, he had to "waste" an entire Saturday morning getting a new one. He decided, in the end, that the new one was pretty decent and had several nice features the "old piece of crap" did not.

When it was impossible to couch a purchase as a necessity, residents might issue what I call, again borrowing from a Keillor tale, the pontoon boat disclaimer. That is, they found another way to justify a purchase that was an obvious luxury as when Lake Wobegon's Wally bought a pontoon boat. As proud of it as he was, he told his tavern patrons that the boat was nothing but trouble: "I sort of wish I hadn't bought it—I bought it as a favor to this guy I know." I heard one example of a pontoon boat disclaimer when Fred and Sheryl, regular patrons at the Legion, bought a mobile home near Potato Lake as a vacation spot. They brought photos to the bar and showed them around, and Fred talked about how relaxing it was going to be to spend weekends fishing at the lake. In the same breath, however, he pointed out that they had already started to find out how much trouble the place was going to be. The previous owner had "left it a real mess."

Similarly, when I interviewed Main Streeters Mark and Marcia Andrew, I asked if they had ever made decisions about purchases that were influenced by the worry that they might appear to be "flaunting" wealth. They said no but that one of Mark's colleagues at the hospital just had to have fancy cars as a younger man. And he "got in some trouble for that" Mark said, but he just had to have them. I then asked if the doctor to whom he referred was the owner of the red Porsche 911 I'd seen in the hospital parking lot many times. No, he was not. The Porsche, it turned out, belonged to another doctor, and Mark explained, "and the first thing he'll tell you about it is that he bought it used and that he got a good deal on it."

What all of these disclaimers had in common was that they were, in a sense, conspicuous displays of rationality. Purchases could not be interpreted as "flaunting" as long as the purchase was based on rational decisions. At the same time that it was important not to be perceived as a flaunter of wealth, it was perfectly acceptable, and even good, to be someone with knowledge of and opinions about products, even products one did not own. Being able to participate in discussions about purchasing was an important means of being sociable. In many social settings, the ability to weigh in on particular experiences with brands or products provided one with a entrée into discussions.

Consumption and Belonging

Consumption is a prominent theme in both ethnographic and literary treatments of small towns. Despite all the pressure against consuming, Viroquans of all stripes participated wholeheartedly in "the cultural sea change to an aesthetic pleasure in consumer goods" (Zukin 2004, 38). The second set of findings reported in this chapter centers on the fact that Regulars, Main Streeters, and Alternatives consumed different kinds of items and that they attached different meanings to practices such as trading, recycling goods, and shopping "locally." The goods and services people consumed were clear markers of the social group to which they belonged.

In their insistence on the rationality of their purchasing, Viroquans conformed to the behavior of Americans more broadly. The prevalence of these conversations made a great deal of sense in light of the growing sociological literature on consumption, and particularly on shopping. Much of this literature argues that consuming has become a key part of contemporary American culture and is closely tied to our sense of ourselves as individuals. Americans experience the choices they make in the process of consumption as empowerment, in which, as individuals, they are entitled to exercise knowledge and make demands and judgments about items in the marketplace (Zukin 2004). Their deliberation in selecting items is based not only on material necessity but on how those items will reflect on the purchaser. This was not anything new. As Warner and Lunt found in "Yankee City" over half a century ago:

> All men and women in Yankee City as physical organisms needed food and shelter, but the values which dictated their choice of a house or of food for a meal were socially determined and also expressed the demands, needs, and limitations of their social personalities in a status system....
>
> When a man in the lower-upper class rented a house...he rented a house which he believed would correspond with and reflect his family's way of life....Many people in classes below the two upper ones earned more money, but the things they purchased were part of a different system of values and were used differently....
>
> All this reduces to the fact that the budget of an individual or family is *a symbol system,* or a set of collective representations, that *expresses the social values of a person's membership in a group life.* (1966, 287–8, emphasis added)

Returning to the example of cars, at the American Legion, patrons often commented on their own and others' cars: their quality, relative value, states of repair. I heard very similar conversations in the Common Ground. In each context, speakers discussed more and less desirable cars, who owned cars of high desirability, and the kinds of cars individuals aspired to own. The difference was that the kinds of cars being discussed in each context were completely different. Among the Alternative residents whose conversations I heard in Common Ground, foreign cars were highly valued, particularly Volkswagens, Subarus, Hondas, Toyotas, and Volvos. Alternative individuals recognized and discussed distinctions among these vehicles. Said one, "The yuppie-hippies drive new [Subaru] Outbacks, and the hippie-hippies drive the old clunkers." But the "clunkers" were of the same makes preferred by the Alternative folks in general.

In neither the Alternative group nor the Regular group did most individuals seem to own the kind of car they would have most liked. I heard many, many discussions in which people compared their own vehicles to "better" ones they wished they owned. But when Viroquans made judgments about the relative desirability of their cars, their reference points were mostly the cars owned by people they knew: people within their immediate social circles—that is, with reference to their "membership in group life" (Warner and Lunt 1966, 288).

In the past, buying an item such as a car might have been a matter of choosing a car that approximated, as closely as possible, some standard set by a local elite (Lynd and Lynd 1929; Blumenthal 1932). Today, the selection of an item like a car is bound up with the rest of a buyer's orientation to meeting life's material needs and a particular set of taken-for-granted ideas about how the world works and one's place in it. The reference points for evaluating purchases were not only local ones, but were further limited to comparisons made within groups of people one considered to be like oneself. In other words, the blue-collar Regulars compared their material achievement to that of other blue-collar Regulars, and perhaps to middle-class or upper-middle-class Regulars, while ignoring altogether (insofar as they dismissed them as irrelevant) the consumption practices and patterns of the Alternative and Main Street groups.

In other words, as in "Yankee City," a car in Viroqua was not simply a means of transportation but part of a system of symbols through which Viroquans confirmed for themselves and for others their membership in certain social groups. While all Viroquans needed to purchase basic goods such as foods, clothing, and shelter, the lifestyle strategies they used to meet these needs varied considerably. These variations reflected, and to large extent reinforced, the social distinctions among residents.[5]

The literature on material culture and consumption has tended to assume that the discretion to consume according to some calculated "lifestyle" is a luxury available only to those with some critical amount of discretionary wealth and with enough cultural capital to see purchasing as a matter of political or aesthetic will. But it was not just Alternative or

---

5. The result is what sociologists in the United States and Europe have already noted in urban areas: a kind of "lifestyle consumption" in which consumption is an activity engaged in to express the user's identity and social affinities. Comparison to "urban lifestyles" (Zukin 2004a): There is a good fit between the desires of the Alternatives and the kinds of retail activities that are attractive to tourists (attractive historic storefronts, handmade goods, etc.); "a new aesthetic appreciation of traditional products with a nostalgia for traditional social spaces outside the standardized core of mass production" (Zukin 2004b, 184).

Main Streeters for whom consumption practices were informed by this kind of aesthetic reflexivity. Everyone in Viroqua made decisions about the classes of items that were worth the extra attention befitting an aesthetic decision, and they assumed that everyone else did the same. Residents felt safe in assuming that the material items consumed by others could serve as effective markers of group status. So, in addition to consumption's serving as a means of self-expression, as it is usually understood, an individual's material possessions were read by others as deliberate aesthetic decisions, no matter how deliberate they actually were. Viroquans therefore thought that they could easily express their own sense of social belonging by using material markers and that they could accurately gauge others' sense of social belonging as well.

What I found in Viroqua was that the social distinctions expressed in consumption were not simply a matter of a hierarchical status system, nor simply markers of subcultural, or "tribal," belonging (Featherstone 1991). Instead, consumption practices reflected different orientations to small-town life that coincided with social distinctions and social groupings that were no longer treated as hierarchical, at least not in the sense that residents continuously aspired to move up in status or to change groups. Ideas about consumption were intertwined with moral ideas about living a "good" life, and I saw little evidence of any desire among residents to engage in consumption practices associated with another group. Some general differences in consumption practices mapped pretty neatly onto Regular, Main Streeter, and Alternative lines. Rather than using material goods and services to demonstrate wealth or class membership, Viroquans used consumption in ways that reinforced their approaches to making community.

These findings complicated another set of assumptions held by many of the theorists and researchers who have examined the production of social distinctions and their relationship to consumption: the assumption that social distinctions are fundamentally a product of economic necessity and power relations among groups that reflect and reproduce existing social inequalities by giving those with the most resources ways to exclude others from acquiring any. This was not the case in Viroqua. The shared ethics of "making do" and pressure against "flaunting" meant that, to a large extent, the goods and services members of each group consumed were widely accessible to members of others, at least in a monetary sense. It seemed that deliberate attempts at maintaining status though exclusive access to particular goods was not a factor either. An effort by an individual to participate in the consumption practices that would be entailed in moving from one group to another would be likely to be applauded rather than resisted—and could be read as evidence of the group's winning a new convert to its ranks. In other words, status-group membership had the potential to be highly fluid, as did access to the material markers of group membership. It would have been relatively easy to shift laterally from one group to another.

I saw very little of the kinds of anxious status work described in earlier studies of small towns—at least across social groups. People consumed what they "liked" without regard to the opinions of any social "betters" outside the group in which they felt they belonged. To the extent that Viroquans aspired to material achievement, the "betters" they emulated were members of their own social groups. Why didn't Viroquans cross the social lines defined by tastes? Because doing so would not be consistent with other parts of the identity individuals developed for themselves. Viroquans sought "to maintain a consistent moral and aesthetic quality" (Zukin 2004).

Part of the ability to do so lay in surrounding oneself, not only with appropriate material possessions, but with people who had similar moral and aesthetic tastes who could validate one's own choices. As a result, individuals' consumption practices not only reflected but reinforced social distinctions, as individuals attempted to maintain consistency. A consumer choice departing from such consistency would not be validated by one's primary social group. Consuming was not only a matter of individual identity but about belonging to the "communities of taste" that demarcated the social distinctions that mattered in Viroqua.

We can see how communities of taste were produced and reproduced in cases in which Viroquans shared some consumption practices across group lines. Even when Viroquans used the same consumption strategy, they often related to it in a different way, and this was clear in the ways that Alternatives and Regulars thought about recycling and reusing items. Alternatives and Regulars had a lot in common when it came to consumer practices. There were four thrift shops in Viroqua, and both Alternative women and some Regular women I knew patronized them regularly. Shopping for clothing for Regulars was a matter of cost, while for Alternatives, it was also a matter of avoiding mainstream markets and clothing made by underpaid workers across the globe, and a matter of style as well.

I knew many Regulars and Main Streeters who hunted deer in the winter, and some Alternatives who did so as well, despite the perceptions of other residents who assumed that Alternatives were uniformly opposed to hunting. For Regulars and Main Streeters, hunting tended to be an enjoyable hobby with a long tradition in the area and in their families. The Alternatives I knew who hunted did so, not because they saw it as sport, but because it was part of a set of larger goals. One Alternative explained that his family was trying to harvest as much of its food as possible from their land, and hunting on the land contributed to the family's self-sufficiency.

Recycling was alive and well among members of both Regular and Alternative groups, and it worked because within each group everyone had so much detailed knowledge about one another. When I mentioned to Bjorn Leonards in the winter of 2002 that I might need a new furnace, he suggested I call Bill Townsend. He and Bill had salvaged a gas furnace from a house they tore down in order to salvage lots of the other materials in it. Sure enough, Bill had the furnace in his barn, and they could sell it to me cheaply if it turned out that I needed one.

For Alternatives, reusing materials was important because it combined their ethics of environmental conservation and of limiting one's participation in wasteful consumer culture. In addition, using recycled goods was part of an aesthetic that included not only a visual style but beliefs about authenticity. The furnace was not the only thing that Bill and Bjorn had salvaged from that house. More important, they salvaged wood and other building materials. Part of the appeal of these materials for them, and for the customers who purchased the furniture Bjorn made from them, was visual. The marks and patinas of the aged woods had more "character" and visual interest than new materials. Both the craftsman and his customers valued the knowledge that they were using materials with history. Main Streeters appreciated this aesthetic too—especially those with an interest in preserving physical pieces of Viroqua's history. For the Alternatives, recycling goods and materials was not only something one does out of necessity but was part of the aestheticization of everyday life, in which the values of authenticity, craftsmanship, environmentalism and a distaste for consumer capitalism were intertwined. Similarly, when I interviewed organic dairy farmer Paul Deutz and his wife Patti, Patti served breakfast on a table surfaced with hardwood strips that had once been a part of the home's floor. Paul had built the table himself.

The furnace in Bill's barn was not the only furnace I was offered. Tony Bakkestuen also gave me a lead on one. He had recently helped Jeff Sandwick replace the furnace in his home. There was nothing wrong with Jeff's old furnace, Tony explained, he just wanted to replace it with a more efficient one. If I wanted a furnace, he said, I ought to call Jeff. Recycling by Regulars was not a matter of taste or politics, but about practicality and cost. People like Tony and Jeff, who were lifelong residents, had intimate knowledge of one another's cars, homes, and the other details required to connect people with recycled things they could use. In this sense, "making do" was still a big part of consumer culture in Viroqua.[6]

Reasons to Shop Locally

The fact that many Viroquans went first to local merchants to purchase things was evidence of the commitment to local shopping many residents spoke about. The commitment was not universal: I met a couple of families who did the bulk of their shopping for all items in La Crosse.[7] However, Regulars, Main Streeters, and Alternatives alike told me, "You can get pretty much everything you need here." What is most interesting was the ways in which different groups of Viroquans patronized the same local merchants for somewhat different reasons that reflected their mode of community making. As we saw in chapter 3, Main Streeters' commitment to shopping locally reflected a commitment to Viroqua's business community, and sometimes to particular business owners, with whom they had commercial relationships. Like the Steiners and Solversons, Trina Erickson, the news director at WVRQ, couched her reasons for shopping locally in terms of loyalty and ongoing mutual support. "The businesses that advertise on WVRQ are really paying my salary," she said. "It wouldn't be right not to support the businesses who support me."

---

6. In the end, I did not pursue acquiring either furnace.

7. "You have to understand, though," said the husband of the couple who told me this, "that we're shoppers. [My wife and I] enjoy going up to La Crosse together on my day off, buying the groceries and other things, maybe having lunch. Making a day of it. We enjoy that." The same family did, however, make an effort to purchase nearly all of the materials needed to build a new house locally, and they hired a local architect and contractor.

I heard references to this commitment to shop locally many times, from many different people, and in a wide variety of contexts. At Good Shepherd Lutheran's Fat Tuesday pancake supper, for example, one of the older men sitting at my table commented on how delicious the vanilla ice cream being served for dessert was. He then wondered aloud whether it had been purchased from the Viroqua Dairy, and added that he hoped the organizers of the breakfast had purchased everything locally. In planning the Vernon County Historical Society's pancake breakfast fund-raiser, board member Marlowe Nelson went out of his way to try to make sure that as many ingredients as possible were purchased from local producers and suppliers.

Many of the supplies for the breakfast that Marlowe secured from local businesses, such as the sausage patties, butter, and maple syrup, could have been purchased inexpensively (and conveniently) in "institutional" quantities from a large grocery or discount chain. Marlowe went to a great deal of extra work to secure good prices on locally made products, and then included the names of the businesses that had supplied the goods in the advertising for the event. Giving credit to businesses that either sold or donated supplies for the event was important, not only to provide some publicity for them in exchange for their support, but also, said Marlowe, because the knowledge that the sausages came from DW Meats and the cheese curds were from the Westby Creamery would provide added incentive for many members of the public to attend.

Marlowe's logic was premised on the assumption that publicity for the breakfast would be reaching an audience knowledgeable enough about the area to recognize and appreciate the products being advertised. Longtime residents were kind of accidental connoisseurs of the area's retailers. "Everyone" knew that the best meats came from DW, and the best cheese curds could be purchased on Wednesdays at the Westby Creamery (because that was the day on which they were made).

Alternative residents, since most of them were relatively recent arrivals, were still cultivating a local sense of connoisseurship. Decisions about where to shop were bound together with the larger aesthetic and political decisions around which their lives revolved more generally. For example, the Mobile gas station and the Jubilee supermarket had the biggest selections of rental video tapes and DVDs. However, the owner of the locally owned Box Office Video speculated that it was largely Alternative residents who kept the shop in business. The shop was on Main Street, and the Alternative residents who lived in town were "willing to walk" there in order to cut down on their use of gasoline. (The truth of this theory was impossible to verify—I knew Alternatives who rented movies at the locally owned grocery store and some who subscribed to services such as Netflix.)

Alternatives' aesthetic sensibilities meant that they were more interested in purchasing items that were not mass-produced. So while Blumenthal (1932) found that Mineville's local bakery was teetering on the brink of extinction due largely to the ability of large bakeries to truck their goods to grocery stores, Alternatives were desperate for a bakery. The ability to shop locally and purchase products that were produced by hand was part of Viroqua's draw for these people, the same way that the galleries and coffee shops were consistent with urban lifestyle gentrifiers in particular city neighborhoods (Zukin and Kosta 2004).

But Wal-Mart was also "local" in the sense that it was literally located in town. Wal-Mart has had particular significance in shaping consumption in small towns and rural areas (Trimble 1990). Whereas the variety chain stores and five-and-dimes that were its predecessors were located in central cities, Sam Walton went out of his way to construct Wal-Mart stores near small towns, where consumers were eager for easier access to new products that they saw advertised in the national media but which were not available nearby. In addition, competition in such areas could often be easily overcome.

In Viroqua, views of Wal-Mart were mixed. Many Main Streeters and Alternatives alike often said that they tried not to patronize Wal-Mart unless it was absolutely necessary. Even so, there were always cars in Wal-Mart's parking lot. Nearly everyone who told me that they tried to avoid Wal-Mart acknowledged that there were times when Wal-Mart was the only place to purchase some items, or when they could not justify purchasing an item from a local retailer at a higher cost. When these Viroquans did have to go to Wal-Mart, many of them said they felt that buying at Viroqua's Wal-Mart was at least better than making purchases outside the community.

But there were also Viroquans, particularly Regulars, who shopped at Wal-Mart unapologetically. Some said they shopped there out of necessity—Wal-Mart's prices were just lower and that was the primary factor in their decision making. Others said that shopping anywhere other than Wal-Mart was simply unnecessary. A conversation at a toddler's birthday party elicited both of these views. Among other gifts, the birthday girl, turning three, was given a coordinated pants-and-sweater outfit by a relative. The toddler's Regular working-class mother held up the outfit and asked if it had been purchased at Center Stage, the locally owned clothing shop on Main Street. It had. As her daughter continued happily unwrapping gifts, her mother said that she never shopped at Center Stage because the children's clothing there was just too expensive. "I can't afford to shop at those ritzy places," she said.

"I buy all my clothes at Wal-Mart," her husband added. "I don't need nothing but jeans and T-shirts anyway. Wal-Mart is fine with me." Shortly after this exchange, the little girl and all the guests were led to the family's garage for the unveiling of her "big" present. It was a wide-eyed, slightly overwhelmed birthday girl who was placed atop the pink motorized toddler version of a Harley-Davidson "motorcycle" for which she had asked.[8] The whole family applauded as she took her first spin around the garage, and her mother captured the event on video. Perhaps because of the audience, the birthday girl became somewhat self-conscious, and after timidly riding once around the garage, dismounted the motorcycle and ran back inside to play with her cousins.

As I watched, I thought about the other parents in town I knew who would have also appreciated the gift—parents cultivating brand loyalty to Harley-Davidson with clothing and toys. I also thought of other birthday gifts I'd seen in which parents gave children either homemade gifts or gifts purchased in some of Viroqua's smaller shops, like Center Stage or Art Vision, which also carried a selection of toys. While much literature about children and consumer culture has examined the way marketers and advertisers (Quart 2004; Schor 2005) have cultivated children as buyers, in Viroqua I saw how parents themselves strove to impart messages about the meaning of consumer choices to their children. Not surprisingly, they did

---

8. The Power Wheels Harley-Davidson Cruiser was battery operated and capable of speeds up to five mph. Molded plastic "exhaust pipes" concealed the pair of back wheels so that it looked like a real motorcycle with just two wheels rather than the three it actually had to enable a toddler to ride it safely. Pressing a small button near the handlebars caused the bike to emit a recording of the distinctive sound of a real Harley. It retailed for $199.99.

so in ways that were meant to perpetuate their own senses of social belonging. I knew one little boy, for example, whose parents named him after his father's favorite brand of firearm. As we will also see, Main Streeter parents tried to cultivate in their children, not brand loyalty, but a sense of consumer loyalty to the community. I also heard Alternative parents commiserate with their teenagers about the times they were "forced" to shop at Wal-Mart, though they deplored having to do so.

"Comparison" Shopping

Viroquans present some complications for current ideas about consumption. If residents in this small town have access to more stuff, do they buy it? Have they been swept up in the "new consumerism"? In Juliet Schor's view, "keeping up with the Joneses" used to mean keeping up with one's neighbors, people who were probably very much like oneself. Today, she argues, our reference points are wider, and we compare our material possessions to those of people who may make much, much more money than we do. The result, she says, is that the "conspicuous consumption" that Veblen found among members of the upper class in the 1910s and 1920s is now a common practice for most Americans, especially those who are middle-class and upper-middle-class earners, and there is a constant ratcheting up of our perceptions of what we need and what we should be able to afford. Schor points to massive increases in overspending, evidenced by indices like the increase in consumer debt, especially credit card debt.

On the whole, new consumerism still did not apply to most Viroquans, and where it did, it is not for the reasons of expanding reference points that Schor thinks matter. Schor is right to point to the relative nature of our satisfaction in consumption. Drawing on the work of social psychologists and economists, she points out that new consumerism is driven by our perceptions of what other people have, and what we are entitled to in relation to others. Money buys happiness only in so far as we believe that we have what we deserve (Frank 1999). If our reference groups expand to include people who make much more money than we do, we spend more, thinking that if others have these things, we should be able to have them as well, even if our resources are fewer. These unrealistic comparisons, according to Schor, are the source of the explosion of consumer debt. Cultures of consumption in Viroqua certainly rest on people's comparisons of their own possessions relative to what others have, though not in the way that Schor describes.

David Brooks (2001) argues against Schor, pointing out that the overall lower cost of living in "Red America" obscures existing economic inequality in predominantly rural, blue-collar heartland areas. Residents there, he claims, don't compare themselves to wealthy movie stars, and don't care to. Brooks assumes that part of the reason is that rural places are still places where "there's nothing to buy." No matter how hard he tried, he reports, he couldn't spend twenty dollars on a single meal anywhere in Franklin County, Virginia.[9] Though Brooks uses this observation to make a specious argument about economic inequality in general, he adds an important correction to Schor's argument: that reference points for consumption comparisons are, in places like Viroqua, still relatively localized.

Both Brooks and Schor are a little bit right, and a quite a bit wrong. Schor misses that in a small town where everyone knows everyone else reference points for consumption are extremely immediate. Everyone has intimate knowledge about who owns what, where they got it, and how much it cost. For Regular residents, these tight and immediate comparisons had some of the effects of overspending that Schor predicts. Viroquans did not need to compare themselves to millionaires on TV to overspend. It was enough for many to feel that if a co-worker or family member, perceived to be similar to oneself, could afford a new ATV or a wide-screen TV, so could he or she.

What Brooks missed in his brief jaunts into the Virginia countryside was that while small-town residents may not be tempted daily by the luxurious window displays of stores like Restoration Hardware and Pottery Barn, those same displays were available on the pages of these companies' mail-order catalogues and websites. In addition, there was no shortage of expensive items available to small-town residents. The difference was that rather than home décor shops, Viroqua's residents passed equipment dealers' displays of snowmobiles or ATVs on a daily basis. During the time

---

9. Brooks argues that the uneven distribution of economic resources across regions in the United States is essentially not problematic, as long as those on the losing end of the national economic stick don't perceive themselves to be deprived. Brooks then overlooks how localized comparisons can draw some residents into debt, foreclosure, and having goods repossessed.

I was in Viroqua, I knew half a dozen Regulars who bought new or nearly new large trucks or SUVs and lost them to repossession within six months. A common topic of discussion at the Legion bar was who had bought something he or she couldn't afford, or speculation about how an individual could possible pay for something he or she had just purchased on his or her salary. In 2002 and 2003, when retailers of big-ticket items like cars, furniture, and electronics started offering many low- or no-interest and no-money-down deals to boost lagging sales, it was a boon to many of the blue-collar residents I knew, who bought items like large-screen TVs, furniture, and recreational equipment, such as ATVs and snowmobiles. By the end of the winter some were struggling to meet the monthly payments that were starting to come due. One family I knew that acquired a pair of snowmobiles in the early winter sold them in the spring when they realized they could not make the payments on them.[10]

It would be easy to criticize such people for poor fiscal decision making, but snowmobiles and other expensive recreational items were not simply a matter of private enjoyment. Regulars bought snowmobiles for the same reason that Alternatives bought artisanal cheeses from their farming friends and Main Streeters bought all their clothing locally. For members of each group, specific consumer choices integrated them into the social groups of their choosing in ways that matched their logics of commitment and ethics of agency.

Connecting to the Community

Even thinking about commerce was linked to Main Streeters' thinking about their commitments to the community. The Main Streeters valued local businesses not just as economic entities but because they believed that locally owned businesses would be more responsive, and responsible, to Viroqua. The question for Main Streeters was whether or not the businesses and institutions with out-of-town ownership had as much valuable

---

10. Overspending is not a new phenomenon in small towns. In Mineville, for example, Blumenthal found that some residents purchased automobiles on installment plans and in tight financial times made "payments on their automobiles even though the grocer and the butcher bills remain unpaid for months" (384).

connection to the community as locally owned ones. When, for example, I asked Garith where he thought Viroquans would have to go for health care if Vernon Memorial were not there, he said, "If this hospital didn't exist...there would be some kind of urgent-care kind of setting, or some emergency care provided. Some [large health-care institution based in] La Crosse or Madison would come in and do something like that. But I don't know how connected to the community that organization would be."

Some Main Streeters thought of the commitment to shopping locally in light of mutual obligations among individuals. As Odell Solverson put it, "If people do business with me, I try to do business back with them." On the other hand, many viewed local shopping less in terms of individual obligations than as actions connected to the health of the community as a whole. Said Julie Steiner, "We firmly believe that if we want people to come to the hospital and use our services, then we need to shop here in town. Unless we are taking a trip or we're off for a little entertainment or something, then we don't do it, but..."

Garith interjected, "A lot of times we'll buy the groceries here and pack the lunch."

Julie finished, "But we try and recirculate as much of our money here in town as possible."

Garith said proudly:

We get all of our care here, all of our vehicles, everything here. The only time we don't is if we are looking for something we can't get here in town.... There was a car I wanted to buy at one time, but they didn't have one at Peterson's, and they went scouring the country for it, and they found one. Then it ended up that I bought something else, but we really do believe in it. Julie hit it right on the head that for us, in particular, this is where we make our money, this is where we spend our money.

"And our kids know it too," added Julie. She rolled her eyes a bit as she said this, and I asked why.

"I just was thinking of instances, like the whole senior [yearbook] picture thing. They wanted to have it done in La Crosse, and I said, "Why?" And they said, "Well, because of [friends who were doing it]." And I said, "That's too bad. Here's your choices [names the photographers in Viroqua].... When there's no real reason, too bad." Their girls did most of their clothes shopping in town, especially at Center Stage. I asked where they themselves shopped.

"Wherever Julie buys my clothes," laughed Garith. "I'm not into clothes."

I laughed as well, thinking of the number of times men in Viroqua had answered my questions about clothes shopping exactly the same way. "I don't think any guys in this town buy their own clothes," I said. The Steiners laughed. Garith said:

> I did surprise her one time. I needed a new suit, so I went right to Felix's, and that's where I got it. I really avoid—I don't even feel a need—to go anywhere else [to shop]. So the only time we spend our money somewhere outside of town is if we're on a trip. And once in a while, now that Nate's [restaurant] is closed down, now and then we'll go eat in Westby, which is still in the [hospital's] service area, or Coon Valley, which is still in the service area, for dinner. We don't even go to La Crosse very much to go out to eat.

The Steiners' linked their ideas about the "local" area in which they tried to spend money to the hospital's service area, which made sense given their concern about fostering the connections between the hospital and the boundaries of the local community it served. "Yeah," explained Garith, "we just try to circulate [money] around the [hospital's] service area. It's important to do that. If those businesses weren't there, if people didn't have those jobs, they'd be somewhere else, and we'd have less people coming into our business, and less people to talk to and socialize with."

The Steiners saw their jobs (Julie also worked at the hospital as its public relations director), the quality of their social life, and the monetary health of the community as interlocking. As we saw in chapter 2, the Alternatives also imagined various facets of their lives—their politics, parenting, work, consumption, the fate of the environment—as intertwined. Members of both groups imagined that their actions in one area of their lives had direct impact on the health and vitality of other institutions or people they depended on, so they worked hard to make sure that their actions in every arena in which they participated would benefit the rest of the arenas in which they lived.

Their image of the elements and amenities in the local community as being interlocking came through even in the joke Garith made in response to my question about whether or not there was anything he would wish to add to Viroqua. "A Krispy Kreme doughnut place!" he exclaimed. Laughing, he continued, "We may have one over at the hospital when we build our new building—we're working on it. It'd be a good feeder for our cardiac rehab program and weight-reduction [program]!"

Epilogue and Conclusion

By 2009 many things had changed in Viroqua, though much was the same as well. The locally owned pharmacies closed after the arrival of a Walgreens. The Macasaet family transformed the Clark/Peterson building into an indoor "European style" market in which a number of local entrepreneurs opened new businesses. The Blue Diamond Café closed, and the building was reopened as a Mexican restaurant. Controversy was stirred by the proposal of an Illinois company to place a high-density dairy operation on sites relatively close to residences and smaller farms near Viroqua's border with Westby.

After Common Ground coffee shop closed, the Associates of the Restored Temple Theatre were able to purchase its space, which adjoined the theater. The purchase allowed them to fully restore the facade of the theater building. Just as the café and other shops were negatively affected by the economic downturn, so were a number of the town's manufacturing businesses. Several laid off their workers indefinitely or closed their operations in Viroqua; these closures promised to deeply affect the area's blue-collar workers. When the largest of these industries, National Cash Register, announced its plans to close its plant in 2009, the Viroqua Partners held an emergency meeting and reached out to county and state officials to see what possibilities might exist to jump-start economic restructuring in the area. It seemed that Viroquans were going to continue their tradition of facing economic change head-on.

The differences that Viroquans perceived as existing among themselves persisted. In 2007 Tim Hundt, a reporter for the *Broadcaster,* wrote a column entitled "Townies and Ridgers" in which he explored these social divisions, but he argued that both longtime residents and relative newcomers could find plenty of common ground that would allow them to work together for the good of the community as a whole. The column generated a great deal of response in the form of comments posted on the newspaper's website, which suggests that the topic was a hot one. The Townie/Ridger categories were used in the same way that I'd often heard Viroquans use the old-timer/newcomer categories: basically this meant Alternatives versus everyone else, without giving attention to the differences among non-Alternatives (or even the variety within the Alternative crowd).[1] While the responses represented a wide range of views on the topic, no one suggested that the differences among Viroquans weren't real.

Though the Townie/Ridger vocabulary was specific to Viroqua, the debate echoed others that continue to be heard in popular culture about dichotomous social categories that divide Americans. Debates about whether or not there are deep factions among Americans—Red, Blue, Townie, Ridger, or otherwise—might be fruitfully understood by recasting these differences, not simply as ideological, but in terms of our ideas about how

---

1. One respondent elided the Alternative group in town with "Rainbow People," which prompted an emphatic response from someone who considered himself or herself an actual member of the Rainbow Family. Only a handful of families associated with Pleasant Ridge Waldorf School would have described themselves as Rainbow People. Another respondent was very critical of Rudolf Steiner and Waldorf education, which she likened to a cult. Pleasant Ridge parents varied widely in their knowledge and adherence to Steiner's "anthroposophic" teachings, and most of the parents whom I knew were not very familiar with Steiner's original writings (some of which are fairly esoteric and unconventional). Instead, they liked the school for features such as its deliberate attention to community building and the incorporation of a great deal of hands-on learning and art in the curriculum. Similarly, no respondents discussed variety among Viroqua's "Townies," though, as we have seen, people who were equally committed to Viroqua as a place expressed that commitment in some very different ways.

we go about living together with others in the world. Viroquans' different logics of commitment and different ethics of agency meant that they had very different ideas about how to make community, and even about its very purpose. Viroquans were all working hard toward goals, but toward different goals. Sometimes their differences made their goals compatible, but in other instances, these differences made it hard for Viroquans to make sense of one another at all.

It was their deep sense of individualism and agency that gave the Alternative community its form, and it is one that is not unique to Viroqua. As in other small communities, Alternatives

> [seek] a particular form of communal life which they *believe* exists in rural areas [and] move into places which would seem to favor the existence of appropriately rural communities. Once established in such places, these new middle class residents act to enhance, or bring into being, the qualities they value; in the process, they may indeed attempt to impose their own exclusive definitions of community upon others. For example, they create institutions which allow certain types of activities to be conducted which act to bring together many of the recent in-migrants.... While these institutions allow certain types of resident to participate fully in village life...they may also, wittingly or unwittingly, exclude others. (Murdoch and Day 1998, 192)

Murdoch and Day capture both the opportunities and some of the questions that arise in the Alternative approach to community. Their deliberate making of community that fits their image of what a better society would be is reminiscent of the prefigurative politics as described in literature on socialist, New Left, and, more recently, direct-action environmental and pacifist movements (Epstein 1991). These social-movement groups are organized deliberately to reflect (to actively prefigure) the kind of political and community life members believe desirable. The question is whether prefiguring such a desirable community would necessarily spread egalitarian ideals to those outside such groups.

The community the Alternatives made for themselves and the organizations they have established, such as the Waldorf schools and the Food Co-op, were based on their desire to enact a vision of community they believed would ultimately benefit everyone, directly or indirectly. They were trying to prefigure a society in which Americans consumed less, worked fewer hours away from home, were environmentally aware and concerned about social justice, and shared a sense of local community in which individuals counted on one another to be equally committed to making the world a better place.

The depth of their sense of agency allowed Alternatives to take big risks, not the least of which was moving to a town where they often did not know anyone in advance of their arrival, trusting that they could make a living and find a place to live, and believing that if they worked hard enough, they could enact the kind of community they had in mind. They were willing to be innovative, and they were willing to sacrifice material comfort for values they believed were more important for their families and the world at large. They examined their own actions in broader contexts, such as how their purchases and other choices affected the world. They assumed that their personal lives and their political goals were inseparable. Alternative people attempted to practice small-town and rural life in ways that reflected their values, for example, by shopping at thrift stores in order to recycle clothing rather than buying new clothing or supporting a system in which textile workers are paid substandard wages. They tried to be a community as they envisioned an ideal of community, and they worked at caring for one another and generating a community where it had not existed before.

But Alternatives also ended up facing some of the same tensions that Epstein's prefigurative activists faced. Being prefigurative meant that not everyone else would follow their example. The Alternatives did not really expect anyone else to follow their example, anyway, it seemed. Maybe getting others to do so was not their highest priority. The point, at least for the time being, was to prefigure a community for themselves. Anyone who wanted to join in was welcome, but the point was for Alternatives themselves to live the kind of moral lives in which they believed, not necessarily to get others to do the same.[2]

The irony was that Alternatives tended to be, in the words of one woman, "save-the-world types," but in their efforts to create institutions of

---

2. In this sense, we might compare them to the local Amish settlements. The local Amish live according to moral principles, but probably don't think of themselves as setting an example for non-Amish, nor would they expect non-Amish to join their settlements. It is extremely difficult to become Amish by conversion.

their own design that fit with their beliefs about making the world a better place, they often ended up withdrawing from the world they'd like to save. They save themselves, in a way, but their limited contact with others would seem to limit their ability to make any "difference" outside their community.[3] Alternatives also underestimated the degree to which their institutions seemed unwelcoming to others. One respondent to Tim Hundt's "Townies and Ridgers" column, identified by the username "Townie 1," said, "One point of view omitted [by Hundt]... is the fact that some of the 'townies' may be interested in learning more about the 'ridgers' and have not felt comfortable doing this because *they* feel like the outsider."

Some might argue that prefigurative community as it was practiced by the Alternatives in Viroqua is something of a cop-out. Rather than just prefiguring in their own social circles, they should have been out working to change existing institutions, or at least spreading the word politically, or jumping in and getting deeply involved in aspects of the local community beyond the ones inhabited by people like themselves. But trying to get the rest of the town to live as they did would also have been a disaster and would have exacerbated the sense expressed by another respondent to Hundt's column that the Alternative lifestyle was being "shoved down [people's] throats." Alternatives realized that expecting others to join them or even for them to actively proselytize was not realistic and, on some level, would have been disrespectful of others. Alternatives, after all, did believe deeply in the importance of individual choice.

In addition, the Alternatives did not always recognize the degree to which their strategies for resisting mainstream institutions and practices reproduced certain inequalities. The formation of the kinds of new organizations and institutions Alternatives have created required the work of people with high levels of cultural capital (Hundt 2004). For example, Pleasant Ridge's progressive tuition structure attempted to make the school affordable for all families, but enrolling a child there also entailed a significant commitment of time on the part of parents, who were expected to engage in many hours of volunteer work. Parent involvement reduced

---

3. Jacob's (1997) study of Canadian and American back-to-the-landers presents a similar dilemma. Despite their relatively high levels of education and cultural resources, Jacob wonders if "the smallholders can possibly have time or energy, much less the disposition and interest, to devote to community organizing after the last of the homestead chores are completed" (16).

the school's operating (and thereby tuition) costs, but it was also central to the school's community-oriented approach to education in which parents, teachers, and students themselves collaborated with equal responsibility for the organization.[4] Most of the Alternative parents I knew had some flexibility in their work and weekday schedules that allowed them to engage in volunteer activities. Parents with less-flexible work schedules, such as those who worked in local factories or who needed to work full time or more to make ends meet, might not have had the time to participate in such activities.

Another open question was the degree to which Alternatives, while so willing to take responsibility for the ways their actions impacted others in a global sense, would take a more permanent stake in Viroqua. Some members of the Main Street and Alternative communities expressed the concern that Alternatives' commitment to community organizations or projects might be fleeting or superficial. When I asked a member of the Kickapoo Valley Friends Meeting if the arrival of so many Alternative residents had increased membership in the Quaker meeting, the member said that it had increased only a bit. I expressed surprise, as the egalitarian organization of this pacifist religious society seemed like it would be very compatible with the values of many Alternative Viroquans. The member of the Quaker meeting said that I was right about that compatibility, and that they had had a number of visitors who came to meeting to "try Quakerism out," but that most had not stayed. The reason, the member suspected, was that Quakerism was "a lot more work than many people think and are really ready for."[5]

In another instance, Dave Ware and Tamsen Morgan, Alternatives themselves, talked in an interview about how they were making a deliberate effort to "put down roots" in the community even though they were relatively new to it. Some of the people they had gotten to know

---

4. The Pleasant Ridge parents with whom I spoke about their role in the school indicated that the high expectations for parent involvement was an attractive part of the school's philosophy for them and a big part of what made the school truly "alternative" to public schools, which, they believed, discouraged parents from getting involved in the school in any more than superficial roles as volunteers.

5. It is also quite possible that, for a number of Viroquans, the distance to the meeting was a factor that discouraged long-term participation. The meeting was held each Sunday at the Kickapoo Exchange building, a food co-op and community center about half an hour away from Viroqua.

particularly well were elderly members of the community, whom Tamsen met through her job as a physician's assistant at one of the town's clinics. They valued their relationships with these people because it was through people who had deep roots in the community that they could learn about the area's history and become connected to it themselves. They contrasted their efforts to do so with some of their friends in the Alternative community whose social lives didn't include many connections to people outside that group. They used the phrase "woo-woo" to describe a related potential hazard of Alternativeness. I asked what they meant by it, and Dave explained he thought that there were a fair number of people who couldn't commit to anything, who "were sort of the flavor of the day."

The Alternatives were proud of all that they had accomplished in Viroqua, and this pride made them feel that their deliberately made community was distinctly superior to other organizations and people in town. Recall the Pleasant Ridge Waldorf School official who described the school as a "little pocket of enlightenment out here in the middle of nowhere."

This was precisely the attitude that rankled the Main Streeters, who also felt extremely proud of the work they had done in the town. The Main Streeters' combination of a logic of commitment particular to Viroqua itself and their highly individualized ethic of agency encourages them to work to improve the community and to accomplish it by relying on personal ties and their particular knowledge of the human and other resources nearby. They were coalition builders—they knew who to "bring to the table" people to accomplish certain kinds of projects and were willing to reach outside of their own social circles, particularly into the Alternative community when they believed that they might find allies there. The Main Streeters had a long-term stake in Viroqua and an ability to get things done with people who were not necessarily exactly like themselves. They were the dedicated people who rushed through family dinners to sit through endless hours of meetings, those who gave substantial amounts of time and money to the community because they believed in making Viroqua a wonderful place to live.

There was some concern that the Main Streeters' logic of commitment limited their attention to their own community, allowing them to set aside the larger structural questions that affected communities other than their own. Indeed, there was evidence that a narrow focus on Viroqua was problematic. By 2009 a new economic development organization had been formed at the county level with the goal of coordinating the development efforts across Vernon County communities.

Like the Alternatives, the Main Streeters' sure sense of their own efficacy meant that they imagined that people who were not as involved in public life were simply not motivated enough to get involved, or were content with "mediocrity." Neither the Main Streeters nor the Alternatives could really imagine that there were Viroquans who did not experience life as an endless series of opportunities, or that not all Viroquans assumed that their contributions would be taken seriously. In other words, it was easy for both the Alternatives and Main Streeters to disparage Regulars for being "apathetic" without considering some of the reasons why they might not be so eager to "get involved." In one instance, when some Alternatives were asking why "locals" seemed to resent them, I tried to articulate something like the argument that I have made in this book. I tried to explain that new schools and alternative institutions seemed like an insult, a rejection of the people who were already here. "Why?" responded an Alternative with a sharp edge in his voice. "They resent anyone who lives their life in any kind of deliberate way?" It was "reprehensible bullshit," he thought, to go "drifting" through life without taking things "into your own hands." The importance of self-actualization as a moral boundary was never so clear to me as it was in that moment.

But it was precisely their sense that neither Alternatives nor Main Streeters took them seriously that enflamed Regulars' rejection of the ethic of agency that defined the other two groups. Alternatives and Main Streeters ran around "tooting their own horns," as one Regular put it, and for what? It seemed obvious to many Regulars that most of the Alternatives' and Main Streeters' activities were mostly about showing off. Indeed, one respondent to Hundt's column argued that "public school should be the only school. If you dont [sic] use it you are teaching your kids that your group is better! Waldorf or homeschool or whatever else they come up with here." According to this logic, it is hard to imagine very many collective efforts that would *not* be construed as showing off. The Regulars adopted an orientation toward community making that was the opposite of showing off. Community was about coming as you were, and being accepted that way. The virtual assurance that one could be folded into this relaxed kind of social life made being around Regulars easy. Of course, you had to be ready to come to the aid of your kin and friends if they asked you to, but you could count on them to do the same. It was sometimes a relief to find that a tractor race was just a tractor race.

Of course, Regulars constructed community as actively as anyone else in Viroqua, though their ethic of agency prevented them from acknowledging that they were doing it and prevented them from seeing what they might have in common with others in town and the potential value in what others were doing. The idea that community life should emerge spontaneously obscured possibilities for agency—possibilities for getting together and getting something done if something needed doing. If the Regulars were to recognize how much work they actually did put into making community, they might not have been so hostile to the efforts of the Main Streeters and the Alternatives or suspicious of their motives.

They might also have taken their potential (as individuals and as a group) to have an impact on the world around them more seriously. When I told a Regular friend that I had recently purchased a wool rug but was a bit concerned that its low price might mean that it was made with child labor and perhaps I shouldn't have purchased it, my friend said, "You think too much." The Regular approach to community prevented them from seeing how effective they actually were, the amount of work they actually did in cultivating community, and the potential effects their actions had beyond the circle of their private lives. The problem with this was that Regulars used their sense that "real" community should not require any work as a reason not to do much, yet they still complained about changes in the town that they did not like.

It would be possible to read these three orientations to community as attempts by different groups to protect particular privileges or resources. The Alternatives could be seen as creating a set of institutions that both required and conferred a useful kind of cultural status. The Main Streeters' actions might have been more about protecting their own businesses, jobs, and prestigious positions in the community rather than the good of the community itself, though in all likelihood, it involved both. The Regulars, in rejecting in essence the idea that community could be made, might have been protecting their most valuable resource: their long-standing networks of family and friends that enabled them to secure jobs and other advantages. If anyone could simply make community, it might have meant that the Regulars' local histories and ties were not so valuable after all.

I don't think these explanations are particularly convincing, at least not insofar as I think each group really believed their own proverbial press. Each of the three orientations to community I studied in Viroqua came with particular opportunities and some serious constraints. In this book I have not only tried to illuminate some features of community making in Viroqua but, I hope, have demonstrated the utility of remaining agnostic about what community is and focusing instead on understanding how community is made.

Appendix

Study Methods

This appendix contains greater detail about the intertwined theoretical and methodological aspects of my study of the impact of social change on community life in Viroqua, Wisconsin. There is a long tradition of using community studies to understand the ways that meso-level and macro-level social changes impact the lives of individuals and the communities in which they live. The community study approach remains a vital source of data about how people live. The analytical tools provided by recent developments in the sociology of culture improve our ability to articulate the means and goals of the community-study approach, and to improve them in ways that expand our ability to unpack the logics by which people organize their lives and coordinate their actions.

Culture and the Community Study

While social theorists and macro-level research provide information about generalized social processes, community studies remain interested in "their concrete embodiments in specific communities" (Stein 1960, 5). Community studies look at the ways broad social processes manifest themselves in day-to-day lives and interactions. The American tradition of community studies represents a set of specific attempts to understand the impact of change on American life (Stein 1960). Park and his students studied the effects of urbanization in Chicago; the Lynds examined the transformation wrought by industrialization in Muncie, Indiana; while Warner and others examined the impact of bureaucratization in Newburyport, Massachusetts. The point of these studies was "not that Chicago, Muncie and Newburyport were representative communities in any statistical sense, but rather that they were undergoing processes of structural transformation that affected all American cities and towns to one or another degree, and therefore could be used as laboratories in which to study these representative social processes" (Stein 1960, 94). These broad social processes manifested themselves in massive rearrangements of the places and ways in which people worked, the places they lived, the ways they spent their time, and the interactions they had with one another. Stein (1960) captures the kind of information a community study can yield about social change:

> Community studies cannot provide information about the men and events on the national scene that influence historical processes so decisively, but they do describe the effects of these processes on the everyday lives of ordinary men and women. They fill out the historical record by giving the intimate meanings that large-scale changes had for a limited segment of the population. (3)

With the notable exception of Blumenthal's (1932) *Small-Town Stuff,* most of the community research on which Stein draws from the first half of the twentieth century involved the impact of change in the context of urban life, leaving small-town life largely unexplored, or, as Brekhus (1998) says, "unmarked." For a number of reasons, small-town life seemed like something that could be taken for granted, as everyone understood what it was like.[1] Small-town social life seemed relatively unproblematic (Blumenthal

---

1. The novelty of large segments of the population living in cities required attention since cities seemed to breed social problems and therefore needed scholarly attention more urgently than small communities. The Chicago school researchers did not actually observe the transition from rural to urban life. The transition from rural to urban occurred in Chicago long before Park and

1932), even though, as Blumenthal demonstrates, the same phenomena that produced changes in cities and large towns also had dramatic effects on smaller communities. Because of my interest in "marking" the kinds of communities we usually take for granted, I purposefully selected a community in which change was not an obvious source of strife, at least not on the surface (see also Stein's [1960] discussion Warner's selection of Newburyport as a site for studying bureaucratization). Mine is not so much a study of how a community responds to crisis or how change precipitates crisis in a community (e.g., Erikson 1976). It is a study of the daily cultural work of adapting to change.

I was interested in understanding a small town as a whole community— how its parts fit and worked together. As a cultural investigation, the examination of these "parts" was guided by a variety of clues about what community *meant* to its residents, their assumptions about how social life works and their practices through which they constituted community. Community studies generally begin with the "parts" of the community that are institutionally recognizable, and mine is no exception. An example of such a study is the Lynds'(1929) *Middletown.* The Lynds approached the whole community through the institutions that make it up—schools, churches, clubs, workplaces, families. But these are not the only important "parts" of a community. In addition, social lives and orders are informed by patterns of meaning, shared understandings that have become the focus of cultural sociology in the last fifteen years. So while I began work on this book by investigating the key institutions of the community, the analysis of the data focuses on the cultural practices through which the community is continuously constructed. These are parts of the community we would not necessarily know much about unless we approached them from a perspective that allowed the salient segments of the community to be discovered in the process of research rather than determined by the researcher ahead of time.

The "community" in community studies has always been more than a physical location, and more than the mechanics of sets of institutions in that location. The idea that part of studying a community is understanding

his students began their work, so theirs were studies of communities that were already fully urban (Stein 1960). Park and many of his students, like most Americans at that time (Pedersen 1992), had at least some experience living in small towns.

the model of social life that members follow is key to understanding the interests of Chicago-style investigations of cities. Cities were not just densely populated locations, they were a "mode of life" (Wirth 1938) that had to be understood as "a system of social organization involving a characteristic social structure...and a typical pattern of social relationships; and...as a set of attitudes and ideas, and a constellation of personalities engaging in typical forms of collective behavior and subject to characteristic mechanisms of social control" (19). Community "refers to a certain way of perceiving the relationship between human beings, a peculiar manner of defining society that is itself dependent on a certain definition of the units involved" (Varenne 1977, 158). In other words, "community" is a shared set of ideas about how the social world works, a "model" of the social world on which we base our interactions with others, as opposed to the content of any particular model. Viroquans' sets of ideas about how the social world works and what constitutes community influenced not only how they enacted community but who they did it with.

Prior to the emergence of the sociology of culture, community ethnographers had only one set of analytical tools to use to understand the connection between communities and the experiences of individuals in them: the tools of social psychology. Variations in the forms of community life were attributed to changes in "personality" and other social-psychological adjustments that researchers believed were connected to the size of the community in which a person lived (Wirth 1938; Redfield 1955). Vidich and Bensman (1960), for example, explained features of interactions among community members with reference to the personal psychological adjustments individuals made when their lives in Springdale did not match their self-defined level of success.

The link Vidich and Bensman posited between psychological adjustment and community life was that of "public ideology" and its "illusory" relationship to community life. They offered a basic view of culture in which illusions are derived from such things as the economy, and people are more or less dupes if they believe these illusions and will become trapped in misery. Everyday activities like work and the avoidance in interactions of pointing out one's own failures were taken to be strategies of psychological denial—ways in which individuals could avoid "coming to terms with [themselves]" (312).

Concepts from contemporary sociology of culture give us a way to avoid speculating about individuals' psychological motives and also to articulate important aspects of what community studies have been doing all along. For this reason, I called my approach a *culturally grounded community study,* the point being to explore the ways in which residents negotiated community life in the course of day-to-day interactions, vocabularies, and practices. Until recently, when sociologists used the word "culture" they usually meant something like values, beliefs, or ideas. Sociologists doing community studies have always been interested in more than the content of values and beliefs, however. They have wanted to understand how communities work. Certainly values and beliefs have a role to play in this regard, but more broadly, community studies have observed how social order is created in practice—as individuals move through formal and informal institutions and other settings where they live their lives.[2]

That these practices *are* culture is an insight that has only recently been explicitly articulated by sociologists in the burgeoning field of cultural sociology. As put by Hayes (2000), "culture encompasses languages, symbols, rituals, everyday practices, values, norms, ideas, the categories of thought and knowledge and the material products, institutional practices, and ways of life established in these" (597). Some of the work in sociology of culture has retained a focus on linguistic practices, discourses, and dialogues, frames, or vocabularies (see Alexander and Smith 1991; Steinberg 1994; Snow and Benford 1988; Wuthnow 1991). Other work focuses not only on language but the context-specific practices in which language is used (see Lichterman 1996; Eliasoph 1998). Sociology of culture asks both how these practices are constituted and what role they play—in addition to and separately from social-psychological and structural factors (Alexander and Smith 1991)—in the unfolding process through which communities are

---

2. An important part of what sociologists of culture have been working to establish over the last decade or so is that "culture is not reducible to power relations, nor does it function simply in the service of rational calculation. Culture operates according to socially constructed logics that are no less 'real' than the built environment they permeate. And cultural structures are no more malleable or inaccessible than the long list of social forms that have been referred to as 'social structure,' including capitalism, bureaucracy, the state, social networks, social classes, status groups, population dynamics, and the distribution of material resources. These 'other' structured social forms, while often treated as analytically distinct from culture, cannot be separated from it" (Hayes 2000, 597).

constituted. Others focus on how meanings inform interactions (for example, La Pradelle and Lallement 2004).

My data collection began with the "institutional" categories used in traditional community studies, such as *Middletown*. However, the lens of cultural analysis made it possible to enter a dialogue with these categories and to analyze them using the cultural categories that were negotiated in the daily life of the community itself. My approach to initial data analysis was influenced by Glaser and Strauss's (1967) grounded-theory approach, which advocates a researcher's drawing categories from the data themselves, which then guide the subsequent analysis. I began with my observations of respondents' own vocabularies and practices, and used these as clues about how residents of Viroqua themselves make sense of their community. Important salient categories and practices to Viroquans that warranted further investigation—including their various conceptions of community—emerged from the community itself. These categories then guided subsequent engagement with theory and with existing empirical work, as well as the collection of additional data. By that point, the process of research began to proceed along the lines of Burawoy et al.'s (1991) extended-case method (Eliasoph and Lichterman 2003), with the important difference that the goal was not necessarily to speak to theories of power and oppression,[3] or to adjudicate between opposing concepts with a third alternative.[4]

---

3. Why do I not simply say that this is an extended case study to begin with? Unlike that method, in which researchers "start with our favorite theory" (Lichterman and Eliasoph, 1999), mine is not primarily a theory-driven study, in the sense that I do not start with the aim of intervening in particular debates or extending particular theories. On the contrary, my aim is to look at a whole community first, to get a snapshot of life in a small town today, and *then* to bring appropriate sociological theories and insights to bear.

4. Bell's (1994) study of the English village of "Childerley" provides an excellent example of the way that understanding a community through the categories used by its residents can give a researcher a theoretically engaged way into the center of a community. Living "close to nature" is a value that residents of "Childerley" seemed to share, and a sociologist operating on the Parsonian definition of culture as beliefs and values would stop here. Using an expanded understanding of culture, we can see that "nature" lay at the heart of a complex of cultural practices that permeated the village's routines, its institutions, and its residents' conceptions of themselves. Residents were aware that their town had undergone some significant changes: the class structure was less rigid than it had been just a few decades earlier, and an increasing number of moneyed Londoners were willing to trade a lengthy commute for the privilege of living "in the country." A shared discourse about living close to "nature" provided "Childerley's" residents with a way to continue to understand the community as more-or-less unified. However, different members of the community had

Logistics

How does one study an entire community? In the methodological appendix to *The Urban Villagers,* Herbert J. Gans (1962) lists six major approaches to data collection in a community study. Using these as a basic framework, I employed a wide variety of strategies for collecting data in Viroqua.

Use of [the Community's] Facilities

For Gans, this meant living in the West End of Boston, shopping in its stores, and availing himself of its "institutions and other facilities as much as possible. This enabled [Gans] to observe [his] own and other peoples' behavior as residents of the area" (337). Viroqua's local facilities were the principle sites through which I initially collected data, and they remained important throughout the study. These facilities included living space, the Laundromat, the post office, and the public library, as well as restaurants, civic clubs, and recreational facilities such as the Landmark Center's gym. I patronized businesses in town for as many of the goods and services I needed as possible.

Selecting a place to live in Viroqua was a challenge, but my choice was ultimately guided by an interest in trying to avail myself of as many different kinds of spaces in the community as possible. After looking at several apartments, I narrowed the choice down to two. One was a large apartment on Main Street that seemed like the perfect ethnographer's nest above insurance and title company offices. I could keep an eye on Main Street constantly, if only on the segment of it half a block south of where most of the Main Street action was. From that apartment, I would have been able to see Gary's Rock Shop, the Sports Corner, the Cheese Corner,

---

different relationships to the idea of nature and went about day-to-day life and related to other residents differently as well.

In practice, these relationships to "nature" played themselves out in the unfolding process in the community's institutions such that they reinforced existing class divisions. Upper-class and working-class villagers belonged to different organizations and socialized at different pubs. In the end, we have a much richer picture of the *process* by which class divisions are reinforced than we would if Bell simply began by assuming that the category of class, for example, would figure centrally in the village's social order, or if he had assumed that "living close to nature" was a "value" to which all residents related in a uniform way.

a gas station, the Dairy Queen, the south-side Kwik Trip, and the hospital. Personally, I was attracted to this apartment because it was enormous, had a dishwasher, and because while the front of the building looked over Main Street, the entrance and parking area were in the back of the building, which might afford me some privacy.

The other apartment was on Independence Street and was owner occupied. Though only three blocks from Main Street, it was located in a strictly residential neighborhood. In the end, I chose the Independence Street apartment. Gans and other ethnographers have found neighbors and landlords to be important informants, and in the apartment on Main Street I would not have had any residential neighbors. I would have been surrounded by commercial establishments. It would be easier, I thought, to have access to this more public part of town at any time than it would be to have to find an excuse to stroll through neighborhoods, the parts of town that seemed more private.

While I will never know how living on Main Street might have affected my project, living on Independence Street was wonderful. I still spent a great deal of time keeping my eyes on the streets below. From my living room windows, I could see the county courthouse and one of the town's two medical clinics. Because I was only blocks away from the public schools, it was easy to see how the school calendar changed the rhythms of the town as I watched students come and go to school and observed high school students amble up my street during their lunch hour and back toward school at the end of it. I got to see neighbors interact with one another. Most of these interactions were positive, as when I walked home one evening to find neighbors from several surrounding houses gathered at the edge of my next-door neighbor's garage, looking intently at something that my neighbor was illuminating with his car's headlights. It turned out that they were looking at a variety of lily whose large blossoms opened only at night.

I also saw some less positive interactions among neighbors. A family around the corner had an energetic dog that frequently escaped from its yard and whose escapades in neighborhood gardens led to the exchange of some tense words. The rather reclusive elderly woman who lived in the house just up the street accused me of trying to put snow from "my" section of sidewalk into her yard. Later that year, the local police department called to say that she had complained that the dog for which I was caring had been in her yard. I explained that I knew it could not be true, and the police officer informed me that the woman often called to complain about a variety of things, many of which were not so. It was easier for them to follow through on these complaints than to argue with her, they explained. It made me sad to think that perhaps I had somehow upset this woman, but the incident gave me insight into some of the ways that local officials of various kinds used the particular knowledge they often had of their constituents in order deal with them.

In general, I went out of my way to use community facilities to a degree that residents of the town probably did not, including leasing a mail box at the post office so I could make regular visits there. I made a point of rotating my visits among local restaurants and the local grocery venues, while most of the Viroquans I knew patronized one or two most of the time. Making extensive use of the community's facilities was not always easy, for two reasons. First, many facilities are commercial enterprises to which one gains access through one's status as a consumer—that is, one was expected to make a purchase. Second, use of public facilities occasionally made one conspicuous in ways that worked against the research.

Despite perceptions among many social scientists that ethnographic research is inexpensive apart from the cost of the researcher's time, a researcher's ability to use community facilities often depends on being able to spend money. I found that I lived a more expensive lifestyle in Viroqua than I did in places where I was not conducting research, as I spent money on a larger variety of things. Though I could have had my mail delivered to my home in Viroqua free of charge, I opted to rent a post office box, which cost $50 for six months, to have a reason to make regular visits to the post office. I ate in restaurants far more frequently than I normally would have in order to spend as much time as possible in the community's public places. Spending time at the American Legion or other places where people consumed alcohol had the potential to be even more expensive than eating a meal in a restaurant, because it not only entailed an obligation to purchase a drink or two for oneself, but I had to be prepared for the possibility of becoming entangled in a string of reciprocal drink purchases. In order to meet residents and spend time in additional community facilities, I found that I needed to purchase a number of services that were not a part of my life when I was not conducting research, for example, manicures at the local nail and tanning salon, $15 per visit, and gym membership, $25 per month—although both were bargains by urban standards.

Scholars (e.g., Lofland 1998) have argued that many of our urban public spaces are now privatized commercial spaces, and their privatization limits access to those who can afford to buy access to them. While I am not convinced that there are fewer noncommercial public spaces in Viroqua today than in the past, it was not easy to spend time in public without spending money, especially in the winter when it was too cold to sit outdoors for extended periods of time. In addition, though it may have been a product of my own assumptions and my sense that as a researcher asking for cooperation from a community in which some residents were less privileged than I, I felt it behooved me to be able to be the buyer of drinks or coffee (depending on the setting) whenever possible.

In addition, the use of some of the most accessible public spaces such as sidewalks and parks were governed by implicit norms about needing a reason to use them. Initially, I spent a great deal of time in Viroqua simply walking around town, and sometimes I sat in public places like Eckhart Park behind the courthouse, which included picnic areas, a large children's playground, wooded areas, and volleyball courts. I sometimes felt quite conspicuous doing these things. Except when the students were out of school during their lunch period, I was sometimes the only pedestrian on the sidewalks in residential parts of town during a typical weekday. I persisted in these activities, convincing myself that I certainly couldn't be the only person in town who walked, for recreation if nothing else. When I began working at the American Legion bar in October 2001, two patrons independently made comments that confirmed my sense that my activities were unusual. One asked if I did "a lot of walking around here" and said that he'd seen me doing so. Another said she's seen me strolling around and at first assumed that I was one of the developmentally disabled people who lived in the community housing across from the newspaper office.[5]

My walking drew attention, but it did so partly because I had no apparent reason for walking around town. For part of the following year,

---

5. Though I had noticed that I sometimes shared the sidewalks and the park with individuals whom I later came to understand depended on community living services due to their disabilities, the comment by this Legion patron ignores that many of them have jobs at the VARC assembly plant and so are generally not walking around town during the business day.

I cared for Tony Bakkestuen's dog, Lucy, for several months. Caring for the dog meant that I again did much walking around town, but I no longer felt conspicuous in any way. The dog provided me with a purpose for walking—a reason to be occupying public space. Because she was very friendly and an unusual breed, she attracted attention from residents we passed who struck up conversations by asking questions about her or asking to pet her. Lucy effectively entangled people in conversations with me (Duneier 1999), and this was particularly true of adults with small children. Children who wanted to pet Lucy would point at her, exclaiming what a big, hairy dog she was, and they would sometimes run toward her, causing parents to follow. Because she was so gentle and well behaved, I had complete confidence allowing strangers, including children, to pet her. Lucy turned out to be an important methodological innovation, and I wished I had had a dog with me from the beginning of the study.[6] Of course, this strategy for engaging people in conversation was only feasible at all because Lucy was so well behaved.

Attendance at Meetings, Gatherings, and Public Places

Gans "attended as many public meetings and gatherings as [he] could find" (337), as did I. I volunteered regularly at the Vernon County Historical Society Museum, particularly during my first winter in Viroqua, and then I began serving as its vice president. I attended dozens of city council meetings, seven school board meetings, and one forum for school board candidates. I visited the elementary school as a volunteer and attended the high school's musical productions and athletic events. Each week, the newspaper was full of announcements about fund-raising events and gatherings organized by a wide variety of local groups, including the Masons, the VFW post, churches, parents/teacher groups, and the Viroqua Partners. I spent many hours at the Vernon County Fair each fall as both a spectator and volunteer. I went to tractor pulls and car races, concerts, and golf courses. Public meetings, places, and events provided good initial contacts with many residents.

---

6. When Lucy was bred two years later, I was given one of her pups.

Over the course of about a year and a half, I worked a total of nearly eight hundred hours at the American Legion bar. Bartending was an ideal entrée into the world of working-class Regulars (middle-class Regulars were harder to get to know, because they tended to avoid the town's bars and did most of their socializing in private). Because all of the patrons in the bar had to interact with the bartender, standing behind the bar provided an ideal way, not only to get to know the customers, but for customers to get to know me and learn why I was in town. It was easy to immediately inform patrons on their arrival that I was there as a researcher, because their first interactions on entering were usually with me. Eventually, the patrons who spent a great deal of time at the Legion bar became so familiar with my short speech about being a researcher studying Viroqua that they would give it to new patrons for me! I did not need to worry that anyone in the bar was unaware that they were being observed for the purposes of research.

Occasionally, however, the word about a researcher in the bar could become a bit garbled, sometimes to humorous effect. One evening during deer-hunting season, a time of year when there were often visitors in town, two men came into the bar in the early evening. One of the patrons who routinely spent time at the Legion, a man whose real name was Wendel, but who everyone called "Windy" because of his propensity to talk a lot, had already heightened his verbosity with a few drinks and took it upon himself to welcome the newcomers to town and to the bar. He pointed to me and said in slightly slurred speech, "She's a doll, but you have to watch out, because she's studying you." He made a sweeping gesture of the room with his arm. "In fact, she's studying all the assholes in this place. But she's a sociologist, so she's putting 'em into categories of assholes!"

Informal Visiting with Neighbors and Friends

Like Gans, I eventually became acquainted with people I met in public settings, who then introduced me to more residents in the context of informal social gatherings. Informal social settings were also key sites for data collection. An interesting finding, as well as methodological challenge, was that not all Viroquans were equally easy for me to get to know in such settings. Alternatives and Regulars were the people I had easiest access to when it came to informal gatherings. This may have been because Main

Streeters were so often engaged in public meetings and gatherings that they seemed to have less time left over for hanging out.

Formal and Informal Interviewing of Community Functionaries

Like Gans, I did not conduct formally structured interviews. I hardly planned on doing much interviewing at all, but I found interviews necessary for several reasons, one of which was the disparity in the amount of time for "hanging out" members of different groups had. Interviewing was particularly important with Main Streeters, because the only way to spend time with them was to make an appointment to do so. However, I also did a great deal of informal interviewing. Over the bar, I asked patrons at the Legion many of the same questions I asked others in their living rooms. In addition to interviewing residents, I observed as many of them as possible in the context of their regular routines, including shadowing some at their work places, accompanying people on shopping excursions, and attending family events.

Use of Informants

I had no idea how receptive Viroquans would be to a researcher when I began my project, and wondered if I might ultimately need to rely on one or two informants for most of my information. Although I did rely heavily on a few members of each of the three groups in town, and on several other people who had feet in more than one group, Viroquans, to a person, were very helpful to me. The only thing like an impediment I ever ran into in my research was two interviewees who preferred that I not record our conversations, but who were willing to be interviewed and happy to have me take written notes. Many Viroquans brought events to my attention that I was unaware of and went out of their way to include me in informal gatherings, even facilitating contacts with other residents they believed could help me.[7]

---

7. In some cases, Viroquans helped me secure informed consent from others as well. This was particularly true in the Legion bar, where established patrons often let new customers know that the bartender was also doing a study.

Observation

The success of the project depended on my ability to keep "my eyes and ears open at all times...to learn something about as many phases of [Viroqua] life as possible, and also looking for unexpected leads and ideas" (Gans 1962, 337). I attempted to be diligent in my observations at all times, and while I got lots of good advice about doing fieldwork before beginning it, no one warned me how thoroughly exhausting the constant vigilance would be. The most difficult thing about doing a community study was finding ways to observe everything and observe my own role in each setting as well.

The other big challenge was keeping track of all of my observations. Like most ethnographers, I took extensive field notes by hand. Initially, I recorded almost everything that happened each day. As time went by, I was able to become more selective, but I still spent hours each day writing notes in my notebooks and taping to their pages receipts, pamphlets, event programs—any paper items that added information about things I had seen, heard, or attended in Viroqua. I used a MiniDisc digital recorder in many public meetings, in interviews, and at other events where I had permission to do so. When it was not possible to make recordings, I took notes during the event if it was appropriate and unobtrusive. In many settings, such as informal get-togethers or parties, and in settings where I had other work to do, such as volunteering or working at the Legion, I had to take notes retrospectively when the event was over.

Confidentiality

Because I selected Viroqua for this study largely because of its notoriety, I knew it would also be impossible to disguise the town itself, so I have not done so. "Everyone knows everyone's business" in Viroqua. As such, it seemed ludicrous to try to offer Viroquans confidentiality in this study. Even if I had disguised respondents' names, in many cases it would have been very clear to others in the community who was being identified. I did, however, disguise respondents' names in a few cases, particularly when the individuals were not people I knew well enough to locate for permission to recount a particular story.

Using the real names of people and town has yielded a mixture of interesting results. On one hand, because I was free to tell people where I was doing my research, I stumbled on many sources of data and contacts I would not have had had people not known which town I was studying. The strength of this study has certainly been improved by those sources. On the other hand, as I wrote up my findings, I felt a great deal of responsibility to make sure that I did not expose respondents to social embarrassment or sanction. Therefore, I have often not identified respondents simply by not naming them or by using pseudonyms, which are noted as such in the text. I have done this most often in cases where a respondent's statement or action might cause others in the community to look negatively on them. In other cases, I decided not to describe events that, while they might have strengthened my argument, might have caused embarrassment to the respondent if fellow Viroquans figured out who I was writing about. I therefore have not discussed some types of incidents I witnessed in which Viroquans often drew most heavily on their community-making capacities: incidents such as evictions, arrests and incarcerations, or grave personal illnesses.

REFERENCES

Agnew, Eleanor. 2004. *Back to the Land: How Young Americans Went to Nature in the 1970s, and Why They Came Back.* Chicago: Ivan R. Dee.

Alexander, Jeffrey C., and Phillip Smith. 1991. "The Discourse of American Civil Society." *Theory and Society* 22:151–207.

Anderson, Sherwood. 1919. *Winesburg, Ohio.* New York: Penguin.

Arensberg, Conrad. 1954. "The Community Study Method." *American Journal of Sociology* 60:109–24.

Akst, Daniel. 2001. "Why Chain Stores Aren't the Big Bad Wolf." *New York Times,* June 3.

Bangsberg, Roy L. Ca. 1950–1970. *Seven Miles to Viroqua.* Two copies are in the permanent collection of the Vernon County Historical Society Museum.

Barry, Joseph, and John Derevlany, eds. 1987. *Yuppies Invade My House at Dinnertime: A Tale of Brunch, Bombs, and Gentrification in an American City.* Hoboken, NJ: Big River.

Baumgartner, M. P. 1988. *The Moral Order of a Suburb.* New York: Oxford University Press.

Bell, Michael Mayerfield. 1992. "The Fruit of Difference: The Rural-Urban Continuum as a System of Identity." *Rural Sociology* 57:65–82.

———. 1994. *Childerley: Nature and Morality in a Country Village.* Chicago: University of Chicago Press.

Bellah, Robert N., Richard Madsen, William M. Sullivan, Ann Swidler, and Steven M. Tipton. 1985. *Habits of the Heart: Individualism and Commitment in American Life.* Berkeley: University of California Press.

Bender, Thomas. 1978. *Community and Social Change in America.* New Brunswick, NJ: Rutgers University Press.

Bloom, Stephen G. 2000. *Postville: A Clash of Cultures in Heartland America.* New York: Harcourt.

Blumenthal, Albert. 1932. *Small-Town Stuff.* Chicago: University of Chicago Press.

Bonner, Kieran. 1997. *A Great Place to Raise Kids: Interpretation, Science, and the Urban-Rural Debate.* Montreal: McGill-Queen's University Press.

Bourdieu, Pierre. 1987. *Distinction: A Social Critique of the Judgement of Taste.* Cambridge: Harvard University Press.

Brekhus, Wayne. 1998. "A Sociology of the Unmarked: Redirecting Our Focus." *Sociological Theory* 16:34–51.

Brooks, David. 2000. *Bobos in Paradise: The New Upper Class and How They Got There.* New York: Simon and Schuster.

———. 2001. "One Nation, Slightly Divisible." *Atlantic Monthly* 288(5): 53–65.

———. 2004. *On Paradise Drive: How We Live Now (and Always Have) in the Future Tense.* New York: Simon and Schuster.

Brown-Saracino, Japonica. 2004. "Social Preservationists and the Quest for Authentic Community." *City and Community* 3:135–56.

Burawoy, Michael, et al. 1991. *Ethnography Unbound: Power and Resistance in the Modern Metropolis.* Berkeley: University of California Press.

Burgess, E. W. 1932. Introduction to *Small-Town Stuff,* by Albert Blumenthal. Chicago: University of Chicago Press.

Clemens, Elizabeth, and James M. Cook. 1999. "Politics and Institutionalism: Explaining Durability and Change." Annual Review of Sociology 25:441–466.

Cloke, Paul, Martin Phillips, and Nigel Thrift. 1998. "Class, Colonisation and Lifestyle Strategies in Gower." In *Migration into Rural Areas,* ed. Keith Halfacree and Paul Boyle, 166–85. New York: Wiley and Sons.

Coffin, R. J., and M. W. Lipsey. 1981. "Moving Back to the Land: An Ecologically Responsible Lifestyle Change." *Environment and Behavior* 13:42–63.

Corrado, Marisa. 2002. "Teaching Wedding Rules." *Journal of Contemporary Ethnography,* 31:33–67.

Croll, Nora. 2005. "Selling Sustainability: The Adventures of an Ideal in Mainstream Consumer Magazines." Master's thesis, University of Wisconsin, Madison.

Dobriner, William M. 1963. *Class in Suburbia.* Englewood Cliffs, NJ: Prentice Hall.

Dollard, John. 1957. *Caste and Class in a Southern Town.* Garden City, NY: Doubleday.

Dube, Arindrajit, and Ken Jacobs. 2004. *Hidden Cost of Wal-Mart Jobs: Use of Safety Net Programs by Wal-Mart Workers in California.* Berkeley: University of California, Berkeley, Center for Labor Research and Education.

Duneier, Mitchell. 1999. *Sidewalk.* New York: Farrar, Strauss and Giroux.

Duneier, Mitchell, and Harvey Molotch. 1999. "Talking City Trouble: Interactional Vandalism, Social Inequality, and the 'Urban Interaction Problem.'" *American Journal of Sociology* 104:1263–95.

Eliasoph, Nina. 1998. *Avoiding Politics: How Americans Produce Apathy in Everyday Life.* Cambridge: Cambridge University Press.

Eliasoph, Nina, and Paul Lichterman. 1999. "'We Begin with Our Favorite Theory...': Reconstructing the Extended Case Method." *Sociological Theory* 17(2): 228–34.

———. 2003. "Culture in Interaction." *American Journal of Sociology* 18:4735–94.

Elkington, John, Julia Hailes, and Joel Makower. 1999. "The Green Consumer." In *Consumer Society in American History, A Reader,* ed. Lawrence Glickman, 333–37. Ithaca: Cornell University Press.

Erikson, Kai T. 1976. *Everything in Its Path: Destruction of Community in the Buffalo Creek Flood.* New York: Simon and Schuster.

Epstein, Barbara. 1991. *Political Protest and Cultural Revolution: Nonviolent Direct Action in the 1970s and 1980s.* Berkeley: University of California Press.

Featherstone, Mike. 1991. *Consumer Culture and Postmodernism.* London: Sage.

Fischer, Claude S. 1977. *Networks and Places: Social Relations in the Urban Setting.* New York: Free Press.

———. 1982. *To Dwell among Friends: Personal Networks in Town and City.* Chicago: University of Chicago Press.

Fischer, Claude S., Robert Max Jackson, C. N. Stueve, Kathleen Gerson, Lynne McCallister Jones, and Mark Baldassare. 1977. *Networks and Places: Social Relations in the Urban Setting.* New York: MacMillan.

Fowler, Robert Booth. 1991. *The Dance with Community: The Contemporary Debate in American Political Thought.* Lawrence: University Press of Kansas.

Frank, Robert H. 1999. *Luxury Fever: Money and Happiness in an Era of Excess.* Princeton: Princeton University Press.

Frantz, Douglas, and Catherine Collins. 2000. *Celebration, U.S.A.: Living in Disney's Brave New Town.* New York: Henry Holt.

Gans, Herbert J. 1962. *Urban Villagers.* New York: Free Press of Glencoe.

———. 1991. *People, Plans, and Policies.* New York: Columbia University Press.

———. 1995. "Urbanism and Suburbanism as Ways of Life: A Reevaluation of Definitions." In *Metropolis: Center and Symbol of Our Time,* ed. Philip Kasinitz. New York: New York University Press.

Garcia Canclini, Nestor. 2001. *Consumers and Citizens: Globalization and Multicultural Conflicts.* Minneapolis: University of Minnesota Press.

Glaser, Barney G., and Anselm L. Strauss. 1967. *The Discovery of Grounded Theory: Strategies for Qualitative Research.* Chicago: Adline.

Grasmuck, Sherri. 2006. *Protecting Home: Class, Race, and Masculinity in Boy's Baseball.* New Brunswick, NJ: Rutgers University Press.

Green, Gary Paul, Anna Haines, Adam Dunn, and Daniel Monroe Sullivan. 2002. "The Role of Local Development Organizations in Rural America." *Rural Sociology* 67:394–415.

Greenhouse, Carol J. 1986. *Praying for Justice: Faith, Order, and Community in an American Town.* Ithaca: Cornell University Press.

Halebsky, Stephen. 2004. "Superstores and the Politics of Retail Development." *City and Community* 3:115–34.

Halfacree, Keith, and Paul Boyle. 1998. "Migration, Rurality, and the Post-Productivist Countryside" In *Migration into Rural Areas,* ed. Keith Halfacree and Paul Boyle, 4–35. New York: Wiley and Sons.

Harris, Chauncy D. 1943. "Suburbs." *American Journal of Sociology* 49:1–13.

Hart, Joseph. 2005. "Just a Small-Town Boy: A Writer Gives Up the Rat Race and Finds Peace in the Country. *Utne Reader,* May–June issue. http://www.utne.com/pub/2005_129/promo/11642–1.htm (accessed May 9, 2005).

Hayes, Sharon. 2000. "Constructing the Centrality of Culture—and Deconstructing Sociology?" *Contemporary Sociology* 29:594–602.

Heiney, Paul. 1998. *Home Farm.* London: Dorling Kindersley.

———. 2002. *Country Life: A Handbook for Realists and Daydreamers.* London: Dorling Kindersley.

Hillery, George A., Jr. 1977. "A General Typology of Human Groups." In *New Perspectives on the American Community,* 2nd. ed., ed. Roland L. Warren. Chicago: Rand McNally College Pub. Co.

Hundt, Jacob S. 2004. "Potluck Schools: Alternative Education and Civil Society in Viroqua, Wisconsin." Master's thesis, University of Chicago.

Ivanko, John, Lisa Kivirist, and Bill McKibben. 2009. *Rural Renaissance: Renewing the Quest for the Good Life.* Gabriola Island, BC: New Society.

Jackson, David Dale. 1992. "It's Wake-up Time for Main Street When Wal-Mart Comes to Town." *Smithsonian* 23(7): 36–46.

Jacob, Jeffrey. 1997. *New Pioneers: The Back-to-the-Land Movement and the Search for a Sustainable Future.* University Park: Pennsylvania State University Press.

Jacobs, Jane. [1961] 1992. *The Death and Life of Great American Cities.* New York: Vintage Books.

Johansen, Harley E., and Glenn Victor Fuguitt. 1984. *The Changing Rural Village in America: Demographic and Economic Trends since 1950.* Cambridge, MA: Ballinger.

Keller, Suzanne. 2003. *Community: Pursuing the Dream, Living the Reality.* Princeton: Princeton University Press.

Kotkin, Joel. 2001. *The New Geography: How the Digital Revolution is Reshaping the American Landscape.* New York: Random House.

Lacroix, Jean-Guy, and Gaetan Tremblay. 1997. "The 'Information Society' and Cultural Industries Theory," trans. Richard Ashby, *Current Sociology* 45:1–162.

Lamont, Michèle. 1992. *Money, Morals, and Manners: The Culture of the French and American Upper-Middle Class.* Chicago: University of Chicago Press.

La Pradelle, Michèle de. 2006. *Market Day in Provence,* trans. Amy Jacobs. Chicago: University of Chicago Press.

La Pradelle, Michèle de, and Emmanuelle Lallement. 2004. "Paris Plage: 'The City is Ours.'" *Annals of the American Academy of Political and Social Science* 595(1):134–45.

Lareau, Annette. 2003. *Unequal Childhoods: Class, Race, and Family Life.* Berkeley: University of California Press.

Lasch, Christopher. 1991. *The True and Only Heaven: Progress and Its Critics.* New York: W. W. Norton.

Lasch, Christopher, and John Urry. 1994. *Economies of Signs and Space.* London: Sage.

Leach, William. 1993. *Land of Desire: Merchants, Power, and the Rise of a New American Culture.* New York: Pantheon.

Levy, Frank, and Richard J. Murnane. 1992. "U.S. Earnings Levels and Economic Inequality: A Review of Recent Trends and Proposed Explanations." *Journal of Economic Literature* 30:1333–81.

Lewis, Sinclair. 1950. *Babbitt.* New York: Harcourt Brace.

———. 1980. *Main Street.* New York: Penguin.

Lichterman, Paul. 1996. *The Search for Political Community: American Activists Reinventing Commitment.* Cambridge: Cambridge University Press.

Liebow, Elliott. 1967. *Tally's Corner: A Study of Negro Streetcorner Men.* London: Routledge and K. Paul.

Lingeman, Richard. 1980. *Small Town America: A Narrative History, 1620–the Present.* New York: G. P. Putnam and Sons.

Lofland, Lyn H. 1998. *The Public Realm: Exploring the City's Quintessential Social Territory.* New York: Aldine de Gruyter.

Lynd, Robert S., and Helen Merrell Lynd. 1929. *Middletown.* New York: Harcourt Brace and World.

———. 1937. *Middletown in Transition: A Study in Cultural Conflicts.* New York: Harcourt Brace and World.

MacCannell, Dean. 1989. *The Tourist: A New Theory of the Leisure Class.* New York: Schocken.

Massey, Douglas, and Nancy Denton. 1998. *American Apartheid: Segregation and the Making of the Underclass.* Cambridge: Harvard University Press.

McAdam, Doug. 1988. "Micromobilization and Recruitment to Activism." *International Social Movement Research* 1:125–54.

McKibben, Bill. 2004. Foreword to *Rural Renaissance: Renewing the Quest for the Good Life,* by John Ivanko and Lisa Kivirist. Gabriola Island, BC: New Society.

McMillan, David W., and David M. Chavis. 1986. "Sense of Community: A Definition and Theory." *Journal of Community Psychology* 14:6–20.

Melucci, Alberto. 1996. *The Playing Self: Person and Meaning in the Planetary Society.* Cambridge: Cambridge University Press.

Melvin, Bruce L. 1951. "Rural Sociology in a Chaotic World." *Rural Sociology* 16:57–62.

Mitchell, Stacy. 2000. *The Hometown Advantage: How to Defend Your Main Street against Chain Stores…and Why It Matters.* Washington, DC: Institute for Local Self-Reliance.

Monti, Daniel J. 1999. *The American City: A Social and Cultural History.* Oxford: Blackwell.

Monti, Daniel J., and Michael Ian Borer. 2007. "Community, Commerce, and Consumption: Businesses as Civic Associations." In *Varieties of Urban Experience: The American City and the Practice of Culture,* ed. M. I. Borer, 39–62. Lanham, MD: University Press of America.

Morris, Paul. 1996. "Community beyond Tradition." In *Detraditionalization: Critical Reflections on Authority and Identity,* ed. Paul Heelas, Scott Lash, and Paul Morris, 223–49. Oxford: Blackwell.

Murdoch, Jonathan, and Graham Day. 1998. "Middle-Class Mobility, Rural Communities and the Politics of Exclusion." In *Migration into Rural Areas,* ed. Keith Halfacree and Paul Boyle, 186–99. New York: Wiley and Sons.

Nearing, Helen, and Scott Nearing. 1970. *Living the Good Life: How to Live Sanely and
Simply in a Troubled World.* New York: Schocken.

Newman, Katherine. 1988. *Falling from Grace: The Experience of Downward Mobility in
the American Middle Class.* New York: Free Press.

Norman, Al. 2004. *The Case against Wal-Mart.* St. Johnsbury, VT: Raphael Marketing.

Norris, Kathleen. 1993. *Dakota: A Spiritual Geography.* New York: Ticknor and
Fields.

Park, Robert. [1925] 1967. "The City: Suggestions for the Investigation of Human Behavior in the Urban Environment." In *The City: Suggestions for the Investigation of
Human Behavior in the Urban Environment,* ed. Robert E. Park, Ernest W. Burgess,
and Morris Janowitz, 1–46. Chicago: University of Chicago Press.

Pedersen, Jane M. 1992. *Between Memory and Reality: Family and Community in Rural
Wisconsin, 1870–1970.* Madison: University of Wisconsin Press.

Putnam, Robert. 2000. *Bowling Alone.* New York: Simon and Schuster.

Quart, Alissa. 2004. *Branded: The Buying and Selling of American Teenagers.* New York:
Basic Books.

Redfield, Robert. 1955. *The Little Community: Viewpoints for the Study of a Human
Whole.* Chicago: University of Chicago Press.

Ricoeur, Paul. 1992. *Oneself as Another,* trans. Kathleen Blamey. Chicago: University of
Chicago Press.

Roberts, Ron E. 1971. *The New Communes: Coming Together in America.* Eglewood
Cliffs, NJ: Prentice Hall.

Salamon, Sonya. 2003. *Newcomers to Old Towns: Suburbanization of the Heartland.* Chicago: University of Chicago Press.

Schor, Juliet B. 1991. *The Overworked American: The Unexpected Decline of Leisure.*
New York: Basic Books.

———. 2005. *Born to Buy: The Commercialized Child and the New Consumer Culture.*
New York: Scribner.

Smith, Nicola, and Geoff Hansen. 2004. *Harvest: A Year in the Life of an Organic Farm.*
Guilford, CT: Lyons Press.

Snow, David A., and Robert D. Benford. 1988. "Ideology, Frame Resonance and Participant Mobilization." *International Social Movement Research* 1:197–217.

Stein, Maurice Robert. 1960. *The Eclipse of Community: An Interpretation of American
Studies.* Princeton: Princeton University Press.

Steinberg, Mark. 1994. "The Dialogue of Struggle." *Social Science History* 18:505–42.

Taylor, Charles. 1989. *Sources of the Self: The Making of the Modern Identity.* Cambridge:
Harvard University Press.

Tocqueville, Alexis de. 2000. *Democracy in America,* trans. Gerald Bevan. New York:
Harper.

Tolbert, Charles M., Michael D. Irwin, Thomas A. Lyson, and Alfred R. Nucci. 2002.
"Civic Community in Small-Town America: How Civic Welfare Is Influenced by
Local Capitalism and Civic Engagement." *Rural Sociology* 67:90–113.

Trimble, Vance H. 1990. *Sam Walton: The Inside Story of America's Richest Man*. New York: Dutton.

Ukens, Carol. 1991. "Wal-Mart Not the Enemy after All, Small Town Finds." *Drug Topics* 135(17): 21–23.

Urry, John. 1990. *The Tourist Gaze: Leisure and Travel in Contemporary Societies*. London: Sage.

Varenne, Hervé. 1977. *Americans Together: Structured Diversity in a Midwestern Town*. New York: Teacher's College Press.

Venkatesh, Sudhir Alladi. 2000. *American Project: The Rise and Fall of a Modern Ghetto*. Cambridge: Harvard University Press.

Vidich, Arthur J., and Joseph Bensman. (1968) *Small Town in Mass Society: Class, Power and Religion in a Rural Community*. Princeton: Princeton University Press.

Warner, W. Lloyd, and Paul S. Lunt. 1949. *The Status System of a Modern Community*. New Haven: Yale University Press.

———. 1966. *The Social Life of a Modern Community*. New Haven: Yale University Press.

Waters, Mary C. 1990. *Ethnic Options: Choosing Identities in America*. Berkeley: University of California Press.

Weiss, Michael J. 1989. *The Clustering of America*. New York: Harper and Row.

———. 2000. *The Clustered World: How We Live, What We Buy, and What It All Means about Who We Are*. New York: Little Brown.

Whitehurst, Robert N. 1972. "Back to the Land: The Search for Freedom and Utopia in Ontario." Conference paper for the Annual Meeting of the Canadian Sociology and Anthropology Association.

Willits, Fern K., Robert C. Bealer, and Vincent L. Timbers. 1990. "Popular Images of 'Rurality': Data from a Pennsylvania Study." *Rural Sociology* 55:559–78.

Wirth, Louis. 1938. "Urbanism as a Way of Life" *American Journal of Sociology* 44:1–24.

Wolfe, Alan. 1999. *One Nation, after All: What Middle-Class Americans Really Think about God, Country, Family, Racism, Welfare, Immigration, Homosexuality, Work, the Right, the Left, and Each Other*. New York: Penguin.

Wuthnow, Robert. 1991. *Acts of Compassion: Caring for Others and Helping Ourselves*. Princeton: Princeton University Press.

Zukin, Sharon. 1982. *Loft Living: Culture and Capital in Urban Change*. Baltimore: Johns Hopkins University Press.

———. 2004. *Point of Purchase: How Shopping Changed American Culture*. New York: Routledge.

Zukin, Sharon, and Ervin Kosta. 2004. "Bourdieu Off-Broadway: Managing Distinction on a Shopping Block in the East Village." *City and Community* 3:101–14.

Index

Residents of Viroqua will be found under the entry "Viroqua residents." Businesses and other public venues in Viroqua will be found under the entry "Viroqua businesses and venues."